THE *Question* OF ETHICS

Studies in Continental Thought

John Sallis, general editor

Consulting Editors

Robert Bernasconi

Rudolf Bernet

John D. Caputo

David Carr

Edward S. Casey

Hubert L. Dreyfus

Don Ihde

David Farrell Krell

Lenore Langsdorf

Alphonso Lingis

William L. McBride

J. N. Mohanty

Mary Rawlinson

Tom Rockmore

Calvin O. Schrag

Reiner Schurmann

Charles E. Scott

Thomas Sheehan

Robert Sokolowski

Bruce W. Wilshire

David Wood

THE *Question* OF ETHICS

Nietzsche, Foucault, Heidegger

CHARLES E. SCOTT

INDIANA UNIVERSITY PRESS
Bloomington and Indianapolis

©1990 by Charles E. Scott

All rights reserved

No part of this book may be reproduced or utilized in any form or by
any means, electronic or mechanical, including photocopying and
recording, or by any information storage and retrieval system, without
permission in writing from the publisher. The Association of American
University Presses' Resolution on Permissions constitutes the only
exception to this prohibition.

The paper used in this publication meets the minimum requirements of American
National Standard for Information Sciences—Permanence of Paper for Printed
Library Materials, ANSI Z39.48-1984.

Manufactured in the United States of America

Library of Congress Cataloging-in-Publication Data

Scott, Charles E.
    The question of ethics : Nietzsche, Foucault, Heidegger / Charles
E. Scott.
        p.   cm. — (Studies in continental thought)
    Includes bibliographical references.
    ISBN 0-253-35123-5 (alk. paper). — ISBN 0-253-20593-X (pbk. :
alk. paper)
        1. Ethics—Methodology.   2. Ethics, Modern—20th century.
3. Nietzsche, Friedrich Wilhelm, 1844–1900—Ethics.   4. Foucault,
Michel—Ethics.   5. Heidegger, Martin, 1889–1976—Ethics.
I. Title.   II. Series.
BJ37.S35   1990
170—dc20   89-46341
                                                            CIP

2 3 4 5   94 93 92

"We will never be done with the question, not because there still remains too much to question but because the question, in this detour from the depth that is proper— a movement that diverts us from both profundity and self—puts us in contact with that which has no end."

Blanchot

Contents

Acknowledgments

I am indebted to the philosophy faculty and students at the University of Essex, England, to the participants of the Collegium Phenomenologicum, Perugia, Italy, in 1987, 1988, 1989, and to the faculty and graduate students at Vanderbilt University for discussion and criticism of parts of this book. I am especially grateful to David Farrell Krell, Susan M. Schoenbohm, Charles Shepherdson, Susanna Thiele, and Andrew Young for their exceptionally helpful suggestions, research aid, and conversations. Holley Roberts provided valuable editorial assistance and prepared the index. Judy Thompson and Stella Thompson typed the manuscript in its several versions with patience and kindness that went considerably beyond the staff support that one might reasonably expect.

I acknowledge with gratitude permission to use all or portions of the following publications:

"The Middle Voice of Metaphysics," *The Review of Metaphysics* 42 (1989). Reprinted by permission of *The Review of Metaphysics.*

"Heidegger and the Question of Ethics," *Research in Phenomenology* 17 (1988). Reprinted by permission of *Research in Phenomenology.*

The Language of Difference, chapter 2, section 4 (Atlantic Highlands, N.J.: Humanities Press International, 1987). Reprinted by permission of Humanities Press International, Inc.

"The Horizon of Time and Ontological Difference in *The Basic Problems of Phenomenology,*" *Hermeneutic Phenomenology: Lectures and Essays,* ed. Joseph J. Kockelmans (Lanham, Md.: University Press of America, 1988).

Selected Works Cited

Nietzsche

GM   *On the Genealogy of Morals,* trans. Walter Kaufmann and R. J. Hollingdale (New York: Random House, 1969).

WP   *The Will to Power,* trans. Walter Kaufmann and R. J. Hollingdale (New York: Random House, 1967).

Z   *Thus Spoke Zarathustra,* trans. Walter Kaufmann (New York: Viking, 1966).

Foucault

CS   *The Care of the Self,* vol. III of *The History of Sexuality,* trans. Robert Hurley (New York: Pantheon, 1987).

DP   *Discipline/Punish: The Birth of the Prison,* trans. Alan Sheridan (New York: Random House, 1977).

EC   "The Ethic of Care for the Self as a Practice of Freedom, an interview with Michel Foucault on January 20, 1984," *The Final Foucault,* eds. J. Bernauer and D. Rasmussen (Cambridge, Mass.: MIT Press, 1988).

LCM   *Language, Counter-Memory, Practice: Selected Essays and Interviews,* ed. Donald F. Bouchard (Ithaca, N.Y.: Cornell University Press, 1977).

MC   *Madness and Civilization: A History of Insanity in the Age of Reason,* trans. Richard Howard (New York: Random House, 1973).

OT   *The Order of Things: An Archaeology of the Human Sciences* (New York: Random House, 1970).

PK   *Power/Knowledge: Selected Interviews and Other Writings, 1972–1977,* trans. Colin Gordon, Leo Marshall, John Mepham, Kate Soper (New York: Pantheon, 1980).

UP   *The Use of Pleasure,* vol. II of *The History of Sexuality,* trans. Robert Hurley (New York: Pantheon, 1985).

Heidegger

AH   "Aletheia Heraclitus, Fragment B16," *Early Greek Thinking,* ed. David Farrell Krell and Frank A. Capuzzi (New York: Harper & Row, 1975).

BDT   "Building Dwelling Thinking," *Basic Writings from* Being and Time (1927) *to* The Task of Thinking (1964), ed. David Farrell Krell (New York: Harper & Row, 1977).

BP   *The Basic Problems of Phenomenology,* trans. Albert Hofstadter (Bloomington: Indiana University Press, 1982).

BT   *Being and Time,* trans. John Macquarrie and Edward Robinson (London: SCM Press, 1962).

ET   "On the Essence of Truth," *Basic Writings.*

LH   "Letter on Humanism," *Basic Writings.*

THE *Question* OF ETHICS

ONE

Introduction

The Question *Concerns Ethics*

"And thus we are bound to grow day-by-day more questionable, worthier of
asking questions, perhaps also worthier—of living?
—Nietzsche
On the Genealogy of Morals

The title of this book could just as well be *The* Question *of the Ethical
Subject* as *The* Question *of Ethics.* The prepositional object *(ethics)* is
far less important than the noun *(question)* modified by the prepositional
phrase, for the book's issue is how questioning can occur in a manner
that puts in question the body of values that led to the questioning. The
reader will find that the question of ethics arises out of ethical concern
as well as out of conflicts within structures of value, that ethical concern
and suspicion of ethics qualify one another. The suspicion is ethical because
it is motivated by a desire to recognize and mitigate certain occasions
of human suppression and suffering. The suspicion held by 'the question
of ethics' is that ethical concern has a pathogenic dimension and is composed of values that occasion human suffering in the pursuit of human
well-being. And of course this question itself, as an expression of ethical
concern, may be as pathogenic as the system of values that it questions.
That is the reason why self-overcoming and recoil in the movement of
thought are central to the book's purpose.

This could have been a study of the development and formation of
ethics as we know it today. Indeed, the book's orientation calls for that
kind of study, for a careful accounting of the genesis of ethics in Western
thought and practice, an accounting that would find its own genealogy
in the subject of its study. But the question of ethics has arisen more
recently and is not broadly recognized. It comes out of the dialectical
thought of the early to mid nineteenth century, but finds its most effective
early expression in Nietzsche's writing. That is because in Nietzsche's
thought both Western subjectivity and reason are put fundamentally in
question, and that destabilization of thought concerning subjectivity and

reason is essential to the development of the question of ethics. So we begin with Nietzsche in order to see how the self-overcoming movement of his thought recoils on his own values and, in the context of his account of the ascetic ideal, both reveals the role of the ascetic ideal in Nietzsche's thought and prevents the formation of a normative ethics in his thought. For our purposes, the question of ethics takes its departure from this movement.

Foucault adds considerably to the formation of the question by the manner in which he puts in question ethical subjectivity. We shall also find that the movements of self-overcoming and recoil characterize his thought and give his genealogies an import that goes considerably beyond the specific claims that he makes. The question of ethics unfolds as his own values lose their power to provide axiomatic certainty or to play a constructive role in the formation of a new kind of ethical subject. By treating the question of ethics in relation to Foucault I am thus able to carry the Nietzschean theme to our contemporary world. For us the question of ethics is Nietzsche's question, and Foucault is one of his most apparent heirs.

But neither Nietzsche nor Foucault embodies the problem of the question of ethics with the disciplined power or the revealing ambiguity that we find in Heidegger's thought. I say *ambiguity* with care. I mean that in Heidegger we will find the question of ethics functioning with exceptional force—so forcefully that many commentators have confused his early work with nihilism or a stance that is indifferent to ethics. They fail to see that Heidegger is working from within the values and thought that he puts in question and that he recognizes that the question arises from within the values and thoughts, not from outside them or by virtue of the originality of his own thought. But we shall also find that one of the major formations in Western ethical thought and practice, which Nietzsche described under the name of the *ascetic ideal,* functions unquestionably in Heidegger's thought and leads him to weaken considerably the question of ethics. He reinscribes a quasi-ethical piety within 'the rule of being'—hence, the ambiguity.

The fifth chapter, "These Violent Passions: The Rector's Address," provides a major focus for the book. After showing how the question of ethics is developed and moves in the thought of *Being and Time* and "On the Essence of Truth," I turn to Heidegger's Rector's address of 1933. Like the chapter in which I discuss it, it is short. But it poses a bevy of problems. In the first place, it is an ethical work in which Heidegger's values, commitments, and passions override the question of ethics that he had developed with such care. In the second place, his commitments place him in companionship with National Socialism, although in the address he avoids racist language and argues for the university's independence of state authority. The early version that I read in 1959 ends nonetheless with "Heil Hitler," and Heidegger's admiration for Hitler is as unmistakable as it is badly informed, naive, and chilling. He violates in the address many of the values that I most likely share with you, the reader: He is dismally authoritarian and offers no quarter in his opposition to academic freedom; he is opposed to democracy as a form of government; he wants to mold the university by one overriding interpretation of the history of philosophy; he values institutional control more than free exploration; and his Germanophilia is virtually boundless in spite of a strong critique of German culture. It is an address that intensifies ethical opposition and argument and addresses the question of ethics only by antiphrasis.

In the third place, reading the address now brings to a head our revulsion in the face of National Socialism and makes difficult our reading it as a serious work of thought. Some of the work now coming out on Heidegger and political issues either largely ignores his thought in the pursuit of biographical information or treats the topic of Heidegger's politics with such limited knowledge of his thought as to place in jeopardy the value of the work. My intention, in the context of this book, is to show how the question of ethics functions or fails to function in certain parts of his thought. I intend to show that when the question of ethics governs a discourse, certain types of suppression and pain can be perceived with a depth and range that is not possible in ethical thought. These are issues that find their expression in the way in which thoughts are formed and words are used. Since they are issues of thinking and language, my effort is to follow the language and thought, to think them through, and to develop the question of ethics that arises from a major aspect of our tradition, an aspect that had the effect of overturning the tradition that has raised that question. Our first obligation is thus to be clear on what happens in the Rector's address, and our second is to understand the address in relation to the question of ethics. I believe that Foucault is right when he says that fascism expresses a basic tendency in the formation of Western subjectivity and power, that Western ethics and fascism are far more closely aligned than we want to believe. And I believe that Heidegger is right in saying that the question of the subject is one that we do not yet know how to address fully and critically. To find out how ethics and the ethical subject fall into question is to find as well how fascism falls into question in a fundamental way. Hence, to examine the ethical stance of the address is, in the context of this book, part of the process of questioning the fascism of German National Socialism as well as that of many of its critics. *The* question for us in the process is how to raise the question of ethics without reinscribing—as Heidegger does in the address—the totalizing thought that the question suspends.

National Socialism, world hunger, destruction of the environment—these and other horrors press upon us and drive us to find the values that will address and defeat the major dangers and causes of suffering. This book, however, is based on the hypothesis that one must suspend consideration of the practical application of an ethical position if one is to be able to follow that position in its most characteristic movements, which are occasioned by the conflicts that invest and structure its values. I have adopted this hypothesis because the perceived application or 'ethical relevance' of an option will have as a dimension of its structure the values that the given option puts in question. We can easily be fascists, for example, in the manner we apply or extend nonfascist values. If one applies an option to everyday life in order to see what it 'means' without putting in question the values and histories that constitute the application and its motivation, the practical move of application is vulnerable to all manner of countervalues that constitute it. If, for example, one wants to find out what Nietzsche's account of the ascetic ideal means in our lives in order to judge its ethical merit, one foreshortens Nietzsche's critique of the Western desire for meaning and the inevitably ascetic structure of Western judgment. Then there is virtually no chance that one can appreciate the full range and import of Nietzsche's account. Our strategy is to suspend the practical move, to put it in question throughout this discourse, in order to see whether that very practical movement may be characterized by problems that compound suffering and tragedy. Our normal esteem for commitment and passionate concern may well be among those attitudes that produce values opposite to the values that we intend to cultivate.

I am taking *ethics* to mean the body of values by which a culture understands and interprets itself with regard to what is good and bad. In this usage, *ethics* is not sharply distinguished from *morals,* since it refers to a group of principles for both conduct and value judgment. I have used *ethics* in order to emphasize the operation of these principles in knowledge and theory as well as in nontheoretical conduct. Assent to 'right' principles and interpretations of these principles are not, I believe, finally separable. Their function within a given ethos will ordinarily be operative in evaluations of them within the ethos. Rather than separating thought from the elements in a people's character that determine their feelings of right and wrong, I assume in my use of *ethics* that thought is one kind of conduct that is formed by and subject to the values that determine both the ideals and the operative character of people in a given ethos. The 'question of ethics' indicates an interruption in an ethos, an interruption in which the definitive values that govern thought and everyday action lose their power and authority to provide immediate certainty in their functions. They continue to function in a person's life and thought, but they become optional rather than axiomatic to the extent that they are in question.

To say that ethics is in question is also to say that the complex structures of thought and action that fall under the category of ethics comes to be questionable. Ethics, as the body of values by which a culture understands and interprets itself with regard to what is good and bad, is interrupted. We shall find in those discourses in which the question of ethics takes place that the status of moral judgment, the axiomatic quality of given values, and the polarity of good and bad are also in question. The guiding suspicion is that the self-determination of our culture makes inevitable the suffering and destruction to which it is insensitive not only by virtue of its specific values, but also by virtue of the manner of self-determination that we broadly call ethics. The issue is obscure because we are thoroughly a part of the process and structures of values that fall into question. If it is the case, for example, that the 'other' in its simple occurrence is unthinkable in our heritage, or if some of our characteristic satisfactions that occur under the influence of the ascetic ideal include or make inevitable certain kinds of suffering, the obscurity that accompanies the interruption of ethics will also affect the *medium* in which we must think if we are to consider the question of ethics. When obscurity replaces clarity of valuational judgment, we can expect anxiety. We shall ask whether an intensification of this kind of anxiety allows disclosure of aspects of our shared lives that are made obscure by the very clarity that characterizes ethical commitment and thought.

This study emphasizes the complexity of elements and their conflicts within the values that we often take to be clear and simple. Nietzsche's account of the ascetic ideal will give us one focus for this emphasis. Foucault's study of the ethical subject gives another. Heidegger's account of propriety and authenticity, a third. The issue is not only one of ambiguity. It is one of genealogy and heritage, of the multiple factors that form a value complex, its identity and powers. Values carry with them their formative processes. Undertows accompany their forward movements, and conflicts often define the harmony that they offer. The ascetic ideal, for example, embodies both life-affirmation and life-denial. The ethical subject embodies both autonomy and subjection. Authenticity embodies both self-realization and self-deconstruction. No identity defines a value structure in its range and complexity. The question of ethics indicates this complexity, the insufficiency of the idea of identity in relation to values, and the importance of keeping to the fore the counterforces that constitute the processes whereby we seek both clarity of judgment and consistency in action.

One purpose of this book is to show how and why our dominant manners of evaluation have fallen into question. Since the question of ethics is a question of knowing and thinking as well as of choosing and everyday action, our subject matter concerns the ways by which we customarily establish bodies of knowledge and patterns of reflections, our ways of producing and maintaining certainty, and our styles of good sense. The writers who shall receive our attention—Nietzsche, Foucault, and Heidegger—all devote their primary attention to the Western philosophical canon. Their own movements of thought are derived from the ideas and logics that constitute, whether consciously or unconsciously, the mainstream of our philosophical heritage. Their originality is found in their turning these concepts and logics on themselves, a turning that we shall generally call *self-overcoming recoil,* and in their elaborating by means of the turning ways of thinking that their heritage makes possible, but which are tradition-ally avoided, resisted, or suppressed. They all find the possibility for their own thought in their philosophical heritage and take their departures from the suppression or avoidance that traditionally accompanies it.

I shall have less to say about the canon than about these departures from it and within it. My intention is to follow the ways in which our primary sense of rightness is transformed in the discourses of Nietzsche, Foucault, and Heidegger and to make this transformation the moving thought of the book. The self-overcoming recoil in these readings of our tradition defines also the movement of my own discourse regarding them. The question of ethical thinking takes place in this process. It is a process that maintains the question rather than the values that have governed our traditional senses of rightness. In this process the violence and oppressive anxieties that are constitutive of the values by which we have organized our thought and lives become apparent. As ethical thinking recoils with the oppositions and resistances that constitute it, different ways of thinking emerge and different thoughts develop in which our ethical, pathogenic violence and anxiety are more difficult to overlook. The anxiety that accom-panies the transformation of thinking confronts the suppressive anxiety in our ethical heritage that has resisted transformation. The consequent lightness of mind that develops in the discourse that we shall consider, while giving less customary satisfaction, produces questions, criticism, and uncertainty in those regions of conviction that harbor those inevitabilities of suffering that are closely connected to the ways we go about maximizing our well-being. The continual deferral of ethical certainty allows a decompo-sition to take place in the aggregates of value and sensibility that are opposed to a self-overcoming genealogical investigation of the heritage.

Questioning is privileged in this study in order to contaminate the 'neu-trality' that traditionally provides the mood and presumption of skeptical enquiry. Ordinarily a philosopher questions because he or she doubts or wants to cultivate doubt regarding certain beliefs and practices. One wants to maximize a distance regarding what is questioned. One adopts a question-ing stance before a claim, belief, or practice and finds enough freedom in the stance to consider alternatives to, or to find weaknesses in, the given claim. This traditional neutrality of investigation, however, is invested with the values associated with breaking the power that the claim exercises and with finding alternative and better claims. This stance is itself contami-nated with nonneutral elements, such as powerful epistemological assump-tions regarding perception and mental synthesis, desires for autonomy and truth, and those values that direct one to attractive alternatives and goals. Neutrality traditionally produces truths and standards for conduct that are not subject, within their discourse, to the questioning that produced them. They compose a nonneutral position.

Question, as I use the word, does not suggest neutrality or skepticism, but the thorough enmeshment of opposing values in the lineage of ethics within which both the question and what is questioned take place. A way of life, for example, makes problems for itself as it attempts to establish its ideals because of opposition to the ideals that is in its own makeup. Our attempts to evaluate and establish a hierarchy of values include forces that run counter to such an effort, forces that put evaluating and hierarchizing in question in the midst of the evaluating process. That does not make evaluation wrong or bad, but it functions as a caution to evaluative processes, suggests limits to the processes, and puts them as a whole in question. One is oneself in question as one questions and makes judgments. When Nietzsche finds, for example, that his work of transvaluing values is constituted by the values that he attacks, he can find no haven in neutrality or authority that will establish the value of his claims beyond question. He finds that his being is in question. When Foucault discovers that the objectivity of his genealogy is within the lineage of disciplines that he finds to be passing away, he finds that his knowledge of their passing away is in question. When Heidegger comes to think nonessence and counteressence *in* essence, his own thought falls necessarily in question. In such instances, an ethos—a way of communal living, and not only the individual's way of life—is also put in question by the countervalences that constitute it and make possible Heidegger's judgment and thought regarding it. The questioning stance is put in question by the stretch of question's privilege. It is a privilege that opens to the question of being as well as to the question of an ethos's standards of good and bad. Hence, the subject of the book has to do as much with the questionableness of putting ethics in question as with the questionableness of ethics. The question of ethics does not lead to a new ethics.

In the question of ethics, the emphasis falls on a continuing process of thinking that diagnoses, criticizes, clarifies by means of questions, destructures the components of meaning and power that silently shape our lives together, and also questions the values and concepts that have rule-governing and axiomatic power in our culture. The emphasis does not fall on the possible complete systematic accounts that prescribe definitive solutions to problems, 'right' structures of value, originary or utopian visions of preferred types of personal identity. Thinking and writing, rather, take place in the questionableness and the problems that arise in the constellations of belief, knowledge, and evaluation that constitute us and set the parameters for what we may legitimately desire and the manners in which we normally relate to people and things. The question of ethics does not arise outside of ethics, but from within it. Its thought is disciplined by efforts to maintain questionableness, by learning how to ask questions in given settings, and by finding its own heritage and its problems. Learning to name things anew, to become alert to exclusions and to forgotten aspects in a people's history, to overhear what is usually drowned out by the predominant values, to rethink what is ordinarily taken for granted, to find out how to hold itself in question: these are aspects of the thought of the question of ethics. There is a subversiveness in such processes vis-à-vis the normal and ordinary, a subversiveness not unlike that of poets and philosophers who are routinely excluded or silenced by totalitarian regimes. But subversiveness is neither a goal nor an ideal for the question of ethics. Its goal is to rethink, rework, rewrite, to listen again to the cultural inevitabilities that make us who we are and to affirm the transformative process without sense of origin or teleology. That subversion of ordinary rightness, be it a totalitarian state or a democracy, is a regular consequence of the question of ethics and is one of its miseries in the midst of our normal obsessions for rightness, universality, and security beyond the level that human temporality can provide.

What is questioned is not abandoned. Questioning, as I use the word, is not a matter of indifference and ignorance, but a way of relating to something that holds its fascination or importance while it loses a measure of its authority. What is in question returns in the question, returns without elevation and without the power to produce heroes, returns without being a totality that is protected against the exposure of its limits and the fittingness of its mortality. I am speaking of a disturbed return, one fraught with worry, a sense of danger, ambiguity, and, as we shall see, mourning. When the questioned returns, still in question, no text is *the* text, no tradition is *the* tradition. A body of writing accompanies the questioning return that moves within and away from what is in question. Here, a recoiling movement undercuts the questioning text as well as the questioned one. The difference of this movement from that of self-establishing thought gives rise to the question of ethics without reversion to an ethics of the question.

The present essay also arises from a body of ethical passions that include anxiety in the face of the possibility that 'right' and 'good' are human conveniences. It takes its departure from a desire to give focus to a history of suffering that has had a force of destiny, but one that now appears to have lost enough of its force to allow it to be questioned. I am aware that I want to avoid this destiny and to inscribe within it an alternative. But the alternative that I shall develop moves away from the ethical interest that motivated the search for an alternative. Does this search for an alternative remain the book's desire and goal? Does it return to an ethical identity that promises a new manner of constituting the self? Does it suggest a new spirituality that places spirit beyond question? Or does it allow an 'other' to traditional ethics to come forward, whereby the destructive dimension of ethics is apparent and the 'other', although without name, tempts thought beyond what it can now think? Does it recoil beyond what is questioned? Or does it give ethics a new commencement?

The American appropriation of Continental thought is sometimes characterized by a pragmatic and almost casual use of one or another of the major twentieth-century European philosophers. Such use is frequently made in a context that is foreign to the heritage of the appropriated thought. That can be an acceptable thing to do—unless such use is assumed to interpret what takes place in Continental thought and is taken to be what these philosophers do in their own context. One major issue in Continental thought, and an emphasis in this book, addresses the intimacy of language and thought. The appropriation is superficial and destructive, for example, if Heidegger is read, not in the movement of his own language and thought, but in the context of a Deweyean liberalism and optimism. Similar displacement takes place when Foucault is read in a context of subjectivity and ethical relativism, or if Nietzsche is read in a context of ethical relativism and propositional analysis. In such displacements, the thought of these Continental thinkers is made to appear exotic or oblique to a set of problems that they are not designed to address. The structure and history of those kinds of reading are, in fact, put in question and lose the basis of their appeal in Heidegger's, Foucault's, and Nietzsche's thought. If one wishes to follow their thought, one must get inside it, allow it to mold the questions and approaches, and to hear its moods as the moods take place. I have thus followed the question of ethics as it develops and unfolds in specific texts by Nietzsche, Foucault, and Heidegger. My purpose is to allow the question of ethics to have a full impact on my discussion of it, to undergo its movement, to heed the thought and language in which it arises as well as the thought and language that it helps to form. Once one has gone through this discipline, one may wish to think in a different discipline— not to say *askésis*—to hear and read differently and without the question of ethics. But one will know that for the question to arise and intensify, one must think within the tradition that yields it, because the question of ethics arises from within a certain constellation of values and thought, and does not constitute a quasi-neutral reflection on ethics.

The primary conflict that gives rise to the question of ethics concerns the relation among the differences of value within the given heritage. Do these differences compose many different constellations that form larger dynamic and unstable confederations of meaning and practice? Or are they parts of a unifying, self-realizing reality, something that pervades the gaps among the differences and provides a life fundamental to all differences, one that is unthreatened by the unstable confederations? The question of ethics takes place as the thought and meaning of transcendent presence weakens in the tradition of Western metaphysical thought and as the specific interests and intentions that compose the thought of transcendent presence are exposed in a way of thinking that is not under their control. The differences among values appear from hence in their fragmented juxtapositions, 'other' appears without transcendent connections, and the imposition of transcendental presence appears to be an option that has produced specific kinds of problems that might now be avoidable. One of the questions of this book is whether under these changed circumstances a way of hearing and thinking emerges that, while not prescriptive, is alert to the dangers embodied in our traditionally axiomatic values and forms of valuation.

The question of ethics arises as the following idea loses its discursive power: Although all finite things in their orders are fragile, never absolute, and mortal, and although language and thought in their finitude can never grasp or comprehend anything absolute, we can nonetheless be reasonably certain that there is a positive connection between finite orders and something ultimate, whole, and capable of bestowing meaning. As this thought comes into question, the utter finiteness of all orders seems reasonable. The divisions within unities that define their finiteness become cues for a sense of mere absence without the primacy of either being or life. All values that have in their history the ideas of ultimate order and the ontological privilege of meaning are experienced as questionable. Thought that has been formed in this heritage is equally questionable. Yet we live by the values and thought that are also questionable. How are we to live in their questionableness? How are we to organize ourselves with the sense that organizations mean no more than their specific values? What is the difference between affirmation with a sense of ultimate meaning and affirmation with the sense of the mortality of meaning as such?

In the final chapter I show that Heidegger succumbed to the temptation of letting the question of being turn toward a piety of thought. That move on Heidegger's part may derive from his awe over the range and disclosure of thinking. But there is so much that thought cannot do: it cannot replace or adequately imitate nonthinking life, that is, most of life. And yet philosophical thought is able to recoil, create, adjust, intensify, die away, and to know itself in these and its many other ways of being. The philosopher's privilege is rare. He or she can doubly reflect, can undergo the life of mind, and, in addition, can reflect in and on that process. The privilege's danger is found in philosophical thinking's otherness and difference vis-à-vis everything that it is not. The more it intensifies, the stranger it becomes, the more alive it seems to itself, the greater becomes the likelihood that philosophical thought will look for itself and find itself everywhere, and the greater the difficulty becomes of returning to other-than-thought and finding the elimination of thought. How is thought to allow—to think—this elimination whereby it is put so radically in question? Perhaps a way of thinking will do that takes its measure from what it cannot think. One may let the boundary of thinking come to bear in a thinking activity. We may interrupt thought in its very process or strategically violate the movements that have become normal for it by desystematizing or destabilizing the systematic and stabilizing activities as that activity goes on. Or one may skillfully undercut signification and meaning in the process of signifying and meaningful expression. Lacan, for example, thinks through the breakdown in signification as signification happens, and Derrida writes an unthinkable and inarticulatable difference to literalization.

I do not wish to underestimate these and other recent accomplishments of thought. In them thought has achieved originality and set in motion a way of thinking that has made this book possible. But in their accomplishment, I also find a certain insistence—even obsession—with thought and language that may give us pause. The volubility of our thinking, our cultivation of strategies and styles, the subtlety of interruption and, in the case of this book, the discipline of the question—these are all indications of thought recoiling back to itself and returning to itself as it finds its other. If what I say in this study is accurate, the other to thought takes place as thinking takes place. Its boundary is not at the end of a process but is everywhere in the process, and our opportunity is to think—allow? express? themetize? articulate? write?—the boundary as it takes place when we move in the continuity of our thought. Then in allowing the boundary, the truth of thinking will be found in a way of thinking that is other than thinking the accuracy of its claims.

And yet, the disclosure of other, in relation to which I will use the metaphors of space, horizon, and dying, occurs in and through thinking, and the mere otherness of no thought will be tinctured by thinking as though thinking could go on and on, always bothered and interrupted, always outside of the possibility and immanence of self-realization, but *always* nonetheless. Perhaps thought is infinite in always being bothered and in question. The upsurge of thinking appears to protect this *always* in the obsessions of writing, reading, thinking, and questioning. If I had chosen not to introduce this book so as not to indicate a completed thing with a beginning and an end, or if I had chosen to deconstruct this book by way of an introduction that refused to be a beginning, I would be no less captured by thinking. And if I succeed in giving priority to question in the way this work unfolds, that priority will include the question of thinking and will unsettle the sameness of thinking that persists through questioning. I will not have escaped the sameness of thinking by means of its interruption. I might defer this sameness, not by finding its mysterious upsurge, which seems to enshrine the sameness of thought, but by allowing the play of other-to-thought in thought. The avoidance of piety-with-mystery is then given words and movement and *thought; other* in its disclosure is interrupted by *thinking* and given a certain thoughtful expression in the style and movement of the book. And once again the unthinkable is covered over by thought. That covering over is itself an ethical 'problem'.

At the core of ethics is the question of affirmation. Heidegger and Derrida, in their different ways, think of affirmation as an 'it gives' that comes with thought and language, but remains uncapturable, that remains thought's given unthought and unspeakable. Foucault thinks of affirmation as beyond positivity and hence beyond the grasp of genealogy and knowing disciplines. Nietzsche thinks of it as joy outside of reason and the circumference of meaning. I am less certain of the priority of affirmation, even when, as in the case of these writers, affirmation is never conceived as an unambiguous bestowal or as something like self-positing. Perhaps Levinas's language of other-beyond-affirmation is closer to the point in spite of his reversion to a piety of troubled apology and prayer. Perhaps the issue is one of thought's depth and range, its nearly overwhelming power and beauty within its own territory, its impulse to release things for thought, even its trickery which is part of its *poiesis*. Perhaps thought can hardly doubt its own act and disclosure, the affirmation that yields it and that it yields as things come to thought and are there, inexplicably, to be thought. Perhaps affirmation is neither the first nor the last word, but is part of thought's compulsion to be . . . thought. And perhaps there is other-to-thought without affirmation or denial, and in its absencelike nonpresence we conspire to free thought to the closure of thought's own revelation as though we were always on the verge of affirmation.

What then? *Then* affirmation is not sufficient to put thought in question. Everything might be in question except thought's affirmation, and thought's affirmation leads to an ethics—a piety of thought—in which thought is privileged even in its difference to the systematic structures of expression and grammar. Then neither disclosure nor self-realization is the issue. Thought, rather, finds itself in its interruption without affirmation, without essence or counteressence. And if I am right, that is the point at which its obsession with being begins again, as though eternally again, and one thinks again of being, searches for affirmation in the interruption, and looks for another grouping of concepts or a new art to affirm the affirmation that must be there.

No affirmation. Obsession with being. And yet another turn to ethics?

TWO

▬

The Question Turns on Ethics

*Self-Overcoming in Nietzsche's Genealogy
of the Ascetic Ideal*

The movements of self-overcoming that are found in Nietzsche's genealogy of the ascetic ideal are definitive both of the complex heritage of the ascetic ideal and of Nietzsche's account of this heritage. One of the differences between the ascetic ideal's heritage and Nietzsche's genealogy is that, in the latter, self-overcoming is recognized and accepted as the life of the discourse. By his affirmation of the "necessity of self-overcoming" [*On the Genealogy of Morals,* III.27] Nietzsche finds that the values by which his own discourse is structured, as well as those of our traditional morals and ethics, are in question. Although many of his values—the valences or powers that provide structure and the economy of placement in his thought—are not avoidable for him, their authority is limited to their heritage, and their endurance is defined by their self-overcoming movement, a movement that is not identified with them and one that they do not control. The concept of self-overcoming names for Nietzsche the movement in Western morality whereby one constellation of values is transformed into another by means of forces within the first constellation. The term *self-overcoming* names this movement. Yet the movement of self-overcoming also characterizes Nietzsche's own discourse. I will focus on that movement in his thought.

Since the concept of transcendence is already in question in the tradition that it dominates and since Nietzsche affirms its doubtfulness and the "maliciousness of its fiction," self-overcoming is not, in Nietzsche's thought, within that concept's domain. Self-overcoming does not function like a veiled concept of transcendence. Indeed, if Nietzsche's thought is successful on its own terms, it will die out in ways of living and thinking for which it has helped to prepare, and the power of self-overcoming will itself fade and pass away.

In this discursive situation, what becomes of one's relation to one's definitive values? How is one to think and live with the *question* of values and evaluation, especially since in this genealogically produced knowledge groups of countervalues, differing structures of evaluation, and the questionableness of each grouping of values and judgments are all inherited in our ability to think and act as we do? We shall approach these questions in the context of Nietzsche's way of 'discovering' the functions of the ascetic ideal in his genealogical account of that ideal and his way of holding the ascetic ideal in question by his recognition of it in his own thought.

Self-overcoming in Nietzsche's thought is seen most characteristically in movements of recoil. I shall discuss below the multiple forms this recoil takes. In order to follow and engage Nietzsche's thought—to 'understand' it *in* our reading and thinking—we must undergo these recoils as we work through his discourse. Nietzsche's thought has this in common with Hegel's: The thinking to be followed is in the movement of the given language; it is not in ideas or concepts that can be lifted from their discourse and kept whole to be viewed in a considerably different discourse. Their thought takes place in the movements of their language, and they are not engageable in isolation from the hierarchies, rules, meanings, and styles that function in the structure and movement of their words. If we separate their claims from the way their language moves and takes its form, Nietzsche's and Hegel's thought is lost to the abstraction of a stance or perspective that has its own movement and body of values which differ from theirs. If, for example, Nietzsche's *idea* of self-overcoming is considered in a way of thinking that strongly resists self-overcoming and moves regularly toward its own establishment and reestablishment, self-overcoming will not be thought. An abstract self-overcoming may be considered, but that is different from thinking in self-overcoming movement.

To think in this way is difficult because our dominant structures of language encourage the posture of standing outside of the text, in an interpretive position that is actually quite different from the text, and understanding it from this quasi-transcendent perspective. Such a perspective protects itself from the process of self-overcoming by its seemingly neutral distance. It is *quasi*-transcendent in the sense that the thought stands outside of the process in the text that is to be thought and yet seems to ground or give connective meaning to the text's rendering. As we shall see, this traditional interpretive position is closely related to the ascetic ideal and the experience of transcendence that is affiliated with it. But this transcendence of the interpretive spectator is *quasi* because it does not provide grounds for the text or a condition for the text's possibility. Rather, as we shall see, the spectator-stance adds a complicating distance to the text, a distance that provides the conditions for overcoming the interpretation and its stance.

In this discussion my own position will often be one of quasi-transcendence and will fall repeatedly into question. In the shift from the interpreter's traditional quasi-transcendence—which I suspect is now an inevitable stance for reflective engagements with our tradition—to a movement of questioning and suspicion in which the quasi-transcendent position moves away from itself in its relation to Nietzsche's writing, a way of thinking without grounds or transcendence will develop. This self-over-coming way of thinking is the subject of this chapter. In other chapters we shall follow several other types of self-overcoming thought, but in each the question of ethics leads us to the question of how valuing and thinking are to proceed. How we proceed is thus always an issue for the content of the given section or chapter.

We shall find that in Nietzsche's thought recoiling, self-overcoming movements remove the discursive, organizing force of the ideal of tran-scendence. In this process of renewal, the ascetic ideal appears clearly and its persuasive power is shaken. But the ascetic ideal in Nietzsche's discourse also has a polluting effect in that the ascetic ideal plays a constitu-tive part. I emphasize the part that the ascetic ideal plays in Nietzsche's account of it: It is recognized as a pollutant in our traditional desire to live; it embodies a desire to overcome pollution; and it is characterized by an unconscious movement of self-overcoming that puts in question, and in that sense pollutes, its own positive role in Nietzsche's genealogy. So Nietzsche's stance of interpretation vis-à-vis the ascetic ideal is shaken by the self-overcoming of the ascetic ideal in that stance. We shall have to pay attention to the heritage of *that* shaking in our reading of Nietzsche in order to appreciate how ethics comes into question in his thought.

1. The Functions of Recoil

Recoiling movements in Nietzsche's thought constitute a way of thinking that does not authoritatively reestablish itself or look to a completion of itself in the ways it moves and develops. There are four senses of *recoil* that may be taken to elaborate the notion of self-overcoming: rebound, falling back under the impact of a force, quail or wince, and coiling again.

Recoil in the sense of rebound. Rebounding is a movement of springing back in response to a release of pressure. This movement is evident, for example, in the rebounding effect of subordinated or suppressed values that are released from traditional and opposing pressures in such contexts as Judeo-Christian morality, nationalism, and Platonic and Aristotelian met-aphysics. When suppressed valences rebound in the absence of traditional opposition, they form multiple foci of organizing powers for thought and action. The power of the ascetic ideal is dispersed in its genealogical ac-count, for example, by the powers of what Nietzsche calls "affirmative" uncovering and making public and by the powers of sensuality, self-interest, appearance, and mortality. This kind of rebounding recoil, in dispersing the powers of traditional philosophical ways of thinking, has a destructive effect on the central organizing force of such ideas as linear time, the choosing subject, and essential unity. It has a similar effect on the affiliation of 'unity' with 'reality', on the positive value of the idea of wholeness, and on the explanatory value of the Kantian conception of subjectivity. The positive effect of rebounding recoil is found in the release wherein multiple forces of making, freeing, and affirming take priority over the traditional ways of establishing truth by the exclusion and suppression exacted by the idea of unity. By attending to this recoiling movement we put in question the tendency to think of Nietzsche as either a metaphysician or an antimetaphysician; that is, the content of his claims and critiques is found to be secondary to the self-overcoming movement of his thought. Rebounding recoil is a significant aspect of the self-overcoming movement of Nietzsche's discourse and is a movement to which all aspects of his thought are subject.

Recoil as falling back under the impact of a force. Many of the ideas and values that have positive functions in Nietzsche's thought fall back under the impact of his genealogical approach to those very ideas and values. In *On the Genealogy of Morals,* for example, his own attempt to remember by his genealogical work and his conscience regarding weakness and fear are clearly a part of the ensemble of values on which this genealogical study has a negative impact. Both his memory and his conscience invoke the traumatic suffering that he accounts as part of their formation. Nietzsche's intention of finding the energy common to all forms of life recoils under the impact of his idea that *all* descriptive claims are interpretations within a specific descent as well as under the impact of his claim that the force of all formations—including the formation of the idea of common force—is beyond meaning and sense. The authority of Nietzsche's constructive ideas falls back, recoils under the impact of the descent and the discursive contingency of those ideas. In this recoiling movement they lose their claims to authority except within their own discursive organization. This retreating recoil is a nonauthorizing movement—in this context, a movement without an author—that pervades Nietzsche's writing. His discursive organization as a whole, as a limited organic unity, is characterized by the movement of self-overcoming. There is the falling back from the authority of Nietzsche's organizing ideas and values, and there is the self-overcoming of the discourse as a whole under the impact of the force of dispersion which undermines the authority of the given discursive unity. His genealogies are thus forces under whose impact his own leading ideas fall back from the authoritative position that Nietzsche at times gives them.

Recoil in the sense of quail and wince. Nietzsche's writing recoils before the foolishness of many of the values that have an extremely serious impact in his tradition of thought. Redemption, self-giving love idolized under the name of *agape,* seriousness of mind, honest truth, scholarly objectivity, passionate commitment to God, philanthropic concerns: Nietzsche's discourse repeatedly winces before such values as their internal motivational structure and historical formations come to light. Knowing himself to be under their effects, Nietzsche is driven like Zarathustra by the force of his wincing recoil to parody and ironize them and himself, not in the hope of eliminating them entirely—he, too, is human, all too human—but with the intention of putting into effect a disgust, a quailing, before their refusal of their own secret interests and before their pious blindness. Zarathustra's nausea and self-sickening are not incidental parts of Nietzsche's writing; they are, in part, physical appropriations of wincing recoil. This movement has moment particularly for us who might read Nietzsche without parodying and ironizing him and ourselves, too, in the reading process. To take him with a heavy spirit of seriousness is a violation of the discourse's wincing recoil. If we are unable to mock our own mocking of him, we are unable to follow one of the recoiling strands of his writing and thought.

Recoil as coiling again. We can think of this movement in relation to the ideas of eternal return and will to power. On the one hand, the idea of eternal return involves a series of claims about the meaninglessness of time and the trajectory of will to power. On the other hand, eternal return, which Nietzsche calls "the great cultivating idea," involves *in its conception* a coiling again of traditional ideas, a recollecting and gathering of inherited forces, a type of torsion among them that can release a torrent of nontraditional effects, such as new directions of action, collections of newly formed or reformed presuppositions, different organizations of values and thoughts, and, possibly, beings that are different from traditional humanity and from us who are constrained to think in terms of the complicated metaphors and grammar that collect around 'being', 'thought', and 'time'. On the simplest level the claim of eternal return is that all things repeat themselves in an endless circular movement. But we must ask ourselves how this claim *functions* in Nietzsche's writing. We find a double recoiling action. There is the avowed eternal recoiling again of each event, springing forward again, expending itself, burning out, and slowly coiling again in an unthinkable return of life force to the event's constellation; then there is the coiling again in the constitution of the claim itself of the ideas of eternity and return, of the early Greek image of time, a coiling against the conflict of meaning and meaninglessness, of the peculiar Western anxiety over death and loss, of the twin anxieties over keeping and releasing, and of all the other bits of thought and sense that compose the idea of eternal return. These composing elements are coiled again in Nietzsche's metaphor, but this recoiling movement changes the patterns of force in which all the elements have been combined in their inherited associations, and the idea of eternal return releases these elements to meanings and senses they do not have in their other metaphysical formations. In the second sense of coiling again, the ideas that have led to and made possible the idea of eternal return are themselves released from the ideologies and passions that have held them and now lead to thoughts and passions that depart from and contradict the earlier authoritative structures. In this movement, eternal return also puts in question its own authority as a definitive

concept or meaning and sets in motion a self-overcoming movement within
Nietzsche's thought. This recoiling movement veers from a static maintenance of the thoughts that compose it.

The movement of coiling again in the idea of eternal return, if it is
itself a movement of recoils, is not a familiar one in our philosophical
heritage. These recoiling movements, as we find them in Nietzsche's writing, are not governed by the ideas of same, identity, or self, and the *again*
does not suggest in this context the repetition of some fundamental sameness, such as being, spirit, subjectivity, or energy with a self-realizing telos.
This recoil, rather, promises a 'beyond' that verges on the horizon of
our thought, on an *über*. This horizon does not verge on our dominant
traditions but on the movements by which those traditions decompose.
This recoiling suggested by eternal return is part of the self-overcoming
in Nietzsche's discourse. Thus in *On the Genealogy of Morals,* we find
a coiling again of the ascetic ideal. On the one hand, it is the object
of severe genealogical critique. On the other hand, it plays a major role
in the genealogical critique, and the essay coils again in the power of
the ascetic ideal, now that the ascetic ideal in Nietzsche's discourse knows
its lineage and amoral power. In this movement there is both coiling again
and a springing rebound that pushes the discourse to the edge of its ability
to speak and propels it beyond itself in a self-overcoming movement that
cannot know its future or its effects. I find this the most forceful recoil
in *On the Genealogy of Morals:* it propels itself beyond itself in its genealogical knowledge of its own ascetic ideal.

2. Nietzsche's Self-Overcoming Is the Middle Voice of Metaphysics

I shall emphasize the middle voice because the *movement* of self-overcoming and its recoils, which take place in Nietzsche's thought, cannot
be thought well in the active and passive voices. In the active voice self-
overcoming appears to be a kind of force that is to be understood by
its effects, by what it does. It seems to be vaguely nihilistic in this voice,
which is the primary voice of our philosophical tradition, because it does
not have a telos or a self-realizing nature; it is something like a chaotic
subject. In the passive voice, self-overcoming is an object of thought that
can be grasped by a movement other than its own. It is something to
be defined, broken apart, put back together again, and understood. Each
voice has its own rights and powers, but without the middle voice we
will not be able to speak and think in the movement of self-overcoming,
which is the movement of Nietzsche's thought.

The dominance of the active and passive voices makes inevitable the
priority of the spectator-subject for philosophical thought, whereas the

middle voice yields a different way of thinking that is marked by undergoing a movement rather than by either active assertion or passive reception.

A. THE MIDDLE VOICE

The middle voice has lost a significant part of its meaning, its semantic significance, in Western languages. It survives in a limited way primarily in the reflexive function. In early Sanskrit, where its still earlier use in Indo-European and Indo-Iranian is traced, the middle voice speaks in the sphere of the subject. On the one hand, it may be reflexive, and on the other, it may speak nonreflexively of an action in the action. For example, in a ritual the active voice for 'cleanse' or 'purify' may be used: "Whatever of you the impure have polluted, that do I cleanse for you."[1] In the middle voice its sense might be rendered: "Whatsoever the impure has polluted, as to that for you through this let them become pure." In the middle voice, the impure's becoming pure is expressed entirely in the verb form. Or, in the passive voice, we say, "Let us be purified." In the middle voice, we say, "Let us become pure." In the latter instance we are of the action that reverts to itself. It is a purifying action that makes pure. In the active voice the verb is for another. In the passive voice the verb acts on the subject. The middle voice is used when the subject is in some way specifically implicated in the result of the action but is neither the active subject nor the passive object of the action. *Pacati* in the active voice of Sanskrit means '(the cook) cooks (something) for another'. *Pacate* in the middle voice means '(the cook) cooks for himself'. In the case of the intransitive verb, the active of *drmhati,* for example, means 'to make (something) firm'. The intransitive middle *drmhate* means '(something) becomes firm' or, we might say, 'firming comes of its own action'.[2] The middle voice of the verb 'to die'—*mriyate*—we translate as 'dying occurs (of itself)'. We translate *ayate* 'to be born' as 'birthing occurs (of itself)'.[3] This middle-voiced intransitivity is also found in the Greek middle perfect form, *phainesthai,* meaning 'to appear appearing or appearing appears', and *gegonesthai,* 'to become becoming' or 'to come becoming'. In both instances the activity of the middle-voiced perfect expresses its temporal movement out of itself.

I note particularly the intransitive uses of the middle voice, because that is one form of the middle voice that is difficult to retrieve in our languages now, but one that plays a significant role in contemporary efforts to think outside of the domain of subjectivity.[4] The reflexive form by which we now retain the middle-voice function is not entirely appropriate in the instances I have cited. We need to bracket the implication 'of itself' when we say that becoming becomes, for example, because there is no distance of self-relation or self-objectification. There is neither an active subject nor a passive object, and the peculiarity of that structure for our grammar is lost by the reflexive form. We are inclined by our structures of expression to speak of an action's doing something in relation to itself and thereby to indicate an incipient subject-relation in the verb's action. We are inclined to say appearing shows itself or becoming itself becomes. In that way we intuitively put into the whole occurrence a positing formation, whereas the middle voice in these instances can indicate a whole occurrence's occurring as a whole without self-positing or reflexive movement throughout the event. The reflexive form indicates the whole event, but shapes that event in an expression by means of a self-relational structure that is often missing in the middle voice. In such cases a nonreflexivity is both carried and covered over by the reflexive suggestion of self-relation. The reflexivity has to be overcome to give voice to this middle form.

The middle voice is also carried and covered over in verbs that have a middle-voice form but an active-voice meaning. The Greek *boulomai,* for example, means 'to wish' or 'to be willing'. It can also mean choice or preference in the sense that one desires to be pleased, in contrast to *ethelo,* which implies consent. What remains of the middle voice can be noted as a state of desiring, a state of preference that issues in active choosing. The 'I will', in the sense of I wish, comes from a dispositional state rather than from active deliberation and judgment. In the case of *gignomai* 'to become', the verb is used of the birth of people and animals, the production of things, and the taking place of events. The middle voice is carried in the sense that the activity of becoming is a state that yields of itself. As we have seen, in its perfect aspect *gegonesthai* indicates a temporal process that yields of itself in its process. When *gignomai* is used with the genitive form of a noun, it means 'to come under the control of' or 'to belong to'; that is, it indicates a state that is under the control or in the possession of something else. It is in a larger situation in which the voice of the controlled thing is lost to itself. In such instances, the sense of being in a middle-voice situation is covered over by a passive-voice meaning. *Oiomai* 'to think' is also a middle form and suggests an activity that speaks in its own sphere and reverts to itself of itself prior to a subject's taking charge of it. Thinking in this case would be an activity that enacts itself out of its own processes. This formation is not at all foreign to Western thought, but whether it can be elaborated adequately by the additional thoughts of subjectivity and presence is a question that will recur for us and one that is important for the larger question of the end of metaphysics.

These middle-voice verbs that retain their middle form but have come to have active and passive meaning often suggest that an event yields the subject that is able to act or to receive an action. In *boulomai,* which means 'I wish out of a state of inclination', for example, something is produced—the I that wants something—from a state in which the produced I is not active. Something takes place that is other than a subject's activity directed toward something else. To think of a state that *of itself* is to be pleased is both an awkward thought for us and a mark of the middle voice.

When a word has several, even countervailing, meanings, the middle voice can give expression to the word's multiple values without indicating a common, harmonizing meaning. The importance of exact signification is not in question here. The active employment of words and literal functions allows for useful naming and predicating. But when a word has in its power several emphases and counterplays of meanings, such that none of its meanings can adequately express the other meanings, the word is then able to bring to expression a variety of registers, tones, experiences, and significatory chains as its play finds full voice. The verb 'to end', for example, means both to limit and to terminate. It suggests arrival at a telos (the end of this project is at hand) or incompleteness (the project came to an untimely end) or the continuing presence of a telos (the end of the project guided its process) or delimitation (the project's possibility ends here). If we think of 'to end' in the middle voice, both the conclusiveness of termination and the nonconclusiveness of delimitation become apparent, both the overtone of death and the overtone of self-realization, the presence of both limited identity and possibility at the limit. The middle voice of 'to end', given the variety of senses in the word, does not allow a conclusion to the question of the end of metaphysics, and this question and nonconclusiveness appear to emerge out of the ending that is in question. Ending does not suddenly happen as a new event, as a final point on a line. It can appear, rather, as a multidimensional voice in the very process of metaphysics. Ending and thinking metaphysically are mutually implied. We shall return to this implication by combining the middle voice of 'to think' and 'to end', a combination that inscribes a process of delimiting that can be adequately elaborated by the reflex of reflection only if the *re* is thought in the middle voice, and only if the flexion is a kind of coiling.

We may also refer to events in their middle voice, to situations that occur with many meanings and deeds and that voice themselves in excess of the actions and meanings that constitute them. These events cannot be understood adequately if the objective meanings that constitute the event are used to objectify the event as a whole. We may take Jean-Pierre Vernant's account of the performance of *Oedipus the King* as an example of an event that is filled with conflict, ambiguity, and transition and that shows the value of the middle voice in giving expression to the occurrence of events in their excess of activity and passivity.

[T]he situation at the beginning [of the play] . . . is that of catastrophe. We call it the plague, but it's not the plague; it's a *loimos,* a calamity, a defilement which has caused life to come to a halt, so that the world of human beings no longer communicates with the divine world. The smoke from sacrifices does not rise to heaven, women either do not give birth or give birth to monsters, the herds do not multiply, the earth is no longer fruitful. The human world is isolated in its foulness.

And the play opens with a *paean,* a joyous song of thanksgiving for some happy event, a joyous song, rapid in tempo. One wonders what a paean is doing here. But we have several clues that there is another sort of paean, sung at the change of seasons, at the passage from winter into summer, or at the entry of spring. For example in the festivals of the type of the Athenian Thargelia, at the moment when the impurities of the past season are expelled at the entrance into a new season, there is, at Athens, the expulsion of one who is called the *pharmakos.* This paean, we are told, is characterized by its ambiguity. It is a joyous song, like a song of thanksgiving, and, at the same time, a song of terrible anguish with cries and lamentations. It is no accident that the tragic poet has placed this paean at the beginning of his tragedy. This paean gives us one of the fundamental oppositions in the structure of the work which enables us to understand it. If we compare this paean with what the chorus says at the moment when the tragedy, having reached its acme, takes an abrupt turn, the moment when Oedipus understands that he is damned, understands what he is, we find that the chorus intones a song which is equally astonishing, for it celebrates Oedipus from two points of view. It celebrates him as a savior of the City, as a king almost divine, while saying at the same time that "he is the most unfortunate and the foulest of men." Thus we see that the tragedy is based on the idea that the same man is the divine king (and there we have a reminder of Greek history) on whom the prosperity of the earth, of the herds, and of the women depends, the king who bears the whole burden of the human group depending on him. And, seen from the perspective now shared by the audience and the poet, he is at the same time considered to be something dreadfully dangerous, a sort of incarnation of *hubris,* which must be expelled. Into this opposition, of the divine king who is also an impurity, the one who knows all but is blind, we [find] . . . the idea that this divine king, who belongs to the Greek past, is at the same time superseded; and that, in a way, according to the scheme of the familiar ritual, he must be expelled as a *pharmakos.*[5]

Further, the performance of *Oedipus the King* was a public event which communicated in the crosscurrents of the fourth-century citizenry, in the ambiguities and uncertainties that marked the social lives of the people. The crossroads of decision lying before the hero are shrouded with such profound ambiguity that when the hero chooses the best possible course of action, the very good that he intends and follows becomes the means by which he commits criminal, even heinous, acts. This fateful ambiguity makes of him a *pharmakos,* a poisoning healer whose presence embodies both great social danger and the very ambiguity that his expulsion is intended to eliminate. His attempt to be just has occasioned enormous injustice; his mission as the savior of Athens has brought about a threat of destruction that is worse than the precipitating calamity.

The city that watched and heard the play was itself experimenting with the relatively new system of elected officials who administer justice. They also watched a play that had been judged as to its excellence by the new system of voting by tribunals. The decision concerning the best drama reflects the new and uncertain system of dispensing justice, a secular system that moved away from ancient rituals and practices in which the gods, not humans, appeared to establish the justice whereby a play or an action was chosen. And in the play at hand, the city watched and heard a tragedy in which the uncertainty of being just and good had fateful, cosmic dimensions. A *pharmakos* was also the person whose secular duty was to provide justice for the city. The city's own profound uncertainty in the transitional situation concerning justice was played before it in a tragedy that arose from the very structural ambiguity that was inherent in the world of gods and people. There is a dark Hades quality to justice that appears in its ritual memory in which the light of law is limited and in which a darkness emerges that extinguishes humans' sense of proper place. "Greek law which had just been formulated, unlike Roman law, is not systematized, not founded on axiomatic principles, but is made up tentatively of different levels."[6]

The movement of the drama plays out the historical, changing circumstances and the enormous ambiguity of its place and time. In addition to what it says thematically and the effect that it has on its hearers, the play in its setting enacts of itself—and not in reflexive regard to itself—a texture of ancient and modern practices that are embodied in its culture. In its being played, it and its audience are involved in an event that exceeds the reflexivity of the play's portraying to the Athenians their own perplexity and quandary. In its complex ambiguity it occurs as the question of justice which binds, as a question, both the play and the people with the play in a voice other than action and passion. A complex history and a complex society are voiced in a whole event that is marked by transformation and multiple dimensions of conflicting currents of meaning. It is like a voice that speaks fatefully beyond the totality of meanings and transformations that constitute the play's activity and suffering and that gives that totality a shaking, quivering quality. *Oedipus the King* comes to pass in the diathesis of the play of forces that structure it. Like a middle-voiced verb, the play, as an event in its middle-voiced function, states its own event in its occurrence. It voices itself without the intervention of regard for itself. In this instance the middle voice is one of question, transformation, anxiety, and a play of countervailing forces rather than the voice of the present identity or group of identities. The play's voice puts its totality in question.

We may now summarize our discussion: The nonreflexive value of the middle voice is not expressible in a present indicative mood. It does not suggest predication or subjective intervention in the formation of its movement. Even in the phrase "he cooks for himself," the middle voice suggests that an action occurs which is immediate in its enactment and is not reflexive. The prepositional, object-forming "for himself," a grammatically formed space that suggests activity and reception of activity, is eliminated in the single middle-voice verb. The middle voice suggests something that goes beyond subject-object formations. It is able to articulate nonreflexive enactments that are not for themselves or for something else. As a formation it does not need to suggest intention outside of its movement or a movement toward an other. It does not suggest action by which the subject becomes other to itself. It does not oppose active and passive formations, but it is other than they are. It is the voice of something's taking place through its own enactment. It remains hearable by us in some reflexive functions; we have seen that those functions often lack particularly the middle-voice value of intransitive processes of enactment. We have seen that in the middle voice a certain immediacy of presence can be expressed, but we have also seen that the presence of a complex, ambiguous verb or event, by virtue of its ambiguity and countervalences, may in its middle voice express not the immediacy of simple presence, but transition, ambiguity, and dissolution of presence. In such cases there is an excess vis-à-vis the meanings that constitute the event or word. That excess suggests that the presence of meaning is not a sufficient basis for thinking in relation to the event, that the excess necessitates something other than the language of meaning and presence for its articulation.

To come to understand the middle voice better, we might analyze the verbs that retained a middle-voice structure but took on active and passive meanings. Then we could formulate the various ways in which active and passive meanings have an almost hidden value that is in excess of those meanings. Or we might show how the middle voice expresses temporal aspects in its various tenses. The coming and passing of things in this voice is articulated as the things' own occurrence. Or we might trace the middle voice through Latin deponents and find its excess there. In such work we would need to be alert to the ways in which the loss of the middle voice functions in our account of it, and we would need to find strategies to show how the loss of the middle voice functions in the process of carrying out our account of it. Perhaps our writing could then give expression to its own loss of the middle voice and thereby delimit the inevitability of its loss.

I have discussed the middle voice with two emphases in mind: first, to take note of a power of expression and writing that is traceable in its loss and that by its loss suggests that there are limits to thinking when it is predominantly constituted by the active-passive structures, and second, to prepare a way of interpreting the recoils in Nietzsche's thought that refers recoiling to its own movement without involving the language of causation. We are working on the limits of the active-passive structures as we trace the middle voice in relation to active and passive functions, and, as we saw in the case of *Oedipus the King,* the middle voice can bring to thought a dimension of events, an excess of present meaning, and a situation of conflict, that is otherwise clouded over if not totally obscured. Both the middle voice and its obscurity, in a way yet to be determined, produce or yield thought processes by which the subject-object structure is overcome. We shall look specifically at one instance in which the function of the middle voice in the context of unreconciled conflicts plays a positive role in the formation of thought. In this instance, the excess of meaning that takes place in conflicts issues in a discursive process that overcomes itself. In this self-overcoming the priority of the active and passive voices is also overcome. Finally, we shall think about the limits of thought by means of the middle voice and mark one sense of the 'end of metaphysics' in Nietzsche's thought. We will be considering a way of thinking in which the end of metaphysics, construed now as delimited traditional thought, opens to thinking both in and through that limit. This part of our discussion is preparatory to considering the movement of the question of ethics in Nietzsche's account of the ascetic ideal.

B. THE MIDDLE-VOICED PROCESS OF SELF-OVERCOMING IN NIETZSCHE'S THOUGHT

The idea of self-overcoming brings to expression a movement that both defines and delimits philosophical thought, and in Nietzsche's work the idea of self-overcoming recoils in a self-overcoming manner.[7] He typically works within a given structure of value or thought in such a way that the values or ideas become increasingly questionable because of the countervailing powers that they carry as well as suppress in their own movement. The history of the formation of morality, the fears and resentment, the profound oppression and suffering that are built into the attitudes and hierarchies of morality: these powers have the effect of turning on themselves when those inherent, countervailing powers are released to take their own directions in Nietzsche's genealogy. The *turning* of repressive powers on themselves, their functioning against themselves, which is also the movement of resentment against itself, is a middle-voiced movement of self-overcoming. Nietzsche releases this turning by providing a genealogy of what is both behind the good-evil polarity and nonetheless effective in the practical and theoretical life of the polarity. As he shows how the ascetic ideal establishes its life by repressing its life, the effect of this account is to turn the ascetic ideal against itself through both its own repressive action and its affirmation of life which maintains the repression. On the one hand, Nietzsche looks for the truth of the moral order. He looks for its origins and purposes, for the nature of its energy, for the intentions internal to self-giving love, for the meaning of moral affirmation, and for values that will provide a different order, a different morality. When this aspect of his work is held in isolation from its own self-overcoming, Nietzsche looks like a critical moralist, another modern ethical thinker. On the other hand, he places in question moral thinking as such by maintaining in his language the countervalence of values within morality. Moral values, by their countervalence, undercut and move to overcome their own power to organize his discourse around any of their groups or poles. In this second aspect, the very structure of moral thought develops transvaluationally out of its own movements and interplays and in the absence of domination by any part of its once definitive structure. In *On the Genealogy of Morals,* the process of self-overcoming thus constitutes a middle voice of Western morality.

Just as Zarathustra must fall under the power of resentment and profound self-hatred in his pilgrimage toward possibilities for living without resentment and self-hatred, so Nietzsche's own genealogical thought works within the structures that come to closure and are delimited in his discourse.

We shall take as an example of this self-overcoming the functions of 'will to power' and 'eternal return' in Nietzsche's account of them. My purpose is to show the effect of the middle-voice function of the valences of will to power and eternal return in Nietzsche's discourse about them. In their own middle-voice movement and in the context of their own multiple countervalences, the ideas of will to power and eternal return recoil upon themselves in Nietzsche's writing. This movement breaks the privilege of the active-passive voices and, instead, privileges the movement by which the overcoming of metaphysics overcomes itself. When will to power is read primarily in the active voice, for example, it appears to be a quasi-subject that does something in and to specific situations of choice and affirmation. In the middle voice, however, will to power occurs as a self-overcoming movement of a specific, complex organization of countervailing values. In this example, we have an instance of the ending of metaphysics and a way of thinking that issues from this ending. The two components that hold our attention are internal countervalence and the middle-voice function.

Is it not the function of these two ideas in Nietzsche's discourse, will to power and eternal return, to provide resolution and synthesis? They appear to give synthesizing order in the "junglelike growth" of the genealogist's descriptions and the ideas that tumble through Nietzsche's thinking. Do they not offer a basis of sameness and a holistic image for all things? In preparation for answering this question we shall look first at will to power with two questions in mind: How does Nietzsche describe will to power? How does his account of will to power function in his thinking?

Nietzsche wanted to show that will to power better explains the appearance of things, that is, it explains *things* better than other competing ideas, such as that of a creator-subject. He adopts the scientific approach, which he understands to be governed by number and measurement. He measures phenomena by a quantitative scale. Further, "force is to be found in quantity. Mechanistic theory can therefore only *describe* processes, not explain them" (WP 660). The quantitative scale is a scale of force. He intends to describe degrees of force, not entities that have degrees of force attached to them, and by this process of description he will have interpreted all things by reference to degrees or amounts of force and the interplay of these forces.

The relations and plays among forces are different from the forces themselves, of course: "We cannot help feeling that mere quantitative differences are something fundamentally distinct from quantity, namely that they are qualities which can no longer be reduced to one another" (WP 565). *Quality,* then, refers to the differences-in-play of quantities of force. Nietzsche's discipline is not to single out forces, see them in a totality, and describe the totality as a sum total of its constituents. The qualities of force relations are not reducible to the constituent parts, and Nietzsche proposes descriptions of qualities, of the interplays of forces, as the subject of his discipline.

Will to power has reference to interplays of forces, not to some preexisting essence. On Nietzsche's terms there are no quanta outside of specific organizations: quanta are relationally conceived. So his science of number and measurement is a description of qualities of force produced in the interplay of various factors of force. By not reducing quality of force to quantity of force he in effect claims that quantities of force are "real," that is, they are effective only as nameable elements in some organization. They are contributing elements, and presumably they are independent of *this* organization only to the extent that they occur in other organizations. And the quality of *this* organization could be a contributing factor, that is, a quantity of force, in another organization that has a different quality.

Instead of quanta having a transorganizational nature, they are distinguishable only in virtue of their different effects in organizations. Differences of force in a complex play of forces, not a common nature, constitute their "identity" (WP 1062).

How, then, are we to read "force," if not as a transcending essence that is present in all organizations? The idea of force is the organizing principle of the disciplined discourse that is emerging from traditional patterns of thought. Will to power names the quality of the organization that is expressed in the transforming, transvaluing discourse that Nietzsche joins in its early stages of development. His "measuring" account of force articulates the quality of will to power that empowers, arranges, and distributes this discourse. Modern science, which, according to Nietzsche, is in the genealogy of resentment, the ascetic ideal, and bad conscience, is articulated in a transformation toward a discourse whose estimates and hierarchies multiply unities and disassemble categorical totalities. His own developing discourse produces a *Wesen* of difference that is called "nobility" in *Beyond Good and Evil,* and, finally, this transformation of science foresees a *Wesen* that is beyond (over) the conscious organization of man.

When Nietzsche says in *Will to Power* that "this world is the will to power and nothing else! and you yourselves are also this will to power—and nothing besides," he is holding the world in his "mirror":

And do you know what "the world" is to me? Shall I show it to you in my mirror? This world: a monster of energy without beginning, without

end . . . enclosed by "nothingness" as by a boundary . . . a sea of forces
flowing and rushing together, eternally changing, eternally flooding back . . .
blessing itself as that which must recur eternally, as a becoming that knows
no satiety, no disgust, no weariness: this is my Dionysian world of eternally
self-creating, the eternally self-destroying . . . my *"Beyond Good and Evil,"*
without goal, unless the joy of the circle is itself a goal. (WP 1067)

The differentiating element in this "world," its quality, is will to power
combined with eternal return. Both a group of metaphysical claims and
a countervalence to such claims occur in the paragraph. It contains claims
making up a nihilism from a metaphysical point of view. But when the
paragraph is read as recoiling on its own claims, those claims are known
to be supported by nothing other than the energy of this mirror image,
this organization. Its energy is not to be taken as a part of something
beyond it and universal. It is a self-reflection, not of Nietzsche particularly,
but of a powerful grouping of discursive forces that in desiring to be itself
has no desire for foundations outside of itself. In willing to be itself, the
discourse wills the will to power. In willing the will to power, it wills
an image of a discourse supported solely by its own interplays, the genealogies of those interplays, and the other interplays that they put in motion.

The energy of this discourse, as a qualitative interplay of forces, has
its validity in its effective organizing power. "The will is a creator" (Z,
"Of Redemption"). The will to power originates in a full interplay of
forces—not, for example, from a lack of energy or a need for relation.
Its characteristics are ebullience, fullness, overflow. It frees its participating
forces from that repression of will that has characterized its predecessors:
"Willing liberates: that is the true doctrine of will and freedom" (Z, "On
the Blissful Isles"). It expends forces for creation and self-enjoyment. It
has been fed by the forces that gained strength through opposition and
repression, as we have seen—not the affections of enslavement, but the
hardness and sense of life bred by struggle with the preceding controlling
powers. In its youthful energy it burgeons, rephrases, appropriates, expands, bypasses. Its profligacy is in its affirmation of its energy to be
whatever and however it occurs. Hence the satisfaction of this discourse
happens in self-affirmation, not in the fulfillment of unfinished goals. Intensity, not teleology, is its hallmark.

But Nietzsche also claimed that the destruction of past traditions occurred because of their violations and fears regarding their will to power.
On the Genealogy of Morals refers to the will to power in the entire
sweep of human history. Nietzsche does not think that it is limited to
his own emerging discourse. Will to power is used as an explanatory concept
for the movement of all history, and particularly as an explanation for
the decline and degeneration of its closest "relative," the ascetic ideal.
Like any other discourse of absolutes, Nietzsche's discourse makes its
central idea, its dominant force, the force that dominates other forces

in its discursive appropriation of them. It gives focus, unifying power, and it sets in motion undercutting movements. This relation of metaphysical claims and antimetaphysical effects sets the direction of thought for a significant current of reflection running through the twentieth century. We are familiar with the undercutting effect: it transvalues metaphysical ideas by putting them in play with equally forceful ideas about movement without ultimate meaning.

One way that this undercutting functions is through the observation that will to power has an oscillating rhythm. As the quality of a limited, forceful interplay (that is, as the quality of a discourse), will to power is not an essence that unfolds inherent meanings or an inherent identity as it develops in an historically extensive process. In its discourse it not only interprets itself as a nonsubject without essential identity; it oscillates in the interplay of forces; by this oscillation it creates zones of identity in which one or another group of forces makes hierarchies that exclude other identities and that themselves have a limited number of possibilities for identity. These groupings play themselves out, and particularly in the regrouping and transitional phases the loss of the dominant identities accompanies the manifest power of transformation. There is no center, no anchoring ballast. Centers of willpower are identities. Will to power shows itself particularly as the centers fade out, lose their magnetism. Will *to* power is manifest in its movement without center. The concept of the will *to* power functions in this rhythm of identity formation and identity decline as an ability to give identity and focus in Nietzsche's discourse. On its own terms, this idea also is expected to lose its centering ability and to be overwhelmed. It is a recoiling part of an oscillation, like the movement of a circle that in its movement changes the smaller organizations of movement within its circumference into larger organizations that, in their interplay, slowly change the whole. In this instance the idea of will to power may be expected on its own terms to recoil back on itself and to rebound with organizing concepts that replace its own impact and power.

Nietzsche often speaks of a sense of rightness or honesty that accompanies the individual who undergoes ego sacrifice or identity sacrifice in a process of affirming will to power. A satisfaction peculiar to the Western ego traces the movement from energy with center to the power of energy without center. In language that transvalues Christian sacrifice in the images of crucifixion and resurrection, Nietzsche finds that ego loss without retention of desire for ego gain finds pleasure in returning to a source that is without identity or subject interest. His own happy movement in the course of *Thus Spoke Zarathustra* to the image of the last man who is still all-too-human, and beyond, toward a state that is not a man-state, is also a movement in the power of the idea of will to power toward an anticipated organization that is beyond the will-to-power discourse. There is no expectation that the overman will think of will to power unless he or she looks into a distant and past discourse in his or her lineage.

When this movement through dominant identities is denied by the forces of those identities, the reconstituting trajectory of the movement is diverted. The ascetic ideal, for example, with its repressive force directed against its own destruction, is a return, certainly, but yet a return to the quality of energy without center; it returns to an overwhelming identity, to a particular magnetic center. This kind of return, observes Nietzsche, particularly in the course of *On the Genealogy of Morals,* weakens or sickens the self-identifying complex, viz. the ascetic ideal. The recoiling movement continues its effect even as the identity struggles to maintain itself and represses its own energy in an effort to control or stop the power toward transvaluation and redesign. A turning now occurs, as the internal weakening—the "sickness"—undercuts the power of repression and strengthens, through pressure and forceful concentration, what is repressed. The repressed, with its increased energy, turns out from the identity center, perhaps at first extravagant in its emerging liberation, and turns toward its own constitution and recentering.

If the center of the emerging quality of identity affirms its own generative process and does not identify itself and its valence by reference to endurance and universal validity, and *if* it centrally affirms a decentering momentum, then the recoil of its power will not mean blind repression, self-sickening, and return of energy through regression. It will move "gaily" in its own self-transformations and, *by that kind of movement,* create the conditions for its successors as it moves recoiling away from its own quality and comes under the effect of other qualities.

If Nietzsche's recoiling thought is successful, it gives the conditions for thinking the processes by which it effects its own overcoming and undercutting. That effectiveness is in the function of its ideas—how they encourage their own transvaluation. If one follows those ideas for a time, the process of self-overcoming develops through the organizing power of those ideas. If one thinks these ideas metaphysically without appropriating the antimetaphysical forces and the consequent recoils that constitute self-overcoming, one is in a discourse that is different from Nietzsche's. The transformations that might go on are more likely to be repetitions of those that led to Nietzsche's discourse. At least they are different in the images and visions that they spawn by virtue of the absence of the torsion of self-overcoming recoil. They will not develop in the strain of forces or in the affirmation of the will to power that center and decenter Nietzsche's inheritance. The discipline of Nietzsche's discourse and its transvaluation involve the maintenance of its recoiling tensions until its metaphysical predecessors and its own "all-too-human" struggle transform into a different creature that knows all parties in the current struggle only as an aging or dead paternity. And if one participates knowingly in the transformative process, one will be in it with senses of difference and perhaps of pleasure that are not characteristic of most other modern discourses.

In "The Intoxicated Song" Zarathustra says that "joy wants itself, wants eternity, wants recurrence, wants everything eternally the same." This "deep eternity" *is* recurrence. Nietzsche often describes eternal return as the return of each pain, sorrow, injustice, and so on, and in those statements he emphasizes that the effect of the idea of eternal return is to transvalue the ideas of final telos and ultimate meaning by the force of another idea (eternal return) and image (time as an enclosed, revolving wheel). He is thinking through the idea of existence without meaning or aim. There is not even a finale of nothingness. Recoiling eternity. No completion, but continuous recoiling. And in this thought he finds existence and the world affirmed (he sometimes uses *redeemed*) in their own recoils amid the vacuum that ceaselessly interrupts the texture of judgments that would override their own disturbed vibrations.

The effect of affirming these occurrences of return, oscillation, and eternal return is to reach out discursively for power (WP 675). Reaching out for power is in contrast to reaction and reversion. The move out interrupts the sickening process that prevails in its own ancestry. Thought metaphysically, the claim is that the foundation of all existence is now affirmed in a group of values that have a dimension of noncontingent validity because they are appropriate to the transhistorical nature of the will to power. But when the idea is thought in terms of its discursive effect in its middle voice, it releases the discourse from alignments of self-protection and self-affirmation. Returning returns. It is a recoil that ceaselessly unsettles the thought of both eternity and sameness. No identity controls the process. Identity control is itself transvalued in the recoiling return. And the discourse is free for its multiple, struggling orders. No meaning rules over them in the recoil of eternity as return. There are surging powers in a quality of energy that affirms them all in their countervailing lives. Out of this affirmation—out of this quality, the will to power—the multivalued orders are affirmed strongly so that they move in their recoiling countervalence beyond themselves not in the power of centering self-maintenance but in the power of affirmation of the multiply contradictory occurrence. If the discourse works, the power of negation peculiar to traditional Western metaphysical thought is transvalued into a different quality of forces. Then the idea of will to power is itself transvalued into something different, which Nietzsche's discourse could not, true to itself, imagine. In Nietzsche's work, the middle voice of self-overcoming and transvaluation functions in the text's self-overcoming and transvaluing movements. It is an unaccustomed voice, but one that Nietzsche identifies as a silent movement in and through Western thinking: the movement of this thinking—I choose *movement* instead of *force* or *will*—is unthinkable, aporetic, within the organization of its controlling meanings and values. Yet it is a movement that Nietzsche thinks by means of maintaining the tradition's conflicts without the organizing power of the ideas of consistency and reconciliation, that is, without the organizing power of a pervasive and controlling presence. Without the power of presence, transcendence in Nietzsche's thought occurs as the image of *trans,* of the beyond, of space without presence. We have noted this transcendence in the self-overcoming functions of will to power and eternal return. Both of these thoughts in their multiple recoils dissolve their own discursive authority.

In the discussion of the play of will to power and eternal return in Nietzsche's writing—a play of metaphysical assertion, antimetaphysical assertion, and nonmetaphysical recoil in the process—we discern not only the conflictual directions that are methodically maintained, but also a middle-voiced recoiling function. In the first place, Nietzsche has developed a significant part of his thought in the conflictual play of forces that moves through Western metaphysical thought and that has not been affirmed in that thought. This conflictual play has a middle-voiced function in the sense that it is of the thought's movement, is neither active nor passive, and provides multiple recoils back on the presumptive authority of its organizing ideas. It is not the subject of action nor the recipient of action. Second, the traditional repression of the conflictual play is not only the result of the active force of a metaphysician's thought. Repression of the play of conflictual forces is also of the semantics, the structures of meaning, that constitute metaphysics. On the Nietzschean account, this repression occurs in the semantic movement of metaphysics and also has a middle-voiced function of sickening while it saves meaning. Third, the play of the conflicting forces and the repression of that play constitute the recoiling movement of Nietzsche's thought, a movement in which their repression becomes one among the playing forces and is a part of the movement's transvaluation. Transvaluation of the repression of the constitutive conflicts within metaphysics is a process in which the dominant meanings of metaphysics are composed by opposing powers and in that condition function blindly in a self-overcoming manner. Self-overcoming in metaphysics takes place as the middle voice of Nietzsche's discourse. In *his* discourse, however, it is affirmed, and self-overcoming self-overcomes without inherent resistance. It is a voice that in its recoils exceeds reflexivity, closes metaphysical thought, and prepares for the overcoming of Nietzsche's own thought. It is the voice of differing, moving of itself, without the thought of transcendence.

The strategy we have followed in showing how in Nietzsche's discourse self-overcoming takes place as the recoiling middle voice of metaphysical discourse is to trace the discursive function of countervalences in his thought of will to power in eternal return. These are countermovements *in* the traditional values and thoughts that Nietzsche followed genealogically and that also play significant roles in his own thinking. His discourse changes as the processes of self-overcoming and transvaluation take place. In his thought, the conflicts and groundless chaos characteristic of metaphysical formations become apparent as countervalues are given full rein in their recoiling movement, multiple organizations, and trajectories. We have seen that only by undergoing self-overcoming do we think Nietzsche's thought.

This means that only as we undergo Nietzsche's self-overcoming and that of our own reading do we think in the movement of Nietzsche's thought.

In the section that follows we shall turn to his discussion of the ascetic ideal in Part Three of *On the Genealogy of Morals,* noting that when the *trans* of transcendence is thought without subjectivity or self-reflexivity, when transcendence is thought in the middle voice of self-overcoming, the ascetic ideal stands out with unusual definition in its multiple functions and patterns. We can say initially that without self-*presenting* transcendence, without a concept of transcendence or that of the thinker's own universal presence, the ground for the Western ascetic ideal falls away. The ascetic ideal increasingly functions as a remainder that, while demanding a ground of validity, has no such ground outside of its own heritage. Various images will function as a ground in this remainder.

The images for ground that have exercised the most power on me as I have worked on this discussion have been those of Nietzsche's texts. I have been tempted to hear his words as something like grounds for my words, which would make a complete whole of his self-overcoming work, and thus I have been tempted to eliminate the constant pollution of self-overcoming as it turns to waste the very elements that functioned definitively in his text. I have been tempted to make Nietzsche's passion and suffering definitive of more than their own momentary discourse and to see his passage through metaphysical thought as transcending his passage and opening up a better world beyond metaphysics. By purifying Nietzsche's text in such ways, I have in effect overlooked and humbled their constant and trivial loss of significance, their mundane and qualified— Nietzsche called it their "faded"—truths, the truncation of their spirited leaps and lofty spirituality. I suppose that it is an axiom that when a text becomes the grounds of its own interpretation, when we wash out biography, personal motivation, historical limitations, and the multiple impacts of other nontextual forces—the messy texts that mix writing with the fragmented, semi-conscious disconnections of psychology, language, and cultural life— when we purify texts in such ways and then make texts the basis of our interpretation, we are within the power of the ascetic ideal, now a remnant of other discourses in which the ideal took its power from the images of perfect being and fallen being. We shall be alert to this remnant ideal and its considerable power as we attempt to think in and with Nietzsche's genealogy of it. I hope to remain alert to the recoils in Nietzsche's genealogy that transgress and pollute the circulations of meanings that might otherwise promise a purity of textual self-realization, but which, in their recoiling circulation, turn away from themselves by virtue of multiple, constituting, contesting powers. These powers recombine with each other in the discourse in a context of the concept of will to power that moves in a self-overcoming manner in his thought.

We have seen that the will to power, in its movement of self-overcoming, will not function as a *self-maintaining* discursive force. If we separate the will to power from its movement of self-overcoming, make it quasi-transcendental, such that it provides a position outside self-overcoming, we will have yet another essence in terms of which to understand human life outside human life. But when we follow the will to power in its self-overcoming, it and whatever we find it investing in the text will be subject to self-overcoming. In the case of the ascetic priest, for example, the will to power, which provides the priest with a strange power of life-affirmation, means that the priest and its ascetic ideal are in the movement of self-overcoming, the very movement that this ideal denies. The middle voice of will to power is the voice that is refused by the active, meaning-giving assertions of the ascetic ideal.

And yet . . . And yet haven't I been in the position of the spectator thinker as I have shown the discursive role of the spectator thinker, its recoils, its self-overcoming? Haven't I maintained a subject's power of representation? Haven't I cleared out a space and given it meaning by my interpretation? Have I, too, been an ascetic priest, removed from the interests of fasting, bathing, and supplication, but resistant all the same to self-overcoming? I may know that the semantics of this book are delimited by the vacuum of their horizon and by the position I take regarding them. But I am a knower and a philosopher, and the spectator position of knowing and thinking is what I find in question. This finding may well reestablish a posture that resists self-overcoming. And in knowing this I am turned again, not by the force of my sincerity or of a will to truth, but by the clash of the knowing posture and a movement that will not know or be known by a spectator. Do I undergo a transvaluation? Am I decanted in my philosophical incantations by a discourse that has Nietzsche's genealogy in its lineage?

What happens when I turn again to the ascetic ideal? Am I removed in this turn? Perhaps in the next section I shall be an *Übermensch,* or at least a guiding free spirit, and will bless us all in our release from the polluting herd who seek the assurances of the ascetic priest. Then I would know why I am so wise and why our work here is so significant. The danger, of course, is not only in such self-deception, but in the self-indulgence of speaking this way, in its cleansing power of confession. So I will look again at the ascetic ideal, wincing before its power within my stance, repelled by its traps, caught by its recoils, attracted by the possibility that I shall be purified by a recoiling ferment, and wondering whether the ascetic ideal masters its recoil and whether it masters me who seems to want to master the distance that separates me from Nietzsche's discourse.

The question is whether this knowledge, which includes a recoiling movement with Nietzsche's genealogy, is part of a springing movement away from the components of the genealogy that has occasioned and attracted it. This is a question of whether the spectator's stance on Nietzsche's genealogy in the lineage of Nietzsche's genealogy is—in its vocabulary, values, and the very space of its thought—more distanced from the ascetic ideal than I at first thought it to be. I have been prepared to write that the spectator's stance is a space of asceticism, that it cleansed the body of its density in a profound, middle-voiced self-deception. By moving to the text I wanted to be in a movement that recoiled from the ascetic ideal of the spectator's stance. But now I find that this stance is in Nietzsche's lineage and that the desire to leave the stance as much as possible is at once a desire to purify it by treating the text as though it were self-contained. If I hold this stance, do I stand in the rebound of *On the Genealogy of Morals*? Is this a self-maintaining posture without self-overcoming? Or is this reading of Nietzsche a space of fragmentation which, to use Blanchot's phrase, relates without relation, which is rapport without rapport? An interrupted stance of a fragmented spectator? A broken space in the verge of Nietzsche's recoil? A pollution of Nietzsche's texts without a bad conscience? A stance that recoils in self-overcoming as it views self-overcoming in Nietzsche's writing? A countervalence with Nietzsche's text in the play of Nietzsche's own countervalences, one that gives full rein to countervalences? Does self-overcoming self-overcome in this reading?

3. Genealogy and the Ascetic Ideal

Ascetic means self-denial by means of severe abstinence. Its antithesis, in our tradition, is sensuality and the body's life. Yet, *antithesis* is hardly appropriate for *body:* already an asceticism is at work in my use of *antithesis,* as though body were a thesis that could be 'anti'. Already too much meaning is bestowed on body, already the body's density is denied in its affirmation as the antithesis of *ascetic*. From what does the meaning of the ascetic ideal derive? In part, Nietzsche says, it derives from the unstable equilibrium between the animal and the angel in humans and from the human desire to survive, that is, from the human will to will (GM III 1–2). A stability is imposed on this instability that pervades human mentation and animality, but this stability has fear and the will to will as its progenitors, and fear combined with the will to will is not the hallmark of stability. The ascetic ideal is generated by lack of stability, and it provides stability *in* instability: it promotes the very instability that it means to overcome. We may say that it recoils in its own instability. When we hold in mind that, according to Nietzsche, the ascetic priest generated the space for philosophical thought, we are prepared to see that this unstable stabilization is definitive of our traditional work, that to think genuinely and seriously as a philosopher is to be marked by the ascetic ideal. We find our thinking in question by virtue of the heritage of our endeavor.

The signature of the ascetic ideal is guilt: the felt and affirmed indebtedness of being an animal in association with the "angelic"; the guilt associated with an individual's being an unjustifiable, meaningless breach, an individual's lacking one central essence, an individual's being under the authority of an image of centered unity in one nature that gives and takes life. To be this breach is to be a self in need of fundamental correction within a hierarchy of greater or lesser reality. To be this breach is to be guilty.

The discipline of the ascetic ideal is self-denial in the form of continuous correction and submission of the animal, the chaotic, the meaningless. It is a discipline that subtly humiliates the meaninglessness of life by imposing a meaning for life under the transcending authority of pure life/pure being. This is a discipline that calls for the spectator's distance from the animal, the dense, the confused, the superficial, the vacuous.

The pervasiveness of this ideal in our tradition cannot be overstated on Nietzsche's terms. Aside from its obvious relation to religious morality and practices, it structures both philosophical and artistic endeavor. It is found in the multiple goals of realizing a higher nature or spirituality by means of superior systems of morality, thought, and enjoyment, by the insights of privileged souls. We are naturally inclined by our discourses to find the highest forms of worship, the best forms of criticism, the most subtle wines, the loftiest music, the purest foods, the most salubrious methods of health care, the best causes for social action, the most sterling morality, the formulae for realizing our true and best nature, the best and truest thoughts. We are driven by our discourses to find the truth of ourselves by disciplines of self-realization and self-denial, like the athlete who trains for movement and endurance by austere denial of most satisfactions and by elevating a few severe activities over all others. When such endeavors are attached to the idea of virtue, we have at work the ascetic ideal and the shade of the ascetic priest.

The pervasiveness of the ascetic ideal suggests to Nietzsche the appropriateness of suspicion of our most passionate life-affirmations. He finds, for example, even in Wagner's enthusiastic affirmation of sensuality an unconscious desire for redemption, conversion, and salvation. Wagner's very seriousness betrays his chaste desire for truth in his revolt against the morality of his age: Wagner's pious, driven seriousness is the carrier of the will to truth and the ascetic ideal of that will. We find the same kind of seriousness in the philosophical drive for exact and accurate thought, transcendental grounding for empirical or phenomenological description, and loftiness of spirit beyond the fallen world of everyday desire and occupation. "Every spirit has its own sound and loves its own sound," Nietzsche says, and that sound in willing itself attempts to drive out other voices and to elevate itself in the form of hierarchies of value (GM III 8). Whenever we find exclusively self-authorizing systems of values—even if those values make sensuality primary—we find the ascetic ideal at work. Such structures of value will be poor in things of nonspiritual living; they will be pure and chaste in their discipline of forming hierarchies and humble before the authority of their truth, whatever their truth might be. Our values of careful objectivity, rational explanation, suspended belief in disciplined investigation, and serenity in the face of confusion and uncertainty: these we find, in Nietzsche's genealogy, to be formed by and to express the ascetic ideal.

We are already familiar with Nietzsche's descriptive claim that the disciplines of knowledge and morality are themselves unconscious expressions of will to power, and we note now that these disciplines are expressions of will to power *in* their ascetic ideal. The ascetic ideal is both an articulation of the unbridgeable breach in human existence, a breach that is bordered by what our tradition names spirit and animal, as well as by an expression of will to power. As unconscious will to power, the ascetic ideal is a forceful affirmation of human meaning that enables the human organism to affirm itself in the face of no meaning at all. As unconscious expression of the void of existence, it is an affirmation that radically denies its own occurrence and that sickens itself by willing its own denial in the very illusion of its self-affirmation. Nietzsche's way of stating this paradox is that all willing that takes its direction from the ascetic ideal longs to get away from appearance, change, becoming, and death, and in denying the very elements of human life it denies its own happening and wills nothingness in the illusion of spirituality: the idea wills the void—death—in spite of itself (GM III 28). But it remains will. In spite of its debilitating itself in its self-denying will to truth and meaning, it *wills,* and the issue for us is how we are to think in this will that weakens its own organism by the non-self-conscious strategy of the ascetic ideal.

Such self-consciousness is at once a process whereby the ideal continually perishes. We note first that in Nietzsche's genealogy we are not involved in an antithesis of the ideal, but in the ideal's own development. The genealogy is characterized by recoil before the only self-contradictions that constitute the ideal, by the ideal's lack of ideality in its ideal self-assertions, its dumbness, its impurity, hubris, and accumulation of power and authority. The genealogy's wincing recoil expresses the ascetic ideal and is structured by it. The genealogy seeks—wills—the truth of the ascetic ideal and in this endeavor finds itself submitted to the law of self-overcoming that is found in traditional morality and thought.

But this recoil is compounded by another recoil. The genealogical knowledge coils again in the energy of ascetic self-awareness, now affirmed without repression, and in this compounding torsion it interprets itself by its own paradox and meaninglessness. The genealogy finds that its own meanings are breached by no meaning at all, that its order is always in the horizon of mere lack of order, and that it does not represent an antithetical position to the objects of its critique.

What is this nontheoretical, nonantitheoretical movement? In *On the Genealogy of Morals* Nietzsche names it the "law of the necessity of self-overcoming" (III 27). In the context of guilt, self-overcoming releases and reinscribes its participants in guilt, "letting those incapable of discharging their debt go free" (II 10). Justice is overcome by a mercy closely associated with the Judeo-Christian experience of forgiveness. But that rendering names a quasi mercy that traditionally is itself spiritualized in the cruel and stringent terms of the ascetic ideal. It is a movement of self-overcoming in the history of resentment, but a movement that reinscribes traditional resentment and asceticism in a more stringent, yet more self-deceived, spirituality of justice and mercy.

The law of the necessity of self-overcoming means in part that no spirituality—religious or philosophical or aesthetic—has authority outside of its own configuration, and it means that its own unappropriated chaos will catch up with its own substantial self-deception and explode it like the recoil of a supernova. The will to power never rests in its expressions, and it never stabilizes the authorities by which it comes to stand in a given environment. It, too, is subject to self-overcoming.

For our purposes, an issue arises that has to do with the recoil of this law as it rebounds from itself in its authoritative status in Nietzsche's discourse. Metaphysical readers of Nietzsche take this law, as well as his ideas of will to power and eternal return, to be claims about what is really real, and many interpret his position as nihilistic because *metaphysically read* he appears to mean that what is really real lacks ultimate meaning or sense: Nietzsche's position then has the kind of negative purity that radicalizes the tradition of metaphysical skepticism. But such readings neither recognize the function of self-overcoming in the texts of this law and these ideals nor do they themselves engage in self-overcoming thought.

This law, the discourse of its authority, is part of the process of self-overcoming in the tradition of the ascetic ideal and the will to truth. Or we may say that it has authority on its own terms only in the organism of its own discourse. In *On the Genealogy of Morals*, Nietzsche has shown that self-overcoming functions within Western morality as a law of life. This law presupposes that mere void is suppressed by the meanings of the ascetic ideal as well as assumes the paradoxical, decomposing void of its own meanings. Without the suppression characteristic of Western morality and its accompanying sickening and decomposition, the law does not occur. It is a law within the movement of the meanings of the ascetic ideal by virtue of those meanings' combined refusal and unconscious expression of what Nietzsche variously calls void, nothingness, and breach. The function of Nietzsche's interpretation of the law of necessity of self-overcoming is thus to undercut its own authority outside of its heritage by showing its genealogy and by maintaining the awareness generated by the genealogy.

We can see now that self-overcoming defines the movement of the ascetic ideal as well as of Nietzsche's genealogical account of that ideal. Self-overcoming is not primarily a theory, but a discursive movement that he identifies in Western thought and practice as well as in his own writing. When self-overcoming is treated primarily as a theory or as a paradoxical kind of intentional activity, void and breach appear to be lost in the activity and passivity of the interpretive structures: it becomes another meaning that might perplex us but that we could not be said to think as we undergo it. We are not, however, the subjects or the objects of self-overcoming. As humans, as instances of Judeo-Christian *humanitas,* we are of it and it is a submerged movement as we live out its denial. It is a movement that by reverting to itself decomposes its own theoretical standing and rebounds beyond its possible meanings into nothing that is self-overcoming itself.

4. The Ascetic Ideal and the Ascetic Priest: "There Is Nothing of Virtue in This"

According to Nietzsche's genealogy of the Western philosopher, the ascetic ideal took one of its points of departure from the contemplative men who in early history were viewed by the rest of their society with hostility and mistrust. Their brooding inactivity contrasted negatively with the most valued activities of their cultures, and they needed to instill fear and hence be left untroubled if they were to survive and flourish. They also seemed internally divided and strange to themselves; in order to empower and authorize their misplaced inclination to lives of contemplation, they turned, without conscious strategy, on themselves that cruelty and castigation that normally was reserved for punishment. In becoming objects of their own tortured denials, they appeared to be related to sorcerers, soothsayers, and priests. Contemplation was thus wrapped in a protective mantle of wonder and divine power. By the fear that these proto-philosophers generated, at war with themselves in a struggle of energies that they could neither understand nor even contemplate, these priestly contemplatives provided themselves with both the social and psychological space and energy to "overcome the gods and tradition in themselves, so as to be able to believe in their own innovations" (GM III 10). Nietzsche suggests that the ascetic ideal had its impact in the early life of philosophy—primarily in India in the case of this account—as a power of deception and of overcoming the anticontemplative values that formed major parts of the contemplator's identity: the self-overcoming of both the man of action and the ascetic priest in the contemplative man is part of the heritage and meaning of the ascetic ideal in the philosophical tradition.[8]

We note four points: The contemplative element was at first a peculiar kind of power that was an object of hostile contempt; it survived by becoming mysterious and fearful both to others and to the one suffering from it; the ascetic ideal functioned to overcome the previously anti-contemplative and dominant values and ideals; the combination of contemplative power and the ascetic ideal involved masking contemplation by means of the ascetic ideal, however, and setting in play the incompatibility of the ideal's power and contemplation's power in the values that arose from the combination. We thus expect in the combination of philosophy and the ascetic ideal a process that empowers contemplation and that also attempts to overcome contemplation. Since the ascetic ideal has become definitive for Western philosophy, this overcoming is self-overcoming. As both ascetic and contemplative, Western philosophy is at odds with itself. Self-overcoming, deception, the ascetic ideal, the ascetic priest, brooding wonder, an inclination toward neither activity nor the establishment of meaning, and the mutual incompatibilities of those elements are all constitutive of Western philosophy. Further, Nietzsche says that the power of contemplation has no intrinsic meaning, no roots in anything that has higher value. It is a physiological process that means neither separation from the world nor attachment to things in a predetermined way. It is a kind of power that is other than the belligerent extroversion that dominated the early social and psychological scene as well as other than the cunning, fearful extroversion of the ascetic priest.

The ascetic priest is the central figure in the meaning of the ascetic ideal both for Western philosophy generally and for Nietzsche's own genealogy. In this figure we find both the structure of valuation that is in question *and* the process of self-overcoming by which the authority and meaning of the entire formation of the ascetic ideal loses its authority and meaning. The ascetic priest is the image by which Nietzsche's own values come most clearly into question and by which self-overcoming is interpreted in this section of *On the Genealogy of Morals*. It—the ascetic priest—is like a *pharmakos* in this writing: it is the condition of its own outcasting, it purges a pollution, and it heals the wound that it signifies. It has one further function that we shall explore: its outcasting carries away with it the ideals of purity, healing, and health that give meaning to the *pharmakos* and its outcasting. This last, self-overcoming element is the one most specific in Nietzsche's discourse.

We thus face the ascetic priest when we inquire about the meaning of the ascetic ideal for philosophy. We now come to grips "seriously" with the meaning of the ascetic ideal when we are "face to face with the actual *representative of seriousness*" (GM III 11). A triple recoil: as we return to the ascetic priest in this genealogy that constitutes a rebound from the ascetic priest, we find that our endeavor is wrapped in the kind of seriousness of which the ascetic priest is a representative. "Our" seriousness, however, is already mitigated—not absent, certainly, but diluted already by our manner of return to the ascetic heritage. The ascetic priest, said Nietzsche, is too interested a party to provide its best defense. It will confront us directly with full power, "confuting" *[Widerlegen]* us rather than helping us to trace its meaning. Our ability to ask about the meaning of the ascetic ideal and the ascetic priest shows a weakening of the ideal's power—a daunting power in its full strength that buries questions under an avalanche of forceful meanings. This weakening of meaning and the consequent open space by which we return to the question of meaning in the ascetic ideal shows a power other than that of the ascetic ideal, a discursive power that appears to take place in the gaping of meaning and the alleviation in the demand for meaning rather than in either its perfection or its presence. The energy released in the loss of meaning will help us later to think of contemplation, contemplative thought, and self-overcoming without the hegemony of the ascetic ideal or the ascetic priest. For now, Nietzsche says, our relative distance in relation to the ascetic ideal will help us to "defend" the ascetic priest against ourselves. This is a "defense" that will trace the meaning of the ascetic ideal genealogically without the passionate, assertive *Widerlegen* of the ascetic priest in its desperate and unconscious articulation of will to power. Power confronts power in this genealogy, but the power of the confrontation is no longer controlled by the ascetic shepherd's bestowal of meaning on all reality for the sake of his fearful, depressed flock. The power of this genealogical confrontation expresses a delimitation of the ascetic ideal, the lack of meaning that pervades its bequest of meaning.

"The ideal at issue *[Gekampft]* here is the *valuation* the ascetic priest places on our life" (GM III 11). The ascetic priest finds values in our life only if it turns against itself and by this turning becomes a bridge to another, quite different, invaluable life. This turn against mortal human life by mortal human life is itself a recoil "back to the point where it begins," to the time of some type of straining violation and mistake. By recovering the original mistake or its image, we are able to evaluate correctly our lives whose worth is found only in their recoil to their origins and is found in a consequent self-denial in favor of obligations that originate outside of ourselves. And the profound disgust regarding ourselves, disgust that neutralizes the power of momentary satisfactions in sensuality, possession, and pride—what does this disgust mean? It means that someone is trying to live in spite of the enormous forces exerted against living. The *recoil* against ordinary living and its satisfactions is a *mode of valuation* by which the continuation of living is promoted. The very elements that depress and threaten continuation—affective deformation, decay, pain, ill fortune, ugliness, lack of esteem, the imminence of death, hopelessness, cosmic indifference—these elements in their discord are embodied in self-mortification and self-sacrifice. One finds meaning through them by coiling them again in ascetic ideals, making them the very elements by which human life is turned against itself and is *enjoyed* by grace of a higher meaning that is placed figuratively in relief by affirming the lack of meaning in human life: "triumph in the ultimate agony."

The values of the ascetic priest constitute a process of self-overcoming in which the profoundly discouraging elements of life are turned on themselves in self-mortification; such recoil makes human life, in its self-denial, a "bridge to that other mode of existence" that is posited as an eternal, life-giving presence beyond our stained and forlorn way of being. The meaning of this self-overcoming recoil, in the senses of quailing, coiling again, and rebounding, is "an insatiable instinct and power-will that wants to become master not over something in life but over life itself, over its most profound, powerful, and basic conditions" (GM III 11). But the bridge to higher life is not physiological well-being, nor is that its goal. The bridge is self-denial in multiple forms of social and psychological life in which the agonies of living that show no meaning at all are re-enacted in the names of absent meaning and truth that are other than earthly life. Yet the driving force of asceticism is not meaning, the promise of meaning, or something like a lost homeland. The driving force is instinctual power, a mere urge to exist that means nothing. It is also the energy that enables us to enjoy the meanings of the ascetic life, as well as the energy of the seductive power of asceticism that enables us to go on in spite of meaninglessness, suffering, and death.

Seriousness about meaning suggests to Nietzsche, then, a return to the error, to the ontological erroneousness of human life and to the alleviation of error by a will to meaning that has as *its* meaning an escape from the meaninglessness of its world and willpower. Seriousness about meaning, in the context of the ascetic ideal, is "an incarnate will to contradiction" (GM III 12). It is a wonderful phenomenon that violently wipes out the gods of nature, cruelty, and expropriation—the divine forces of creation and destruction with no hint of ultimate care—in processes of continuous self-denial that produce continuous, if resentful, self-affirmation in the name of a life without contradiction or malice. The ascetic ideal functions by a movement of reversal, like that found in such traditional philosophical claims as "there is a realm of truth and being, but reason is excluded from it," or "things are so constituted that the intellect comprehends just enough of them to know that for the intellect they are—*utterly incomprehensible*" (GM III 12). The reversal is found in claims that things with which we have contact can be known only by an agency that is distant from them and that occupies a purer, less contaminated realm of reason and consciousness. In all such claims, the ascetic reversal is found in affirmation of life or truth or meaning by way of separation from the things to be known or affirmed in traditional ways. Usually the reversal develops in the concepts and beliefs regarding transcendence, whereby human existence is truncated in its difference from what is higher, better, more true, and without perspectival stance. In the heritage of the ascetic ideal the will to live is preserved by the cultivated desire to be in touch with a form of life that is different from our own fragmented lives and by realizing the difference of the desired form by squandering (sacrificing, which is to say, investing) the life one has at one's disposal.

As the mediator of the differences between higher and lower forms of life, the figure of the ascetic priest wields the enormous power of providing hope for us in our misfortune and hopeless pain. By wounding itself through hunger, celibacy, disciplines that counter the body—the disciplines that bring to experience a world different from ours and a life beyond our reach—the ascetic priest provides the miracle of reversing life-denial and profound depression into life-affirmation and the will to live. This kind of resurrection has moved Western metaphysics as few other powers have. Nietzsche's claim is that this figure constitutes the pattern by which contemplative power has polluted itself in both its fear of itself and its fear for its survival. The unconscious tactic becomes part of an unconscious identity, but one that is fissured by contradictions that issue in continuous recoil and self-overcoming. Ascetic self-overcoming is self-destructively obsessive because it regularly loses itself by repeating its own pattern: it repeats itself in a future of repetitions that reinstitute the absent transcendence that both cuts it and delimits it. It is an obsession with and, in the unaccepted, unacceptable absence of its ideal.

Yet, ascetic self-overcoming in the form of self-denial, truncated as it is in its own denial, is self-overcoming nonetheless, and the figures of the ascetic priest and the ascetic ideal are definitive of Nietzsche's genealogy of them. In seeing how this is so, we shall see how the definitive structure of valuation in Nietzsche's discourse is self-overcoming and how the possibility of valuative thinking comes into question. It is Nietzsche's own self-overcoming that raises the question of ethics, and this self-overcoming is simultaneously the self-overcoming of the ascetic priest. Thus, a major aspect in the formation of traditional philosophical thought and evaluation no longer assumes the figure of self-denial but that of self-affirmation. The distance that enables this genealogy to "defend" the ascetic priest and the ascetic ideal is the distance necessary to affirm the ascetic priest in its meaning by affirming self-overcoming—but in this case, self-overcoming without self-denial. It is a distance that allows for a middle voice of self-overcoming that takes momentary priority over the stances of activity and passivity. Self-overcoming without self-denial both permeates Nietzsche's discourse and has its basis in the ascetic ideal's violent, anxious, and blindly combative heritage. In this affirmation the obsession with self-denial in the ascetic ideal's heritage is broken. Self-overcoming comes self-overcoming like a vortex that is finally released to flow no longer in the repetition of self-denying formations, but in a dispersion of possibilities previously withheld from this heritage. Nietzsche's distance from the ascetic priest is a distance of self-recognition in which the seriousness of meaning for life is weakened enough to allow an affirmation of its own self-overcoming movement. In Nietzsche's experience one can think in this movement and not die. One can think it and become more alive.

The movement of self-overcoming in the ascetic ideal in Nietzsche's account thus involves the following aspects:

1. Part of the ascetic ideal's meaning is found in five elements of unconscious will:

(a) Sensual attraction, that is, its seductive charm—"a touch of morbidezza [found] in fair flesh" in women; "the angelic look of a plump pretty animal." The ascetic ideal intensifies the sensual by dissembling it.

(b) Its justificatory power for weak and incapable people: we can see ourselves as too good for this world, "a saintly form of debauch" that provides a sense of significance amid pain, boredom, and flawed activity.

(c) The means of attracting power and justifying it among religious leaders—the Gandhi or St. Francis syndrome whereby an ascetic individual, or, in many cases, the *seemingly* ascetic individual or group, is given enormous leverage because they deny their bodies and in a broken way become the image of both the ascetic ideal and the self-overcoming will to will.

(d) The means of expressing lust for everlasting association with life by self-denial. Nietzsche calls it the cupidity of saints.

(e) Always, in all its forms, the meaning of the ascetic ideal is found in human horror in the face of mere emptiness, the "human horror of a vacuum."

2. The meaning of the ascetic ideal gives expression to the vacuum that it intends to overcome. This "higher spirituality" is a type of willing that fills mere lack of meaning with images, goals, projects, and ideas that mean nothing beyond their own endeavor. They express the vacuum that they propose to overcome.

3. The continuing factor in all types of the ascetic ideal is the will to will. Humans would "rather will nothingness [i.e., the ideals of life-denial] than not will at all."

4. The ascetic ideal developed out of previous, opposite valuations and fear of life as structured by those valuations. The opposite values that Nietzsche finds prior to what we call civilized life or history include cruelty, dissembling, revenge, slander of reason, the good of danger, etc. (III 9). The ascetic ideal developed as an internalizing of these values in forms of denial that inverted love of life into suspicion and malice toward life. Cruelty, for example, turned into love of the weak and sick coupled with a dissembling self-denial and its consequent suffering in the form of weakening and sickening human lives.

5. The meanings and strategies of the ascetic ideal give both form and content to philosophy. They are found in the withdrawn contemplative spirit of wisdom, "nonjudgmental" objectivity, suspicion of the senses and of sensuality, lofty rejection of everyday life, and the priority of representation and belief over creation and assertion.

6. The ascetic ideal in philosophy undergoes transformation by its genealogical account into a different kind of freedom and thinking. We are able to represent to ourselves the seriousness of this ideal in a history of its striving for the rights of representation (III 10). We can describe the ideal's drive to "compel its acceptance," how it promotes its own growth and prosperity in the life-inimical species that it breeds, how it seeks to master life by its life-denial. This drive for mastery that turns against its own life has led to suspicion of its own life-mastery, to questioning

and doubt regarding its own truth. Its self-denial turns against itself in genealogical thought. Its commanding self-absorbed perspective has re-coiled upon itself and produced new genealogical knowledge of itself. Its blind refusal of meaninglessness has been transformed into a reassertion of its own meaninglessness, into a denial of its own meaning. This means that the recoil of the ascetic ideal on itself, with its disgust over life, has transformed its own nay-saying into yea-saying by the transvaluation of founded meaning into meanings that are created and affirmed in the midst of no meaning at all.

7. The self-overcoming of the ascetic ideal is a movement in Nietzsche's genealogy. In this case we can say that self-overcoming, not a perspective, a law, or a form of life that rejects the ascetic ideal, is Nietzsche's thought in his account of the ascetic ideal.

5. "Probably It Infects Even Us"

The ascetic priest's own self-overcoming movement is found in part in the interplay of denial and affirmation that structures the ascetic ideal: "The no he says to life brings to light, as if by magic, an abundance of tender yeses; even when he *wounds* himself, this master of destruction, of self-destruction—the very wound itself afterward compels him *to live*" (III 13). The life of his self-denial compels him to live with intensity and passion and in this sense his life is self-seeking and self-affirming. But the future of this life is severely delimited by the fear of life that moves the ascetic ideal. Fear of life is expressed as continuous repetition of values that embody the ideal. In the ascetic ideal's power a person is repelled by the (self-overcoming) *life* that moves in the denial. Not-this-life is willed intensely: that is the sickness, the nihilism, of Western contemplation as it developed into the mainstream of our philosophical heritage. Denial of the self-overcoming movement that characterizes the life of the ascetic ideal is definitive of this sickness. The move out of depressed fatigue with life in its ambiguity, meaninglessness, and suffering is blocked by the factors of fear and denial, and the yes made possible by the ascetic priest turning denial against itself is lost in the obsessive quailing before things as they are. Until this fear and denial recoil against themselves, wince before their recognized and, in that sense, affirmed self-contradiction, the release of self-overcoming that silently infests the ascetic ideal is lost.

The suppressed movement of life-affirmation in the dominant structure of life-denial makes possible the self-overcoming of self-denial. This is the first of three aspects that we shall note concerning the self-overcoming of the ascetic ideal. The affirmation of life-affirmation, however, which under the circumstances is also an affirmation of self-overcoming, is the missing element of the ascetic ideal. When the ascetic ideal recoils in this affirmation in the movement of Nietzsche's genealogy, the life-affirmation that is suppressed by life-denial rebounds to form a different and productive focus of thought and living. We find this focus at work in Nietzsche's genealogy of the ascetic ideal as he overcomes the ideal through his affirmation of its force within his own discourse. We shall turn to that force after we consider a second self-overcoming element in the ascetic ideal.

The life-affirmation at work through the ascetic priest is found in the exploitation "of the bad instincts of all sufferers for the purpose of self-discipline, self-surveillance, and self-overcoming" (III 16). By the consolation that the ascetic priest and the ascetic ideal provide, those besotted with "guilt, sin, sinfulness, depravity, damnation," those people who are thoroughly defeated in their lives, turn the defeat on themselves by means of practices and disciplines that institutionalize their lostness. One effect of such consolation is to create communities of the consoled, which separate them from those who are able to live without sin or consolation. There are two self-overcoming factors in this part of Nietzsche's description: that of a falling back under the force of life, and that of rebounding in restrained self-surveillance and self-negation. In this instance the self-destructive, depressed self is overcome by its own consoling denial and becomes the life-affirming, life-denying contradiction that we examined in the previous two paragraphs.[9]

We note with emphasis "the chief trick" of the ascetic priest (GM III 20). Nietzsche's clear insight that our traditional experiences of "ecstasy" *[Entrücken]* are affiliated with the maintenance of guilt, both as fallenness from transcendence and as moral failure, will help us to see the structural play of the affections of transcendence within the ascetic ideal. In Part Two (Sections 2–6) of *On the Genealogy of Morals,* Nietzsche shows that cruelty and suffering are components in the formation and functions of memory, that memory is affiliated with a person's promising a future action and affiliated as well with contractual relations in which the debtor is guilty in the senses of being inadequate to some demand or need and borrowing in response to the demand or need. The capacity to make promises, a capacity that is bred in suffering and cruelty—suffering and cruelty are parts of the 'life' of promising—this *capacity* includes an individual's indebtedness to the future in a present inadequacy and by expected completeness vis-à-vis future events. Promising includes the individual's ability to affirm itself in its painful inadequacy. The individual can promise itself in its inadequacy to the future. Part of the self-overcoming of guilt is found in ecstatic—that is, future-oriented—confirmation of guilt, which is now a genealogical condition of the body and mind that could otherwise exist without guilt. This ecstasy is one of standing out into the future and removing oneself from the limits of the present. For Nietzsche, ecstasy is a matter of temporal transcendence based on a capacity to make promises. The ascetic priest's chief trick of providing life-affirmation by means of life-denial is thus unconsciously in the lineage of the cruelty of memory's formation. Paradoxically it embodies the continuing fissure of indebtedness to the future in its own self-overcoming movement as it attempts to overcome guilt. While Nietzsche's account of guilt emphasizes relations of time, however, the ascetic priest's formulation is organized by the idea of the perfect, judging, transcendent being. The ascetic priest takes ecstasy as transcending time by a relation to a nontemporal being. The priest's "trick" is to appear to transcend the temporality that constitutes the ecstasy: to affirm life by negating its dispersing temporality. On the contrary, Nietzsche finds ecstasis in the structure of time: an individual stands out of the present by promising a future yet to be and by remembering a past that is no longer. His is a temporal ecstasis, whereas the ascetic priest's is an ecstasy of standing out of time into a timeless reality. The latter transcendental ecstasy denies the temporality of its own occurrence—denies its life—in its ideal of transcendence.

The strategy at issue here is the principal means of relieving life-threatening anxiety that is unbearable for many individuals. Emotional intensity is cultivated by pulling people away from the senseless suffering of life by "raptures" *[Entzückungen]* of feeling; that is, they are carried away from life *[entrückt]* by the delight *[entzückt]* of affections that embody the idea that everything, and most particularly suffering, has meaning. The enraptured person stands out [ek-stasis] from temporal, physical, sensuous, mortal existence in an "orgy" of meaning-affect (GM III 20). Instead of low-energy melancholy, he or she thus experiences intensity of anger (righteous indignation), fear (those who look upon the face of God shall die), voluptuousness (Jesus the groom), meaning-saturated despair (Where art Thou, O Lord, in my hour of need?), etc. The feelings or morbidity are overcome in the ecstasies of guilt in which one knows oneself to be in the forgiving judgment of a righteous God.

Traversing these feelings are reasons for suffering and injustice: we are guilty before God, shortfallen and inadequate, bound to err, in desperate need of a redemption in which the failures of human life are made good by the healing God. We come to know ourselves in this transaction, this rapture, as beings who find in their guilt reason to live in the light of a transcendent divine meaning for life. The cruelty of this ecstasy is found in its wrenching a person from the conditions of self-enhancing life and projecting them into a structure of fallen, always guilty life, bowed before a higher life. Suffering means just punishment from which one is released by grace. The self-overcoming element of this ecstasy is found as guilt is turned on itself, clarifies itself, and comes to know itself in the processes of its own escape. The "sickness" of perpetuated guilt is the genealogical condition for a return to that "health" in which the meaninglessness of suffering-guilt is affirmed and the 'meaning' of the ascetic ideal is thereby overturned.

We could view this overturning as itself a kind of rapture in which a new affection of life-affirmation takes place. But in that case we must separate it from the ascetic ideal's meaning of ecstasis. For Nietzsche, life-affirmation stands inside, not outside, the meaningless suffering of life; the move to the *Übermensch*, a being beyond guilt and redemption, is not a transcendent ecstasis, but one of living through and going beyond the heritage of conscience. (In chapter 5 we shall consider whether Heidegger's account of the ecstases of temporality avoids the ascetic ideal and its escape from time.)

The second self-overcoming factor is found in the "creation of a chasm between healthy and sick" (GM III 16). In this instance, the countervalence is not internal to the conscience of the ascetic ideal but is the divide between the communities of consolation and individuals who do not need the ascetic ideal's strategies of survival in the face of the meaninglessness of life. The chasm between these differences is itself a gap without meaning, a mere difference that makes possible a coiling again of the energy of those who are not suffocated by resentment so that they are released for creative work beyond the limits of the saved and the damned. This chasm makes possible the development of bodies that are not (de-)formed by the "physiological depression" of life-defeat.

A third movement of self-overcoming is found in the apparent opposition of the ascetic ideal and the disciplines of modern knowledge. These disciplines have embodied opposition to the blind beliefs of the moral and religious traditions, have been nurtured by the values of enlightenment, and generally have "survived well enough without God, the beyond, and the virtues of denial" (GM III 23). But philosophical knowledge in particular is also characterized by faith in the value of truth. "This unconditional will to truth is *faith in the ascetic ideal* itself, even if as an unconscious imperative" (GM III 24). This faith is the moving force of modern knowledge and thought, and is an internalization of the ascetic ideal by which contemplative people protect and explain themselves. Because of it, people search for knowledge and think that they discover meaning and truth everywhere they turn. In this faith, truth appears to have a transcendent status. It stands beyond mortal life, is pure in relation to the tarnish of coming to be and passing away, and makes poor our humble attempts to approach it. This faith requires a sharp division between the sensuous body and its passing achievements on the one hand and the agency whose promise it is to know truth and perhaps become true on the other. In this faith, knowledge and thought are disembodied, spiritualized, and given disciplines of abstraction and separation from the world. The ascetic ideal creates this value. Philosophy and the other disciplines of knowledge are formed by it. In philosophical knowledge and thought, the "affects grow cool, the tempo of life slows down, dialectics in place of instinct, seriousness imprinted on faces and gestures (seriousness, the most unmistakable sign of a labored metabolism, of struggling, laborious life)" (GM III 25).

This unconscious collaboration of the ascetic ideal and modern disciplines of thought and knowledge defines the structure of self-overcoming in Nietzsche's genealogy. The issue is one of meaning—the meaning that generates and maintains abstraction and separation from the living, temporal, and changeable movements of that meaning. Nietzsche emphasizes the negative roles of sensuality, fundamental change, physical processes, and mortality on the one hand, and robust, self-accepting self-assertion on the other. The negative recoils in the processes of abstraction and separation include quailing before the mortal, mutational life of 'truth', quailing usually in the form of fear, disgust, and anxiety; falling back under the impact of meaninglessness; rebounding in types of life-denial; and coiling again in disciplines, ritual repetitions of imposed meanings, petty pleasures, uncritical and unsuspicious obedience, and emotional outpourings that enhance guilt, that is, a sense of fallen and unworthy distance between one's ordinary physical and psychological life and some transcendent perfection such as truth. Nietzsche's discourse takes part in these recoils. His is a genealogy in which the will to truth attains self-consciousness and finds in that process that truth evaporates in a will to will.

"All great things," Nietzsche says, "bring about their own destruction through an act of self-overcoming: thus the law of life will have it, the law of the necessity of 'self-overcoming' in the nature of life. . . . In this way Christianity *as a dogma* was destroyed by its own morality; in the same way Christianity *as morality* must now perish too: we stand on the threshold of *this* event. After Christianity truthfulness has drawn one inference after another, it must end by drawing *its most striking inference,* its inference *against* itself; this will happen, however, when it poses the question *'what is the meaning of all will to truth?'"* (GM III 27). This is the question that controls Part Three of *On the Genealogy of Morals.* It is the question that moves the discourse, and it means that Nietzsche recognizes in his thought the moribund life of Christian morality and the ascetic ideal. He continues, "What meaning would *our* whole being possess if it were not this, that in *us* the will to truth becomes conscious of itself as a problem?" [emphasis added]. The problem of the genealogy of the ascetic ideal is the meaning that constitutes it, Nietzsche, and "us." "As the will to truth thus gains self-consciousness—there can be no doubt of that—morality will gradually *perish* now: this is the great spectacle in a hundred acts reserved for the next two centuries in Europe—the most terrible, questionable, and perhaps the most helpful of all spectacles" (GM III 27). The meaning and truth—the ethos—of Nietzsche's own genealogy is thus in question.

"Our" account of Nietzsche's genealogy of the ascetic ideal has as one of its own genealogical aspects something that Nietzsche's did not have: Nietzsche's genealogy. We have verged on thinking beyond Nietzsche as we have organized his writing in a voice that was not his to control—the middle voice of self-overcoming—and as we have followed the effects of that movement. We have not undergone his pain over the loss of infinite meaning, for example. We have not felt Zarathustra's nausea. We *could* say this is because we have not felt deeply enough or spiritually enough. But we know that Nietzsche has put in question the meanings of both 'depth' and 'spirituality', and we pause before capitulating to their attraction. The ambivalence that Nietzsche experienced between laughter and terror over the loss of founded, teleological time need not be so poignant for us as it was for him when we have undergone the movement of his discourse. Whereas he struggled to find courage to endure the self-overcoming of both religious and moral beliefs, the passage of the monopolizing power of those beliefs has yielded to a much less troubled discursive organization. No matter how frequently we participate in religious and moral faiths, we may know that their meanings are optional and may feel, perhaps with keen alertness, the vacuum of human meaning; we may know this and yet feel no inclination to worship, to search for truth, or to look for transcendent justification of our values or continuity of meaning among our transactions. We know that both religion and morality may well carry not only their own means of destruction, but may well be destructive for us when we live by them. These emotions and this knowledge indicate part of the effect of Nietzsche's self-overcoming. We can be no more than tempted by aspects of our tradition whose passing threatened catastrophe for Nietzsche.

On the other hand, we do not need to look beyond ourselves to register the continuing effects of the ascetic ideal. I have said that one of this ideal's phenomena is found in our own reading of Nietzsche. But we can also trace the effects of self-overcoming in the weakening of those emotions that collect around the loss of foundations, the nineteenth-century ideas of subjectivity, God, and the power of the idea of unity. The traces of Nietzsche's self-overcoming are found as well in the growing attraction of the ideas of breach, division, fragment, scission, void, torsion, recoil, verge, and horizon. There is probably a strong temptation for us to feel satisfaction in intellectual types of humility, poverty, and chastity regarding texts, and one way beyond the ideal is concentration on self-overcoming which recoils and repeatedly occurs without reestablishing a center of focus that escapes the voice of its own overcoming. In this case, self-overcoming does not suggest dominance and exclusion in the name of the traditional notion of right. Alternatives to the traditional ethics of suppression and outcasting, to the insistence on founded meanings, might emerge from this movement. Even that hope, however, may legitimately raise our suspicions. The nonethics of self-overcoming doubtlessly threatens the loss of those satisfactions we feel when we struggle for right and justice understood according to their inherited meanings. But in the recoil of self-overcoming that overthrows morality from within its own genealogy, and in the rebound to options that we cannot foresee, we might expect less of that asceticism that is able to affirm life only by distorting it in the names of meaning and goodness, that remembers only by outcasting its mere vacuum, and that fears its margins even more than it fears its closure to its own voice of self-overcoming.

Has a springing out from Nietzsche's genealogy occurred during the writing and reading of this chapter? Has there been a recoil in our reading of Nietzsche, a recoil that moves in, to, and beyond the horizon of Nietzsche's thought? In *On the Genealogy of Morals,* the ascetic ideal comes to a horizonal awareness in which the genealogical discourse on the ascetic ideal recoils in the discovery that it has given its own lineage and found itself in the ascetic ideal, not beyond it, but aware in it, and this awareness appears to give a different horizon from that of the ascetic ideal, one aspect of which is the *question* of ethics. This genealogy discovers itself as a spectator of the ascetic ideal and as a recoiling part of the ascetic ideal. In willing its own truth, the genealogy wills the self-overcoming recoils that move without awareness in the ascetic ideal. Nietzsche's genealogical discourse moves beyond the ascetic ideal only in the sense that it affirms the recoils that pollute the ascetic ideal and that infect it with self-overcoming and with the vacuum to which self-overcoming bears witness.

I have emphasized this discursive movement, not the experience of a genealogist, not the self-consciousness of an individual, but the discourse that puts the genealogist beyond the reach of any instance of consciousness or experience. Is this reading in the springing movement of Nietzsche's genealogy a different product from what he would or could have done? In recoiling back to Nietzsche's genealogy, are we one step removed from the ascetic ideal that his genealogy found within its own discourse? Or are we still within the penumbra of the ascetic priest, entranced by the play of shadows, less aware of the priest's shadow than Nietzsche was? My dilemma is found in the posture of a thinking and rethinking that distances, disciplines, and purifies Nietzsche's texts. My question is whether there is a recoil *in* this *distance* that is springing from the part played in our lineage by Nietzsche's genealogy, whether in coiling again my own discourse is under the force of Nietzsche's spring which pushed his own language to a place in which the individual's experience could be undone by discourses that move in recoils that are of the language's own making. My clue has been that the vacuum no longer seems so terrible, that Nietzsche's pathos is less intense in a lineage that has sprung from his work, that the space of spectating might be able to will more freely its own pollution of meaninglessness and differences without identity.

I am ending with the question of thought and a question of ethics, with questions that do not demand answers but demand, rather, their own continuation as questions by recoiling on themselves, with the thought that the priority of question recoils in Nietzsche's affirmation of self-overcoming, an affirmation that moved thought through the nihilism of self-overcoming to self-overcoming as a spring for thought without the necessity of asceticism's denial of its own self-overcoming movement.

The distance of our stance is thus in question. Nietzsche might call it the pathos of distance. If this distance moves in a springing recoil of Nietzsche's genealogy, if it is a distance of recoiling "in vain" (GM II 28), then it is not a purified space for meaning but a movement of question without answer, a movement that in recoiling on itself produces neither solution nor moralities, but produces a quality that approaches us as a shade without a will to certainty, a Dionysian quality that is the voice of self-overcoming. The discipline of the distance of our stance regarding Nietzsche is found in maintaining the priority of question. Does *this* discipline recoil on the ascetic ideal of the *Wissenschaften*? By maintaining the priority of question, are we engaged in a self-overcoming of the ascetic ideal in our work as philosophers? Do you find it disconcerting, as I do, that we, by this discipline of distance regarding Nietzsche's texts, have less of the ascetic ideal to live by? Less intensity? Less meaning? Do we find more to will—more will—in this loss of meaning? Can we be philosophers who do not mortar and fill in the cracks among the fragments of values and meanings? Can we as philosophers suffer and parody the 'why'? Know without wanting to be wise? Read with laughter the great thoughts, and live without heroes? Can we maintain the distance of the questioning discourse in Nietzsche's recoils? Or must we once again return to the comforts of the ascetic priest, will meaning among all things, and answer the question—why human existence at all?—in order to have the energy to think and to be?

The question of ethics is found in the self-overcoming of Nietzsche's discourse. It is not a question that is structured by a group of values that oppose another group, but is rather embodied in a way of thinking and knowing that comes to its consciousness as it "affirms" the limits of meaning in the surpassing transgression of no meaning at all. Nietzsche's genealogy does not attempt to find the thought and language that will make its limits of expression or the limits of expressiveness—the difference of no meaning at all—into a nonevaluating 'power' in a discursive organization. That is one of the issues that Nietzsche's self-overcoming left for thought and contemplation. He made the question of ethics unavoidable in his thought and brought faith in meaning and in the will to truth to their own limits in such a way that the question of ethics becomes conspicuous in his self-overcoming genealogy.

THREE

Ethics Is the Question

The Fragmented Subject in Foucault's Genealogy

Foucault's genealogical and archeological studies of both modern and classical practices and discourses give accounts of *ethea* and of our predisposition to establish normative ethics. His language and movement of thought, however, are not ethical. That his discourse could be so filled with lineages of ethical standards and the desire for these standards and yet not be ethical or express desire to be ethical defines the issues to which we now turn. The continuous recoil of ethical thought and desire in his work, whereby the possibility of ethics becomes questionable, is the subject of this chapter.

Foucault's acceptance of his Nietzschean inheritance is clear. Although the ideas of the will to power, *Übermensch,* and eternal return, the specific contents of most of Nietzsche's genealogies, the roles of Schopenhauer and Wagner in Nietzsche's thought, and Nietzsche's readings of most of his predecessors do not play a notable role in Foucault's thought, we shall find the prominence of the ascetic ideal, the replacement in knowledge of logic by genealogy, the refusal of contemplative self-possession, and above all the recoiling movement of self-overcoming in his work. The question of ethics rather than an ethics of liberation is characteristic of his discourse. The distinction is one between the ethical thought that he discusses genealogically and the movement of his own thought in that process. While Foucault espoused many causes in his lifetime and worked always within a framework of values, the self-overcoming movement that characterizes his writing and his view of the nonviability of self-constitution put in question the normative status of the values that find expression in his thought and hierarchies. His is a movement away from a new subjectivization of the self that promotes a "better" way of caring for oneself or for a general population.

Ethics, according to Foucault, is defined by the manner in which selves constitute themselves. Do people in a given culture make themselves into aesthetic subjects, subjects of desire, subjects of pleasure? Subjects of an a priori law? How do they recognize themselves and put themselves to work on themselves? What are their primary problems? Desires? Styles? Lives? Self-actualizations? By what means do they recognize their moral obligations in everyday life? By reason? Divine law? Cultural ideals? Feelings? How do they go about expressing or restraining themselves? By self-examination? Examining nature? Investigating reason? To what end do they constitute themselves? To the end of purity? Freedom? Self-mastery? Authenticity?[1]

Foucault's enquiry is not directed toward a new self-relation, however. In sharp contrast to developing or even suggesting an ethical option, Foucault "defines the conditions in which human beings 'problematize' what they are, what they do, and the world they live in" (UP 10). Rather than arguing for a position regarding what people ought to do, who they ought to be, or how the world should be changed, he engages in a process of "constantly checking" the regulations, procedures, and constellations of power that make up our inheritances for identity and commitment.[2] The Western phenomenon of the ethical self is always in question in his work. "I am not looking for an alternative," he says. "Rather I would like to do genealogy of problems, of *problematiques*."[3]

Foucault's distance from ethical and political self-relation is part of his approach to our ethical and political lineage. His access to this lineage, as he conceived it in the three volumes of *The History of Sexuality,* is found in "problematizations" that occurred as an ethos suffered uncertainty concerning its axiomatic procedures and practices that emerge both on the basis of the meanings and values in the lives of those practices and on the basis of a weakening of those meanings and values. The ethos becomes a problem to itself. In the midst of living in the normal self-relations of a given culture, people begin to experience uncertainty about their ethical lives and step away from themselves by means of reflection on themselves. This distancing, which is neither opposition to nor clear departure from the given self-relations, creates the conditions for transformations of the difficulties and obstacles that have given rise to uncertainty. It provides a space for diverse practical solutions, although the distancing movement itself does not suggest any particular solution.[4]

Foucault uses the phrase "history of thought" to name the study of problematizations. This type of history is distinct from an analysis of systems of representations or one of attitudes and types of actions. Representations—axiomatic ideas, myths, symbols—underlie a group of behaviors. Attitudes and types of actions constitute a group of behaviors. Thought, as Foucault uses the word, "is what allows one to step back from this way of acting or reacting, to present it to oneself as an object of thought, and question it as to its meaning, its conditions, and its goals. Thought is freedom in relation to what one does, the motion by which one detaches oneself from it, establishes it as an object, and reflects on it as a problem."[5] When Foucault analyzes problematizations, he, too, is engaged in thinking as he defines it. In his case, however, thought attends not only to an ethos or to a functioning morality, but primarily to the problematizations by which the ethos comes into question. Instead of re-forming a problemed ethics out of ethical concern, he takes as his primary point of departure the emergence of uncertainty and detachment regarding a complex body of ethical behavior. He maximizes the freedom in relation to what one does, and *this* freedom is the aspect of his own lineage that accents his own procedures.

When we keep in mind that the lineage of distance and detachment define the freedom or liberation of Foucault's thought, we can see that far from an ethics of liberation he is thinking in a way that intensifies transformation without proposing solutions. We shall see that rather than proposing a new form of self-relation (that is, a new kind of ethic), Foucault's genealogical work holds in question the ethical project of self-relation. His genealogical analyses and their multiple recoils constitute a discourse that makes modern ethics and morality optional as a form of human life. The heritage of distance and problematization returns repeatedly to itself in his work in such a way that ethical life as we have come to think of it, and not just a particular ethic, appears doubtful.

Why does he set aside a new self-constitution as a definitive goal of his work? Why does he refuse to engage in political action and to rejuvenate positive virtues in his writing? Why does he undercut his reader's attempts to read his work as an ethics of liberation from inherited confinements? "My point," he says, "is not that everything is bad, but that everything is dangerous, which is not exactly the same as bad."[6]

The locale of danger is found in the traditional practices of making divisions. We find these practices in the divisions of well and sick, sane and insane, the laudatory and mean, the elevated and low, the self-enhancing and self-destructive—in a phrase, in the normal and abnormal, the good and bad—as well as divisions between men and women and authority and subject. Wherever there are normalizing divisions there are ordering powers on which both a given arrangement and a hierarchy of judgment and discrim-ination depend. Foucault's intention in his work on ethics is to show "the different modes by which human beings are made subjects."[7] He finds that in our recent history individuals are governed in a way that mandates interiorization of rules for self-formation and that sovereign powers control an individual by the ways in which a self regulates itself. Ethical meanings as well as regional arrangements of power are found in the very process of self-formation. Foucault cannot put in question the operators of power and the subjection of individuals that they effect if he merely changes the meanings and the authorities. He sees the need, rather, to break the totality that characterizes the formation of self and the power inherent in the formation. Unless this is done, his thought will replace one kind of subjectivation with another, and the process of subjectivation is the thing that he wants to think through, from which he wants to keep his distance and detachment.

We shall see that the process of making divisions recoils on itself in Foucault's thought as he both thinks on the basis of and separates himself from the dividing activity that defines the life and knowledge of the modern self. In this way he puts in question not only the particular powers and knowledge that circulate through the dividing process. He also puts in question the domination that moves in the self-forming circulation. Foucault's intention is to give an analysis that interrupts the subjectivation characteristic of self-formation, without suggesting an ideal of anarchy or another kind of self-constitution. The idea of self is in question.

Hence the importance of his recognition that everything, including of course his own discourse, is dangerous. In his accounts of ethics and morality (for example, in *Power/Knowledge*), the danger of self-formation (that is, of the ethical) is the object of tension. The modern complex of dispersed sovereignty in the form of self-regulating subjects must be distanced. The sovereignty of methodologies that define our knowledge and the values that maintain the silent, invisible infrastructure of disciplinary power must be held in question (PK 105–6). The dispersion of sovereignty in this case is the 'basis' of his thought, which recoils back on the dispersion and displaces the sovereignty that circulates through modern selves. Foucault does not make dispersion an ideal or a regulating principle. He finds it and intensifies it in its function of making subjects; and as he monitors it, putting in question the authority by which sovereignty is dispersed in selves, he exposes the dangers inherent in the principles and identities that are created by its movement.

The kinship among our "best" values and the evils that they recognize and oppose is an important aspect of the danger. Two of the West's recent "diseases" of power, fascism and Stalinism, "used and extended mechanisms already present in most other societies. More than that: in spite of their own internal madness, they used to a large extent the ideas and devices of our political rationality" (PK 209). The madness of these two diseases is not totally separated from the procedures of normalcy by which 'good' orders and orders of 'goods' are arranged. The rationality of good sense, whereby the general welfare of a population is pursued, and the formation of regulated selves are themselves divisive processes. They divide, even as they seek unification, by the excluding and hierarchizing power of their own imperatives. The pursuit of the general welfare and the formation of selves establish totalizing movements by their own activity. These totalizing movements, which are definitive of modern states, institutions, and selves—as well as many other ideas and values that are taken to function for the good of us all—appear to Foucault to create the conditions of fascism and to create those conditions in the process of achieving the 'good things' sought by the state.

If Foucault's thought, in its exposure of the rationalities that form us, has a totalizing movement, or if it is regulated by the best that our culture has to offer, it will have perpetuated the very danger that he hopes to make evident. His intention is to create a discourse that is attuned to its own dangers as it analyzes other dangers. His discourse, which is not a group of rules for self-formation, is governed by recoiling movements that prevent their instantiation in principles of conduct or in self-relation. Our intuitive inclination to look for practical 'cash value' in studies of values, our impulse to make ourselves better by applying the values of the discourse, our hope of improving the world by reading Foucault are the kinds of motivations that his work makes questionable. In these motivations flow the powers of ethics that Foucault holds in question as he constructs a discourse that resists 'practicality' and that holds open a horizon for multiple solutions that might be as far from Foucault's thought as Christian confession is from Greek aesthetics. Freedom from danger is not an expectation in Foucault's work, but ignorance of dangers, particularly the ignorance that is enforced by our finest disciplines, professions, and knowledge, is the object of his analysis.

The ethical disappointment that accompanies the modesty of Foucault's project is one of its threats for his readers. In the midst of terrible suffering and cruel domination, we, at our ethical best, want hope bred of the possibility of relief from the causes of evil. Rather than yielding to this misleading hope, Foucault refers to "the fascism that causes us to love power, to desire the very thing that dominates and exploits us."[8]

He does not look for a specific, pragmatic alternative to fascism, but attempts to put in question the fascism inherent in idealistic, 'good' political movements as well as in the Western practice of self-constitution. Our selves, our identities, want to refuse the openness of this exposure. We naturally want to provide something better, and the disappointment of no clear and operational alternative throws us back, not on ourselves, but on the doubtfulness as to whether we truly are the selves we seem to be. As modern selves we want self-constitution in any case. As ethical persons we want good axioms, beyond question. Monitoring the disappointment and its accompanying anxiety, which come from the question of ethics, and the deep mourning for selfhood are not incidental to reading Foucault. *Everything* is dangerous, and that presumed fact leaves us without an unquestioned arbitrary sovereignty or an internalized discipline of subjectivation to inspire in us overwhelming conviction and ethical passion. Could our passion for full commitment to right and goodness be reflected in the madness of fascism? Could our selves in their strongest sincerity be implicated in the blindness of repressive regimes? Could our positive senses for unity and wholeness forecast the inevitability of the destructions they intend to overcome? "The search for a form of morality acceptable to everyone in the sense that everyone would have to submit to it, seems catastrophic to me."[9] This is not primarily a statement about the relativity of all values. It is a statement about the catastrophic dangers of drives for unity, universality, and wholeness—it is a statement about selfhood. And yet Foucault is not disappointed. If anything, he is exhilarated. How this exhilaration—reminiscent of Nietzschean affirmation—arises out of the self-overcoming recoils of his thought will be a continuing question for the remainder of this chapter.

1. Genealogy's Ethos

An ethos—a living movement of thought—takes place in Foucault's discourse. We have seen that it does not constitute or lead to an ethics. I have suggested that this movement is one of recoil, that the distance and divisions of traditional ethical formations recoil in Foucault's thought in a way that displaces the structures and desires of self-relation, and that Foucault's thought recoils on itself in a way that prevents it from becoming a basis for specific ethical programs. Its middle voice, we shall see, is found in a recoiling movement that keeps ethics as such in question. We shall first see how this recoiling occurs in three of Foucault's specific studies of the formation of the self as we know it and live it. By the recoiling movement of his thought the idea of self-constitution is held at bay, and hence the possibility of ethics is made optional in the ethos of Foucault's genealogy.

A. RECOILING KNOWLEDGES

Characteristically, Foucault's genealogies produce knowledge that falls back on its own inheritance and by this return recoils away from the powers that have ordered things and protected themselves in the given, inherited discourse.[10] The recoil may occur under the force of the genealogical study, as in the case of *The Order of Things* in which the study pushes itself back to the events and disruptions that have led to the attraction and viability of genealogical knowledge. In this case the mutations and disruptions that have been traditionally ignored and are major forces in forming the structures of knowledge under investigation are given power in the order and formation of Foucault's discourse. His genealogical recoil, in the sense of falling back, involves returning to the lineage of his work, uncovering the nonsystematic interruptions in systematic knowledge, showing that these interruptions are motivations toward genealogy within nongenealogical methodologies and epistemic orders, and recasting the reformation and succession of these methodologies and epistemic orders in relation to the mutations and disruptions that they have systematically ignored. His genealogical knowledge falls back on its lineage by the force of factors in the lineage that have been excluded from the lineage's self-interpretation.

There is a second kind of recoil in *The Order of Things*. In it the knowledge developed by the genealogical study has the effect of coiling again the various discursive and epistemic strands and forming a springing, self-overcoming movement whereby the truth of this knowledge is relegated to a lineage that is itself now in question. This recoiling movement includes an appropriation *by the genealogical knowledge* of its place in the lineage of the discourse-specific regularities ("necessities") that order and define the knowledges that it studies. It arises, for example, out of both the rupture of the modern subject of knowledge and the regularities of knowledge that define this rupture. This kind of recoiling movement, in the sense of coiling again in a springing movement, brings to light in Foucault's genealogical knowledge both the regional and permutational formations that constitute the recoiling movement and the space of dissociation that characterizes it.

Foucault's genealogical knowledge is always in a position to critique, mock, parody, and ironize itself. The possibility of parody according to Foucault, for example, arises from "the unreality" that helps produce our images and interpretations of the past—the projections that arise from the confederations of meaning and sense of a specific discourse. As the projective "unreality" that makes genealogy possible in our heritage comes to be "enjoyed" in a genealogical study, the genealogy becomes susceptible to the parody that it exercises on the subject of analysis (LCM 160–61). It finds satisfaction in the instability of its certainties, and this satisfactory instability, as we shall see, is a significant part of its recoil from the orders and practices that it uncovers and that play a role in the uncovering process.

In the context of *Discipline/Punish,* for example, genealogical knowledge recognizes itself in and speaks out of a lineage in which a combination of constraint, control, and punishment are ingredients in the fabric of the genealogical discipline that produces this knowledge. But this knowledge coils itself in a springlike suspicion (as aspect of satisfaction in its own instability) in its process of seeing and recognizing and has the effect of releasing itself from the grip of its own concepts. The paradox of this knowledge is found in its uncertain certainty, its releasing the discipline of its accomplishment at its limits and making part of its discipline a cultivation of the instability that will overcome its own procedures and certainties. This release occurs in part as the confinement of discipline is opened out to other options in genealogical disclosure of the disciplinary heritage. Instead of recoiling into a defensive posture or into a posited originary presence or experience, it is a recoiling motion that embodies no more than the tension of its spring out beyond its established territory. In *Discipline/Punish,* one is driven toward a kind of knowledge that, in its disclosure of the concealing, punishing heritage of discipline, is ill at ease with its own discipline and is left with the questionableness of its own knowledge. This recoil is made in part by the torsion of the concealing and uncovering that go on in Foucault's genealogy.

A third type of recoiling that is typical in Foucault's thought is exemplified in *The History of Sexuality* and combines with the springing motion.

Foucault finds that sexual repression is a major force in our modern discourse on sexual liberation. This is a discourse that he names 'sexuality'. Instead of the pleasure of bodies, sexuality inscribes shame of bodily pleasure in the name of sexual liberation. This genealogy, which is found particularly in the discourse of psychoanalysis and its many progeny, is a part of the lineage of fear and repression in the name of sexual liberation, and it comes to be known genealogically as part of this lineage. This genealogical knowledge recoils (in the sense that it winces) before its own history and coils itself again in a springing movement away from its own 'sexuality' in the direction of pleasures that, as a discourse, it does not know how to embody. Such recoiling is made by the forces of wincing, revealing, recognizing, releasing, and constraining—all of which occur in this discourse.

In *The Order of Things, Discipline/Punish,* and *The History of Sexuality* we can say preliminarily that genealogical knowledge recoils on itself and from itself, without the benefit of origins or essences, in a springing movement that is like self-overcoming rather than like the movements of self-establishment or disciplined self-nurturance. We shall examine *The Order of Things* in greater detail later in this chapter, since in this book the formation of genealogical knowledge develops in the question of its own lineage and without either the thought of truth or the will to truth.

B. THE READER'S RECOIL

We have said that Foucault's thought takes place in the movement of his discourse and that reading it and thinking through it involves one in a process distinct from that of standing outside the movement and observing it from within a different configuration of ordering powers. The recoiling, self-overcoming process is not a law or principle of self-preservation or self-realization. It is not like a principle that gives unity or order or telos to the discourse. 'Self-overcoming' names in part the effect of nonsystematizable randomness that moves through a systematic discourse. This randomness, we shall find, has the effect of recoiling our universalizing and categorizing ideas back on themselves by means of their lineage's heterogeneous and arbitrary formations. The absence of extra-discursive law—for example, in the Western formation of laws that are taken to be universal—that kind of instability has a recoiling force when it is thematized within our common orders of concepts and principles. It is the force of recoil in thinking with organizing principles which in their 'work' show that while they themselves are taken to be universally necessary, they are necessary only in the discourse that they unify. Self-overcoming in this context is found in the effect of the known whose stability depends on a discourse that is intrinsically unstable. One finds a torsion of laws that have their authority by virtue of a given lineage and that order all random things within their jurisdiction as though they derived their force from outside their heritage.

In Foucault's case, knowing is in tension with the categories, logics, and exchanges that form his knowledge. His knowledge is anarchic in the sense that no thought of primal origin, foundation, or continuing presence structures the word patterns. This means that as one follows his thinking in the texts, one undergoes the transformation of the metaphysical patterns and habits of thought that are in the text, and, as we shall see, subtle physical transformations also take place that may occasion a hostile recoil on the part of the reader in the sense of shrinking back, wincing, or quailing in the face of the transformative process. This recoil by a reader is, of course, distinct from the self-overcoming rebound of his text. It is a movement away from self-overcoming, and this kind of recoil is often all the more powerful because it is unconscious.

The interaction of rebound from the given heritage in the text and a heritage-bound shrinking from the text in reading it creates a strange situation of interpretation. In shrinking from the text one may exercise a violence against the text by unconsciously and systematically eliminating the work's own self-overcoming as one interprets it. This reaction is evident in some discussions of Foucault, which reinscribe his work in a metaphysical concept or problem, such as the necessity of a constructive concept of subjectivity, an implicit ethics, or a hidden humanism. Others read him as an historicist or historical relativist by ignoring the fact that the meaning of these orientations derives from a way of thinking that polarizes transcendental and temporal reality, a polarization that is problematized and largely eliminated in Foucault's thought. Those who interpret him as a structuralist, for example, overlook the metaphysical concept of structure that characterizes structuralism, as well as its self-enclosed calculus of interpretation, and also eliminate the self-overcoming recoils that move his thought away from a structuralist orientation.

These ways of reading Foucault have in common a reassertion of metaphysical patterns and ideas that are destabilized in Foucault's thought. These interpretations exhibit a shrinking recoil in the face of the self-overcoming that rebounds in and away from its own lineage and forces itself away from its regional center. It repeatedly falls away from the definitive interests and affections of traditional language, and this falling away *in* the discourse both addresses and repels a reader's inherited discourse concerning world order. This engagement is like a mourning experience. As one undergoes the quiet passing away of a scheme of definitive linkages, a pervasive quailing sends one springing back to familiar ground and motivates commentaries that recapitulate a discourse's metaphysical basis for life and hope. *This* recoiling then becomes the movement in the reader, a paradoxical kind of phenomenon, by which one may understand the turning of Foucault's thought to a metaphysics that his thought has overcome. Writing a genealogy of this manner of perverting Foucault makes possible a reentry into the self-overcoming that is carried negatively in the reaction.

C. GENEALOGY AS EFFECTIVE HISTORY AND CURATIVE SCIENCE

In his discussion of Nietzsche's genealogy in *Language, Counter-Memory, Practice,* Foucault outlines a way of writing history that "introduces discontinuity into our very being as it divides our emotions, dramatizes our instincts, multiplies our body, and sets it against itself. 'Effective' history deprives the self of the reassuring stability of life and nature, and it will not permit itself to be transported by a voiceless obstinacy toward a millennial ending" (LCM 154). "Knowledge is allowed to create its own genealogy in an act of cognition; and 'wirkliche Historie' composes a genealogy of history as the *vertical projection of its posture*" (LCM 157; emphasis added).

As a history projects its position vertically, so that its seams, traumas, and mutational confluences become apparent, like layers of sedimentation on a canyon wall, its process is "curative" (LCM 156). The formation of the patterns of knowing that give it its perspectives are apparent, and the effects of all the constraining factors—such as posited necessary causes, continuing presence, or transcendent laws of formation—these effects lose their power to organize blindly the linkages, multiplicity, and disruptions of things. It is the epistemic demand for constant and transcendent elements, elements that are found *in* the layered sedimentation, that give an aura of pathology to the traditional discourses when they are known in the perspective of their discontinuous, broken, and serially repeated associations. In that sense, genealogy is "curative" as it comes to know the fragments and random associations that function as though they were expressions or discourses of nonfragmented, continuous presence. The genealogy recoils on these claims and procedures within the genealogy.

If we stopped at this point we would appear to have a version of a modern enlightenment discourse. Genealogy would appear to shed light on certain metaphysical assumptions and concepts in terms of discontinuity and to cure us of our illusions in the presence of certain overlooked facts in our lineage. But the effect of this kind of history is to show that the genealogical approach is itself an outgrowth of a series of epistemic and institutional patterns and practices that fail to appropriate their own generative, discursive life. The curative aspect is not found in an illumination of a false discourse by a true one, but in a knowledge that finds itself both repeating and departing from the inheritances that it describes. The genealogical description is not outside of the given lineage, but within it in the perspective of its exclusions, borders, unreconciled differences, and strategies of repression.

This recoil within the lineage and away from it takes place in forces embodied in both a disciplined wincing that develops within a given discourse from the perspective of one or more aspects of the discourse before other of its aspects, and a coiling again in the form of genealogical knowledge, which rebounds away from its own authoritative repetition. This recoiling process cures the stoppage induced by self-maintaining and self-repeating centers of power against generative, exposing language and against the emergence of options that come in the wake of disclosed dangers and failures. The genealogical discourse is opened by its exposure of its own lineage to its dissent from itself and to its own overcoming, to its lack of continuous presence in the form of a transdiscursive subjectivity or regulation, and to its own dangers. It is open, as we shall see, to whatever might emerge as *other than* genealogy, as the lineage of genealogy dies away in the recoiling force of its own knowledge. This type of genealogy is not based on an insistence to be true or on a will to power, but occurs in the force of its own self-overcoming recoil. It consists of the conflicts and coalitions within Western thought and practice; it organizes its lineage by the forces of those coalitions and not by the validity of its principles.

We may summarize the elements of genealogical ethos in the following way:

1. Foucault's genealogy is implicated in what it comes to know and is epistemically involved in what it exposes. The disruptions in a given lineage provide a discursive basis for his genealogy's disruptive, curative aspect as he thinks in the perspective of what is excluded from the discourse's organizing forces.

2. The movement of coiling again includes a torsion or springing counterplay of these elements by: (a) making public a lineage's hidden uses of power; (b) uncovering those uses of power and structures of oppression and exclusion in the genealogy's own knowledge; (c) giving disciplined attention to nonsystematizable randomness; (d) giving focus to accidental formations of universalized values and ideas and to the absence of transcendent regulations in the formation of laws that are taken to be 'natural' and universal; and (e) elaborating the discourse-specificity of the principles, rules, and regulations that are regionally necessary in a given genealogy.

3. The movement of Foucault's thought is not ordered by a will to truth, a will to universal knowledge, or the concept of a self finding itself in self-expression. These elements are present in Foucault's discourse, but within a recoiling movement that mitigates their ordering power.

4. The wincing recoil in Foucault's thought is an effect of the interplay of traditionally peripheral and outcast forces, which have nontraditional organizing power in his work, with the central, organizing forces in the tradition, whose organizing power is weakened when their oppressive limitations are exposed.

5. The conflicts among the various ordering powers, that are encouraged in his genealogies, are empowered and maintained by the prominence that he gives to their divisions and nonsystematizable differences. By maintaining the conflicts without reconciliation—reconciliation effected by means of systematization or self-constitution on the basis of selected, ideal values—the force of the conflicts tends to engender options that go beyond

the conflicts without resolving them. Neither reconciliation nor harmony play significant, ordering roles in his discourse.

6. A negative or hostile recoil by the reader in the presence of the self-overcoming movement in Foucault's thought is usually a movement of thought that eliminates the self-overcoming of its own lineage and re-institutes a self-maintaining, authoritative structure of thought.

The ethos we find in Foucault's thought involves an embodiment of thinking and speaking that does not reconstitute an emphasis on identity and selfhood. In it one is not inclined to reconstitute a *definitive* self. Rather, this discourse is, on its own terms, always optional. One can move in it and then move out of it either by its self-overcoming force, or by the force of a change of direction and orientation, or by one's involvement in a very different discourse. The fear or suspicion that Foucault's genealogies arouse are not only a matter of one's having a different and valued perspective. One may, for example, become a different body in thinking through Foucault and undergo the emergence of different tastes, desires, and expectations. In that changing body a person knows that other embodiments are optional identities, that identity knows no transcendental regulation, that one is a discursive body amidst many discourses and sub-discourses. One may move out of Foucault's ethos—indeed, on its terms one can always move out of it—perhaps rather more marked than Aphrodite or Socrates the morning after an evening's bout, but not so marked as to have lost something essential, not so marked as to have fallen or risen by the standards of a self that seeks fulfillment of an already given nature.

The embodiment of Foucault's ethos includes knowledge of the optional manner of selfhood and identity. One is in a movement of self-overcoming in which the necessity of *this* movement bears witness to the dangers that one has learned to dread and attempted to prevent. In this ethos one has felt the desire to expose those dangers, including the dangers of definitive selfhood and of the best values and selves one has known. One also feels and knows the temporality of the desire to expose, the discursive quality of constituting actions, the discontinuous, mutational quality of discourses, the unprotected standing of values in this discourse, and the vague horizon that promises only options, experiments, and the loss of the one we insisted on being; one knows an ethos without proposing an ethics in such knowledge, knows selves who become doubtful of selfhood because of the totalizing activity that characterizes constituting actions. Lineages are found to recoil on themselves by virtue of the divisions that define them. And one finds no complete prescriptions in all of this because the self-overcoming movement arises from the dangers, ignorance, totalizations, repressions, and conflicts that define the lineage of our possibility of being a self at all. Prescriptiveness, selfhood, and the ecstasy of insight are as much in question as are the limits of representation, the authority of the professional, and the powers that subvert human life in an effort to govern it well. The *question* of ethics is part of the curative effect of genealogy. Our thought and practices are not 'cured' by our becoming better persons, but by exposing the danger of the desire to be better. *This* embodiment, in contrast to self-constitution and the subjectivation that it makes inevitable, is a body of self-overcoming, one that produces knowledge *in* this movement and embodies an ethos of recoil in a lineage that has injured human beings by making them selves.

We shall turn now to three of Foucault's studies in order to see in greater detail how genealogical recoil and self-overcoming characterize thought and maintain the question of ethics by putting in question their own authority. As we think through Foucault's self-overcoming recoil, we are in a process that puts ethics and self-constitution in question. As we consider these three studies, we shall pay attention particularly to the definitive quality of the recoiling movements that lead to self-overcoming within prominent discourses and practices in our recent history. This definitive quality is found in modern thought, in institutions, and governments. It is a regional inevitability that takes its departure from specific disjunctions and failures that are both constitutive of modern discourse and systematically denied or excluded by the confederation of powers that organize them.

2. The Unbearable Lightness of Reason: Reason's Recoil in Madness

In Foucault's *Madness and Civilization,* the movements that hold our attention are found in reason's recoil from its own limits, which are demarcated by insanity, and also in the silent recoil of insanity from rational constraint. Both movements are marked by "the caesura that establishes the distance between reason and unreason." Foucault himself enacts a recoil in this study in appropriating the silence of madness into his account and use of rationality. This appropriation cannot speak or think what it appropriates; to the extent that the analysis thematizes the silence of madness, it cannot make sense of what it thematizes. The aporetic disclosure of the hiddenness of madness generates a kind of knowledge that moves around or toward nonknowledge, toward something quite other than what genealogical knowledge is able to know (MC ix).

Madness and Civilization, which is a "history of insanity in the age of reason," as its subtitle puts it, is also a genealogy of "unreason"—of the experience of no reason at all—within the language and institutions of the seventeenth, eighteenth, and nineteenth centuries. In tracing folly and madness in the classical and modern periods, Foucault traces the unavoidable indications of classical and modern reason's radical limits, which appear in relation to madness when reason's orders, which are taken to be definitive of the world, confront no reason at all in the world. Reason's unconscious anxiety takes the forms of multiple projects to confine madness: madness symbolizes a radical other to reason which, if placed under rational restraint, might be rational at least in a negative sense. Madness gives expression to no rational expression. Madness is not containable or graspable in the language and concepts of reason, and rationality is thus driven, out of self-consistency, to confine and contain madness in a formation of reason's craft, in some institutional order that will give meaning to utter meaninglessness and that will reassure rational standards by the measure of the confining and correcting institution's force.[11]

We note a double recoil in this movement. Reason's drawing back from its own limits as demarcated by the transgression of madness indicates that the asylum's history is in part in the lineage of this particular kind of recoil; further, there is the recoil of madness in its silence within the reasonable processes and structures of confinement. The effort to set rational limits on madness is itself a type of madness, an expression of unreasonable anxiety at the limits of expressibility, of a rational madness that is blind to itself. Reason's own project of confining and containing madness is one in which madness rebounds in reason's very effort to contain it.

Yet the recoil that is most germane to our interests is found in relation to the function of the "caesura that establishes the distance between reason and non-reason" (MC ix). *Madness and Civilization* traces the break that divides reason and nonreason. How does this break occur in the genealogy of Foucault's own study? Does it 'define' the space of Foucault's study? We shall see that it both allows a certain contemporaneity with madness and occasions a recoil of Foucault's knowledge before no presence at all, a recoil of which Foucault takes account in the language of his study.

Unreason names the rational experience of madness from the early modern period through the nineteenth century. Five groups of images aid the rational articulation of this experience: light/darkness, disclosure/hiddenness, fullness/void, truth/error, and order/disorder. *Reason* embraces the elements of light, disclosure, fullness, truth, and order. Beings are accessible in their truth and order by the full, disclosive light of reason. The world comes to human beings in the light of human being. Its order and truth are found in reason. This is an experience of the infinite span of being, its complete abundance, its fundamental serenity and truth. Where there is darkness, there is also encompassing light, where error, always the errant truth, where death, unquenchable and immortal life. Disorder is a matter of ignorance, unenlightened government, or irrational will. Depravity is a question of deviation, straying from an always available truth. Madness, on the other hand, transgresses the experience of eternal sufficiency. It seems to open out to mere void and unredeemable darkness. Its sheer perversion, in this context, is found in its meaningless disorder, its senseless chatter, screams, and sightless stare. The rational person looks into the eyes of the insane and sees emptiness or vacuous hilarity or dumb pain without hope or remorse. Reason's gaze finds something less than immorality. It finds a space without the poles of morality and immorality. Less than animal innocence, it finds *déraison*.

"But," says Foucault, "the paradox of this *nothing* is to manifest itself" (MC 107). The insane use—"explode into"—signs, words, and gestures. There is an appearance of order that evacuates itself into silent emptiness. "For madness, if it is nothing, can manifest itself only by departing from itself, by assuming an appearance in the order of reason and thus becoming contrary to itself" (MC 107). By showing itself, it withdraws from the order of its self-showing and leaves no hint of a self or of the continuation of reason. It is simple transgression in the order of knowledge, morality, and government. If one order transgressed another, one would need only to find the rationality of the conflicting orders to maintain the experience of reason. But the disclosure of madness leaves modern rationality disturbed by the absence of what seemed to be revealed. Reason is brought to the limits of its light and seems to be crossed by no light at all. This is not even a tragedy, with its fullness of sense in the alternation of light and dark in the unity of time, but transgression with no unity, no light, no truth, no contrariety. Reason may contain madness, hold it, as it were, but its containment does not restore comprehension and truth to what is held.

Unreason thus means the experience of a caesura, a radical interruption, in modern reason's fullness. Even if the "cruel sadism" of the techniques of healing are applied to the insane with the loftiest of humane intentions, the seeming and sporadic successes that restore a person to reason's sway do not eliminate the darkness that compromised the infinite reach of order and truth. The dominion of reason is broken by unreason, and the experience of this dominion appears irrevocably in *question*.

The early modern response to unreason was to confine it. One of Foucault's intentions is to show that men of good sense, rational men, and not professional medical men, were the ones who set the standards for freedom and incarceration. At that time madness was not perceived in terms of illness, but as the paradoxical dazzlement of reason in which the absence of light and truth had ascendancy over light and truth in the apparent functions of rationality. In the mad, reason contradicted itself in its employment. In the nineteenth century, the physician became the controlling authority as madness came to be experienced as illness. That history is less our concern than the lineage of a discourse that descended from madness viewed as dazzlement in the sixteenth century to the language and thought that speaks in the caesura of unreason.

When madness is experienced as dazzled reason, it is no longer experienced as a sign of a higher order of truth. The mad do not have the special gifts of discernment that they had, for example, in the high middle ages. Neither are they objects for seers who can discern in them the language of another mysterious realm. In the early modern period, the mad were separated from a world of signs in which everything reverberates with special significance and in which a major human responsibility is to learn how to read the words of God and nature in all connections and all events. No longer are the mad either the messengers or the metaphors for transcendent truth; hence the caesura of unreason vis-à-vis reason. No system of signs brings the two together in their radical divergence. Reason is the region of truth; madness, a void of meaninglessness. The sounds of the mad are as cut off from reason as they are from the messengers of God, and they mean nothing in their radical division from the order of truth. In the delirium of dazzled reason, the transgression of reason *seems* to have expression; it is an expression in which being withdraws and devolves. Void and dissolution reign.

Dazzled reason is in the lineage of language in which the foundational quality of meaning, the plenitude of reason, and the infinity or eternity of life do not order the discourse. What happens when the discourse of this lineage comes to thought? The resulting movement is a major component in the lineage of Foucault's genealogy. How does the language of this caesura compose Foucault's thought of madness?

The practices of confining the mad and maintaining their silence, prior to the medical-psychiatric ordering of the asylum, are separated by explanatory accounts of the physical and soulish qualities of madness and by attempts to heal the disease by medication. The discourse of reason with unreason, however, takes the therapeutic turn of attempting to engage errant reason by reason in its proper function and to restore errant reason to its proper truth. In the latter psychoanalytic instance, the therapist covers over unreason through the art and language of healing talk in order to return it to its rational home. In both lineages—that of confining the mad and that of healing talk—the caesura is systematically overlooked and the breaching of reason is covered by the continuity of reasonable technique and conversation. Unreason is submerged unconsciously by rational language and organization. Reason so dominates the relation that it stands in ignorance of the frightening transgression that motivates it.

The experience of unreason, on the other hand, continues in the work of Hölderlin, Nerval, and Nietzsche (MC 212, 278). In their writing, the experience of unreason as the caesura of reason constitutes a *contratempo* in which time and unreason are affiliated. Time and unreason appear in a common "rootage" in the sense that time also seems to transgress the experience of modern reason in its presumed universal and self-contained movement of truth. Whereas the medicalization of madness and the discourses of therapy maintain the dominance of rationality and rational order in their efforts to cure or overcome madness, the discourses of time and unreason speak in and out of the transgression of reason. In Nietzsche, for example, genealogy shows the partial and broken strands of power that, without reason, fabricate rational orders for the mere enjoyment of exertion, creation, domination, and conflict. We have seen that the recoils of his thought articulate no reason, but rather something like *déraison,* as the rationality of his own thought evaporates in self-overcoming. Self-overcoming 'rules' the time of his heritage and puts in question the meaning of eternal return and teleological evolution. The movement of time discloses no sign by which to discern a fundamental truth or a right order of transcendent sense and meaning. The conundrum of time timing in self-overcoming interrupts the temporal configurations that hold time in the sway of meaning. The knowledge of time is undercut by the timing that traverses it. This *contratempo* functions as a countermemory to reason's narratives, divides them by the 'force' of the caesura of unreason, and leaves without truth or technique the traces of self-overcoming that show neither a narrative nor a reason, but merely the withdrawal of anything at all. In such thought the work of reasonable good faith that seeks to free the insane by making them whole stands out as suppression not of illness but of unreason and its illumination of the darkness in which we, on the presumption of eliminating the vacuity of (un-)reason, restore people to good health. The grounds of our attempts to reconstitute broken selves to good order are brightly displayed in their "catastrophic blindness" to the anxiety that moves them.[12]

The place of Foucault's genealogy in this lineage is clear. "The ambiguity of chaos and apocalypse," of the disclosive effect of unreason's "darkness" in the world of rational "light," forecasts the passing of that order of knowledge and practice which we shall find Foucault naming 'man'. In this passing order, the passage of time is accounted in his genealogical work to be affiliated with unreason, with the transgression of the unity that controls the configuration 'reason'. Time lacks continuous presence just as human being lacks continuous selfhood. The caesura of unreason and the fragmented temporality of mortals that are described and marked in genealogy are modern reason's opening to the limits of reason which traverse reason and show us no reason at all. By giving this fissure an ordering priority in his thought, Foucault is able to give prominence in his language and style of writing to the element most strenuously unregarded in the thought and style that has produced our dominant values of living, knowing, and healing. He works in the lineage of modern reason by thematizing its suppressed rupture, a rupture that is highlighted by the temporality of the modern period. The problem is that this rupture is not a theme and is, on Foucault's own account, susceptible to absurd incorporation within thematic language.

Foucault's work is built on a scholarship and sensibility that are unthinkable without the rational disciplines of the modern period. He crafts a knowledge of this period in terms of its own intelligibility. His language is not the dazzled nonsense of the mad. He makes distinctions, divides practices and attitudes by conceptual structures, arranges theories by categories. He argues a case that can be understood, and he means what he says. As in art, so in genealogy: "There is no madness," he says, "except as the final instance of a work of art—the work endlessly drives madness to its limits; *where there is a work of art, there is no madness;* yet madness is contemporary with the work" (MC 288-89). This statement is applicable to his own work. His is not a work of madness. He brings his work to its limit by the sensible meanings that collapse before madness. In that sense he draws closer to madness than does our traditional language.

Nevertheless, the otherness of madness is contemporary to his work: his study recoils on madness in the sense that his thought continuously returns to madness as the limit of his own expression, and it finds itself cast back on itself by what it would, but cannot, address. He takes his bearings from the transgression of madness, from the *déraison* that puts in question everything he has to say about it. The otherness of madness remains. He can designate its silence in modern discourse, but he cannot make it speak in his own work. And yet madness is contemporary to his work as an other in relation to which his thought, his reasonableness, recoils. As other to his discourse, the caesura of unreason is not covered over in its withdrawal from his discourse. Its nonanswer is traced as Foucault's language rebounds from unreason in a complete and owned inability to grasp it, articulate it, or control it.

Foucault's thought constitutes a question that it cannot answer as it coils again at the limits of its reach. It has no authority before madness—its authority is only in the lineage of modern reason—and in this restriction it is rather more like a clearing for other and different thoughts than a reasonable grasp of the caesura of unreason that is its subject matter. If it takes its departure from this caesura, it has no originary presence, no primal experience, no founding reality. Its own order verges on the incurable nonorder of unreason and the unclosing space of its lineage. Foucault's discourse lacks an ultimate order, and that lack 'produces' the self-overcoming of a constellation of thoughts that have no reason to maintain themselves as though time unfolded in a self-realizing process to which thinking was privy.

His discourse, then, does not lead to attempted cures of insanity, the containment of unreason, or the dissolution of intelligibility. It is curative in the sense that it releases the traditional fissure of unreason/reason from the anxious belief that unreason is 'itself' illness, immorality, or mental weakness. The caesura occurs without resolution, and like chaos, it borders the book's meaning and good sense. The language by which madness is confronted recoils from the confrontation in the knowledge, not of unreason, but of its own limits as rational; it suggests that in facing unreason the tradition of reason may follow a process of self-overcoming or it may reconstitute unreason blindly in reasonable attempts at suppression and cure. In Foucault's own discourse rational incorporation of unreason undergoes the self-overcoming of knowing itself, *in* its reasonableness, to have no power over unreason. It continuously recoils upon the otherness of madness and upon the inevitable overturning of its own good sense regarding the senselessness that it both thematizes and loses by its genealogical intelligence. The withdrawal of unreason, its caesura, engenders the self-overcoming of modern reason's discourse.

3. A Genealogy of Genealogical Knowledge

Madness and Civilization is a genealogical account of the Other to modern reason which transgresses reason and is excluded from rationally founded discourses and relations. In contrast, *The Order of Things* is a genealogical account of the Same, in a lineage from the renaissance discourse of similitude and resemblance in which likenesses are found and organized by comparing like to like, to the early modern discourse in which sameness is found in the processes and structures of representation, to the modern formation of knowledge, which Foucault calls man, in which the transcendental subject of knowledge is also the principal empirical object of knowledge. In 'man' the sameness of knowledge is faulted by a self-founding subject that cannot represent itself or know itself in the positivity that it requires. It is always other to itself and cannot overcome this gap which puts in question its own unity. We shall see that Foucault's genealogy finds its bearings in the fault of modern knowledge and that it forecasts a way of knowing that experiences no necessity for a genealogical approach. The idea of Same and the problematic of identity/difference, which play central roles in *The Order of Things,* also fade out in consequence of this genealogical study.

Foucault argues in *The Order of Things* that modern thought is unable to formulate a clear morality—an applied code of behavior—because its ethics is constituted by thought's relation to itself, instead of to nature or the world, and systematically turns to itself instead of to the world as it formulates its imperatives and values (OT 128). We shall see that the Same, which guarantees a universal system of resemblance, is lost in the fractured movement from renaissance knowledge to modern knowledge and that this loss defines the disturbed problematic of late modern knowing. This problematic is similar to that of self-constitution in the sense that thought attempts to ground itself in its own activity, analogously to the self's effort to define itself by reference to its relation to itself. Any ethical imperative will be one whereby thinking comes to its enlightenment by means of thinking's own enactment. It works on itself to discover its own truth by its action of relating to itself. Thought posits itself in order to recover its laws, its truth, in self-enacting inquiry. If self-enactment fails in its project of recovering itself in a full unity of self-illumination, the possibility of ethics is fatally jeopardized. Having already lost its definitive bonding with nature and the world of nonthought, having defined both nature and world in its own reflexive movement, the failure of thought to complete itself in a union of subject-object means the impossibility of an ethic that defines the meaning and truth of reason-in-act.

Foucault's genealogy of the Same emerges from this failure, repeats it to a certain degree, and overcomes it, not in the form of a new ethic, but in a formulation that makes doubtful the entire discourse of self-relation. Without an origin in nature or any other kind of continuing presence, and with the stimulus of the rupture of the modern self that destroys modernity's best hope, Foucault's knowledge articulates this rupture as an open field for thought. His genealogy emerges from the loss of both the Same and the problematic that originated unwittingly in its loss. He follows the loss, speaks out of it, and adopts the impossibility of definitive self-enactment that characterizes it.

We may say in an anticipatory way that the question of ethics that emerges in this and other of Foucault's writings is a question that is embedded in his own Western tradition of thought; he follows the development of this question as he shows the decline, deterioration, and finally the failure of the idea of the Same. The problematics of self-constitution and the self-relation/self-enactment of reason grow out of the traditional thoughts of 'reality' and continuing presence. Those ideas have lost their power to organize Foucault's discourse by a general and traceable loss of power in our recent history. Self-constitution and rational self-enactment are aspects of the decline of the idea of the Same and hence of the ideas of reality and continuing presence. By tracing this decline and failure, *The Order of Things* indirectly traces the passage of the viability of ethics to the question of ethics, and by developing his own conceptuality and language in response to this decline and failure, Foucault writes a genealogy that resists the repetition of the problematics of self-constitution and rational self-relation. By thinking within the question of ethics rather than within the problematic of self-constitution, Foucault's work puts its own imperative and regional necessities in question and moves in a recoiling and self-overcoming movement that we shall now follow.

A. THE TEMPORALITY OF THE SAME

The word that Foucault uses to name the pervasive, organizing concept of continuing presence is *Same*. Its meaning dominates the structures of knowledge in the renaissance in which the similitude of all things spawns a group of discourses based not on the division between language and beings but on the continuous resemblance of beings and signs. "To search for a meaning is to bring to light a resemblance. To search for the law governing signs is to discover the things that are alike" (OT 29). For renaissance knowledge there are no essential breaks, no essential gaps among things, and hence no imperative for the thought of re-presentation. Language is within the universal field of resemblance in which the world duplicates itself endlessly in a chain of likenesses and affinities.

This kinship among signs and things, between the signifier and signified, was troubled by a growing understanding in the late sixteenth and early seventeenth centuries that language is "restricted to the general organization of representative signs" (OT 42). Increasingly, scholars wanted to know how the signifier is linked to the signified, and the question of linkage made doubtful the epistemic assumption that language merged with things by resemblance. Difference must be accounted for.

The identities of signs and the identities of things constitute differences that need to be known if language and world are to be known. The senses, however, are understood to be deceptive and unreliable, and the project of universally valid knowledge can be successful only if the human intellect functions representatively according to universally valid rules and principles. The identity of human intellect, its difference and particularity in relation to all other identities, is found in part in its universality. In Foucault's genealogy the universally valid identity of intellect proliferates problems for modern knowledge analogous to the proliferation of signs in language designed to represent things in their truth. The emergence of these problems challenges the sovereignty of Same for knowledge. The question of the relation of signifier and signified and that of the continuous dispersion of signs and things in the function of human mentation disenfranchises the Same. Same becomes dispersed among identities and differences.

Foucault's account of this transition from the renaissance to early modern knowledge thus focuses on the fracturing of Same by the questions of signification and representation. Same does not disappear, but it no longer controls the movement of the discourse as it did in the episteme of resemblance in which Same meant the absence of 'real' fissures in the fabric of being and existence. Concurrent with the dispersion of Same by the question of language's relation to the world and its signifying structure is the recurrent issue for knowledge of how Same is to be understood in its proliferation. The question of Same in its emerging *temporality* in modern knowledge is found in its dispersion through identities and differences that do not make evident an easily assured universal kinship between language and things. Whereas for renaissance knowledge, for example, this kind of proliferation is found in madness, which separates language from reality, and in the caprice of imagination, which is lawless fantasy, for early modern knowledge the madman overlooks identities and differences and confuses language and things by seeing resemblance everywhere (OT 49). The distance between these two epistemes thus constitutes the beginning of the temporality of the Same which Foucault's genealogy is designed to know. It is a temporality and knowledge that compound this distance as it functions in the formation of the modern episteme, which is formed by the problematic of representation. Temporality in Foucault's thought is constituted by dispersion and proliferation. We shall see how temporality and Same recoil on each other in modern thought and constitute a self-overcoming movement in Foucault's account of them.

The prominence—indeed, the organizing sovereignty—of representation in modern thought is measured by the discontinuity that becomes evident among things and signs and between language and things. Re-presentation is necessary because identities are not continuous with each other. The difficulty is compounded because the agency of re-presentation is also an identity in difference vis-à-vis other identities and because the signs that constitute language are themselves differentiated identities. In order to establish the resemblance of all things, to establish their sameness which had been a given for renaissance knowledge, people have to use signs that signify things and that signify each other. The problem is that this continuity among signs is expressed in the proliferation of signs, the endless production of differences that cannot establish finally and completely the desired unity of being.[13]

The processes of signifying and the lives of identities were characterized by dispersion and proliferation: they came to be, persisted, and passed away in growing discontinuity in spite of modern discourse's indigenous desire to establish the sameness of being. Modern knowledges thus constituted a temporality that they desired to overcome. In the course of our discussion we shall see that Foucault's discourse overcomes this desire as well as the knowledges that it motivated by giving priority to the temporality of dispersion and the distance that constituted these knowledges.[14]

The division between signs and desire grows to fatal proportions in the episteme of representation and leads to nineteenth-century organicism and historicity. Things are ordered by systems of signs in this way of knowing. Similitude lies beneath thought and is not reached in its unity by "signs [that] have no other laws than those that may govern their contents" (OT 66). One deciphers things by understanding signifying relations. Representation is "the mode of being" that defines the being of all things. But since the "disequilibrium" among signs, by which one knows, and things, which are hidden in their nonrepresentational being, is constitutive of representation, similitude's being—the very unity of being—is made more remote. Such disequilibrium is "contemporaneous" with representing, is part of the "common ground" of representing, and is thus a temporal constituent of the system of signs. Although it could not have been known by the episteme of representation, this contemporaneity had the effect of unsettling representational projects by holding at an infinite distance the goal of unity that defined the projects. Knowledges were condemned to begin again and again—finding their end-point only in the beginning—by the division that defined them.

Further, the power and 'body' of desire occur outside the limits of representation. Although desire can be represented and analyzed, it is not ruled by representation. In this episteme desire is understood as "libertinage" to the extent that it overflows representational structures (OT 209).

Bodies in their mere conjunction express the ungraspable excess of desire. The endless project of containing desire in representation, and the futility of that project, finds its clearest expression in Sade, who writes within the transgressive limits of representation and comes to know the limits of representation in its cruelty and denial regarding the 'otherness' of desire. *Desire* names a moving power of organisms, a power that expresses lives that are outside the circumference of representation. The question is, how are organisms to be known in their power and structure, in their internal relations, as they mark their division from the life and internal structures of representing? In order to answer that question, one needs to know organisms as they function in *their* internal relations.

Organic structures in this episteme are discontinuous and cannot be ordered in a table of unbroken similarities or a system of signs. Their emergence into knowledge creates a "new space of empiricities" within which one develops methods to study functions specific to a given kind of organism, whether it be a living being, an economy, or a grammar. The temporal issue in this late modern episteme is one of succession. How do organic systems lead to other organic systems? What are the influences of one on another in the succession? How does one set of interrelated structures develop or evolve out of others? History, not a field of representation, is the field of laws and regulations within which organic relations appear. Instead of representational duplication, one finds origins, lines of generation, and forms of life that are exterior to representation. Things are understood as "withdrawn into their own essence, taking up their place at last within the force that animates them, within the organic structure that maintains them, within the genesis that has never ceased to produce them. . . . The very being of that which is represented is now going to fall outside representation itself" (OT 239, 240). The problem is to find ways of knowing the source and origin of representation.

One approach to this problem was to determine "the transcendental field in which the subject, which is never given to experience (since it is not empirical), determines . . . all the formal conditions of experience in general" (OT 243). This is a field of synthesis for representations that cannot be known by representations. A second option focuses on the force of labor, the energy of life, or the power of speech, which are also outside the field of representation but which condition whatever is known. In the first option, the subject is divided from the mode of the object's being; in the second, the forms of analysis are divided from the laws that give unity to the organic structure. These fractures are contemporaneous with nineteenth-century organicism and historicism and define its temporality, but they lie outside of what either approach can know.

In discussing the rupturing movement from the episteme of representation to that of organicism and transcendental thought, Foucault is admittedly tentative. He frequently reformulates his account of the rupture, acknowledges that he is still within its power and is unable to get a definitive grip on it (see especially OT 218, 237, 239, 248). The growing distance between the forms that empirical objects take in their analyses and the conditions for knowing them is clearly at work in this book. The importance of linear history is still powerful. Yet Foucault is thinking about the rupturing distances in the ongoing transition from pre–nineteenth-century modernity, distances that continue in the twentieth century and in his thought. He thinks in them by defining his own approach by reference neither to sequence nor to evolution but to the lineage of fractures and the contemporaneity of dispersion. The "structures of positivities" that he finds are themselves adrift from the earlier principles of order that established identity and difference in tables of representation. These structures have emerged in the dissolution of the orders of seventeenth- and eighteenth-century knowledge and are also, by their own account, separated from the very positivities that they structure: life, labor, and language.

In this field, the possibility of synthesis is detached from the space of representation and mathematical tabulation. Foucault's own narrative is one that situates itself in these fractures which cannot be subject to narratives, but which operate to dislodge in his knowledge any predisposition to universalization, organic structural truth, or a priority of narration. One becomes accustomed in his work to know without foundation, without appeal to any continuing natural structures. As a product of fractures, his knowledge proliferates and recoils in the fractures contemporaneous with it. *Power, will,* and *life* do not name the hidden movement or limit of anything. They name the effects of combinations and configurations. *Desire* no longer names a limit or an essence but a movement of certain historical bodies. Foucault's is a knowledge in which the contemporary ending of nineteenth-century thought recoils on itself.

Foucault finds now, in the wake of the nineteenth century, that the disciplines of knowledge are faced with the contemporaneous "impossibility *and* obligation" to locate syntheses in the space of representation and to open up the transcendental field of the subject (OT 250). Contemporaneity in this case is constituted by the loss of the episteme of representation, the fragmentation of the unity of representation by transcendental and empirical divisions, the demand for the synthesis of transcendental and empirical thought, and the impossibility of meeting that demand. Such contemporaneity constitutes what Foucault terms *man*. Man, the knowing being, is the being of time when time is understood as dispersion. These fragments of impossibility and obligation constitute the being of man. Foucault's own knowledge apprehends these structures in their historical development and in their contemporaneity *with* their constitutive fractures. That means that his knowledge of his traditional historical development rebounds away from the concept of development, which has formed a strong resistance to fractures and the absence of the development that they disclose. His use of the concept of development feels the impact of the power-effects of the unappropriated fractures in the discourse of evolution and representation. These fractures put in question the ideas of both origin, linear history, and teleology. Development without origin or telos—fractural development—as we shall see in the next section, marks a break from the nineteenth-century episteme of lawful, ontological history and that of understanding organic structures as unities with natures that are internal to themselves.

What happens to the recent understanding of language in Foucault's discourse? Out of the nineteenth-century study of the historicity of grammar and its organic, self-referential manner come both the divisions among grammatical systems and the break from the continuity of fields of representation. The dominant nineteenth-century knowledge of grammar found the "time systems" of different grammars to be system-specific instead of being derivative from continuous Time, which repeats itself in endless representation. Modalities of formation dominated the chronology of successions. 'History' rather than representational time began to form (OT 290). "The order of time is beginning," Foucault says (OT 293). History is the field within which certain mutations will or will not be able to occur. "The new grammar is immediately diachronic." The central diachronic aspect arises from the dissociation of language from what it represents; it is intelligible, not by representing something other than itself, but by its historical development and "its own particular legality" (OT 294).

This understanding perpetuates the break from representation by the effort to know language in its empirical divisions and in the discontinuous sequence of temporal development. Its intelligibility is made possible in part by the fractures that it incorporates. History is the organizing concept, and unique organic structure is the dominant functional image. Foucault, in seeming continuity with nineteenth-century historicism and organicism, understands language by its regional quality in the power of its dispersions. Conditions for the nineteenth-century study of language, dispersion and proliferation—conditions that are largely overlooked in the nineteenth and twentieth centuries—become Foucault's organizing thought. Hence time as dispersion rather than history and structures of fragmentation rather than organic unities transpose his thought out of historicist organicism. The importance of a universalizing ground is dissipated by this mutation, and with this passage, the question of the transcendental/empirical connection (that is, man) also disappears. The structures of intelligibility regarding things are also in a process of mutation. Instead of a mathematical or anthropological basis, Foucault's intelligibility rests on the dispersion of time, a thought that first begins to take shape in *The Order of Things*.

He does, however, "disturb the words" that he uses, an approach that he notes as an exegetical technique in the nineteenth century. Language has an "enigmatic density" that is excessive of the general grammar that explains it. Disturbing language means "denouncing the grammatical habits of our thinking, . . . dissipating the myths that animate our words, . . . rendering once more noisy and audible the element of silence that all discourse carries with it as it is spoken." Nietzsche and Freud are notable expositors in this tradition. Foucault is like them when he maximizes those phrases that both "support and . . . undermine our apparent discourse, our fantasies, our dreams, our bodies" (OT 298). Syntax, tyrannical modes of speech, and the silent priorities of our thoughts are shifted, pushed off-center, and destroyed in their unquestionable ordering power. Foucault does not "go beyond the frontiers of experience," as both nineteenth-century transcendental thought and empiricism tried to do, but turns rather to the dispersed and fragmented manner of language as he finds it. In this sense he temporalizes language outside the limits of representation, historicity, organic structure, and anthropomorphism.

As he formalizes the epistemic lineages into eras, strata, distinguishable discourses, and delimited transformations, Foucault uses a language that fragments as it formalizes. This is a procedure that is unfinished and unsure of itself.[15] But he clearly eliminates the structure of problems that dominates both transcendental phenomenology and structuralism as he works in a discourse within which the inherited language of meaning, empiricism, and transcendental thought is transgressed by the language of dispersed time. In this sense his language is closer to that of literature, which manifests "a language which has no other law than that of affirming—in opposition to all other forms of discourse—its own precipitous existence" (OT 300), than it is to criticism in its efforts to make the language of literature intelligible by categorical functions that operate in ignorance of its own fractured density.

Foucault's language does not suggest something like an eternal return to its own being. The thoughts of the being of language or of language as a self-enclosed process are foreign to his emphasis on institutions and nonlinguistic practices. Yet his language does hold foremost its own scattered density and returns to this density in the knowledge that this language is transgressed and subdued by it. This language is not universal in its self-constraint or in the unity of its regulations. But writing in the "enigmatic multiplicity" of language that characterizes our lineage and that was given self-conscious expression by Nietzsche, Foucault sidesteps the project of mastery that characterizes both philosophy and philology—"the themes of universal formalization of all discourse, or the themes of an integral exegesis of the world . . . or those of a general theory of signs; or again, the theme . . . of a transformation without residuum" (OT 305)—he sidesteps such projects and writes a discourse of dispersed time that puts in question the language that has promised unity and universal meaning by projecting itself on the world.

Foucault combines Nietzsche's question "who is speaking?" with Mallarmé's reply that the word speaks and means nothing in its "fragile vibration" (OT 305). Foucault notes that the distance between this question and reply has not been thought, but has been overlooked because of a preoccupation with what language is and how it orders itself in its plenitude. His own studies maximize the distance between the question and the response, however, by analyzing the formations of discourses in their languages, institutions, and ways of living. These discourses carry finite inevitabilities and form individuals as subjects. *Discourses* speak, Foucault says to Nietzsche. They speak without origins or foundations. They articulate confederations of power and the fractures carried by such confederations. They effect power and are the consequence of other power-effects. He shows in an enlarged elaboration of Mallarmé that in their transgressions and fractured totalities these discourses mean nothing but their effects and formations. Lacking 'being', they exist as bodies, ways of doing things, rank orders, systems of distribution, means of elimination, and plays of force. The distance between "who is speaking?" and the meaningless existence of the word is found in Foucault's discourse of dispersed time which traces the dispersions that have effected a discourse in which he is constrained to live out the uncertainty of language, its meaninglessness—a discourse whose own heritage is found in the multiple losses of self-understanding, self-reference, and orders of knowledge. These losses arise from the defining structures and engender the dispersion that gives them their temporality. Rather than master the schisms and make language visible in its entirety, Foucault maintains an uncertainty and questionableness that keep the schisms alive in the constraint of having to inquire without knowing origins, being, or ends.

4. Fragmented Man

Man, the subject of knowledge in the nineteenth and twentieth centuries, is produced out of the fractured renaissance and modern epistemes, out of their transitions, ruptures, and emerging problems. It is a subject whose epistemological failure produces the temporality of dispersion in Foucault's discourse in *The Order of Things*. His genealogy arises out of and gives expression to this temporality; it takes form as a knowledge in which ethical thinking is in question. By his account of 'man', the subject of modern knowledge, Foucault exhibits the epistemic structure whose problematic and failure define the space of his account of man. He also provides an account of the way of knowing that is most likely to inform those interpretations which read him as though he were wholly within the broad ethical discourse of Western self-constitution. Foucault's work in *The Order of Things* shows what may be hardest for us to believe: that the way of valuing that inspires us most easily in both secular and religious commitments, that our 'best' interests for the common good of 'mankind', find their credibility in the divided and ultimately suicidal structure of modern knowledge.

Such subjectivity—man—constitutes a division that expresses the inevitability of its own passage out of its 'nature'. If this self-overcoming is repressed or overlooked we may expect repetitions of its mortality in values and value judgments that reinstate in the name of good things their opposites. A spirit of violence accompanies the repression, a sensibility that will not understand its own mischief as it repeats itself and unwittingly resists its self-overcoming. If man in its fragmentation appropriates its fragmentation and affirms its self-overcoming, the cycle of violence prompted by modern ethics may be interrupted and the space may emerge for thought that is genealogical and experimental. This opening can occur in spite of the expectation—which seems intuitive and proper—of passionate commitment and self-constitution. This mix of fragmentation and self-overcoming in our heritage, which we find to be the voice of the *question* of ethics, is also the voice that provides the most characteristic and counterintuitive movement in *The Order of Things*. It is the voice that emerges in the ending of modern knowledge and its ethics.

In the previous section we saw that Foucault's questions regarding language, and his experiments with it, arose out of the fragmentation of language in a movement from the episteme of similitude to the episteme of representation and from thence to the historicist organicism of the nineteenth century. These discourses speak in the formation of subjects of knowledge that are intrinsically fragmented by the discourses and yet are prefigured by the power of the problematic of the Same to overlook their fragmentation. Foucault finds his language and thought emerging out of this overlooked fragmentation, and by that anarchic birth he finds himself in a discourse without an originary presence to link the divided parts. He does not constitute himself in this discourse, but is constituted by it as the project of self-constitution and the ideal of universalization fall apart within it. The subject of knowledge is subjected to processes of thinking that put in question the authoritative subjectivation of totalizing or normalizing authorities; these authorities proliferated knowledges and practices in ignorance of their own dispersion. Hence the aim of definitive and synthetic knowledge, the ideal of enlightenment, is destroyed by what at first appears to be enlightenment through genealogy. The latter "enlightenment" recoils upon the unthought shadow of modern knowledge, to the density and ambiguity of language and the definitive divisions that characterize the subject whose mission is to provide unity. Foucault's genealogy knows itself to lack a basis for unity in the inevitability of fragmentation that moves through its own lineage.

Man is the subject that represents its representations. Instead of a renaissance table of representations in the episteme of similitude, man is the being who folds its own nature back on itself as it duplicates and expresses what it finds through its own activity of representing. Its sequence of representations takes place in its activity, and that sequence of self-repetitions constitutes both its time and the 'place' of all things. If we can know the activity of compounded representations, we can know the presentation of truth and the order of things. But that knowledge would be a representation that re-establishes the rupture of difference by the force of the *re*. Man must be the sole object and subject of such knowledge; that is, the representational chain needs to be broken by pure, self-knowing presentation. And the impossibility of such knowing, of such presentational immediacy, is exactly what gave rise to this subject of knowledge, to this act of representation.

Man, in spite of its goal to provide unity, means discontinuity between itself and what it knows. Foucault calls it the enslaved king who is the sovereign of knowledge and the impossible object of knowledge, the one who must know itself in its immediate unity and who, trapped by its representational activity, knows itself only as a representation, never as the pre-representational unity that it has to be. Man can only know itself by reducing itself by deduction to an abstract necessity. Surely man is the Same, the link between subject and object. But in this rational hope it repeats the question that gave it birth: What is the immediate linkage that unites being and knowledge? Representation assumed this linkage, but needed to find and found it. Man was the intended foundation, but it found itself, as the condition for the possibility of its founding activity, to be at a distance from itself—a distance no less great than that of the nineteenth-century object of knowledge from nature. Being was still a question, lost in the finitude of a repetitive circle of representation.

Man thus composes its own limitation. Its finitude is not defined by external limitations placed on its ability to know, but by the internal limits of self-representation. Finite man is the condition of its own possibility in spite of its project of establishing an incontestable identity for all things. Finitude is the *Same* for man, its representational being, that makes inevitable a continuous succession of images that promise but cannot fulfill a presentational immediacy as the basis for certainty. Rather, finitude is both man's certainty and its failure to be an unbroken truth for all things. The Same recurs ironically as the repetition of the failure of certainty, and the continuous passing away of pure subjectivity marks its temporality. Man's death, in this sense, is the 'nature of its being'.

As Foucault makes his case for the episteme of man in the context of transitions in modern knowledge, he writes in a language that neither returns to itself as a literary absolute nor posits an object that must be known if his discourse is to have validity. He writes in the distance that is created by the movement of representation in the sense that instead of attempting to recover either the retreating object of knowledge or the Same that links subject and object, his thought is organized by the schisms and fractures that constitute modern knowledge. The recoiling movement of modern knowledge occurs as the represented unity rebounds in dispersion. Foucault's recoils occur as the constitutive gaps of modern knowledge rebound, as the distances that positively define his knowledge open as other than distances to be overcome. His knowledge provides no basis from which to project unity on the dispersed things that are known by the inherited divisions of methods and disciplines. Genealogy has no claim to unity of succession or order. Its procedures and regulations coil again and move away from themselves, not with the aim of repeating themselves in an establishing action, but in a continuing, affirmed proliferation that is open to radical transformation and to newly generated styles and thoughts. It recoils in and from the self-identification and the satisfaction that characterize the Western projects of self-relation and self-reflection. Recognizing modern ethics to be a project of self-constitution by means of self-representation, and recognizing *self* to be a discursive, normalizing function with no essence other than the effects that have made it, Foucault's knowledge is as thoroughly self-overcoming as Nietzsche's.

With the *rupture* of representation organizing it, Foucault's knowledge does not look for a return to essence or origin or right. It attends rather to the dissolution from which it emerges and anticipates its own dissolution in the formations to which it gives rise. In his thought no identity seeks itself, is imminent or near to itself, liberates itself by proper self-appropriation, or fulfills itself. His analysis of these characteristics of modern thought is without a teleology. In the *without* we find both his inheritance and his thought of no origin, no essence, no completion (OT 338–40). Modern thought and practice have sought the liberation of people from whatever stifles the realization of their common nature and selfhood. Foucault's liberation occurs in the death of this project.

Both "Man and His Doubles" and "The Human Sciences" in *The Order of Things* analyze the deterioration of man within the force of that deterioration. The episteme of the Same is perpetuated if finitude, desire, or language becomes the new Same by which human being draws nearer to its lost other, if language closes on itself and becomes a single field of relation and lost relation, if experience is its own condition, or if the other is taken as a nearing-distancing Same. The unveiling of Same provides the context for Foucault's efforts. 'Doubles' (e.g., near-distance, being-other, identity-difference) shadow this thinking and put in question the thought of rupture that constitutes both them and Foucault's account of them. Man's self-overcoming passage, its ending, is the force of his thought: "It is no longer possible to think in our day other than in the void left by man's disappearance. For this void does not create a deficiency; it does not constitute a lacuna that must be filled. It is nothing more, and nothing less, than the unfolding of a space in which it is once more possible to think" (OT 342).

What happens in this space? In one development, man is the object of knowledge in the empirical sciences; it is the living being studied in modern biology, the problem of wealth studied in modern economics, and the maker and user of language studied in modern linguistics. Man, the object of study, appeared in these empirical sciences as the basis for empirical, nonproblematic knowledge, knowledge that did not need transcendental founding. Linkages among data are established by causal and structural constants. In another development, mathematical and physical sciences link evident or verified propositions by deductive connections. In a third development, philosophical reflection attempts to provide a common place for empirical investigations, to define the being characteristic of the various regions of investigation, and to formalize thought in a clear and universal language. These developments, in their considerable complexity, intensify the regionalization and proliferation of knowledges. Man the transcendental figure is diminished by figuring in only the third aspect of modern knowledge, and this knowledge is but one of the three major dimensions of the emerging, empirical knowledges of man. It is marginalized by the other knowledges that characterize its time. What enables man to know what life is? What is the essence of labor and its laws? What enables man to speak? The human sciences, in the absence of a clear, founding subject, seek to *connect* the sciences that produce, in their different domains, knowledge of man. In short, the issue for the human sciences is man's ability to represent itself to itself. Is there a unity for the different knowledges? Is man-the-object founded in a common subject?

In attempting to find access to man, now so dispersed by its knowledges, the human sciences experimented with functions, norms, conflicts, rules, signification, and systems. Among these things surely a unifying knowledge could be established that would define the manner of self-representation that is common to man. In the decline of the role of consciousness in nineteenth-century empiricism, in addition to the epistemically mandated distance of man-the-foundational-subject from man-the-object-of-knowledge, a new factor emerged as a possible unity: the unconscious. The activity of representing had remained beyond the grasp of nineteenth-century transcendental thought and in that sense had remained functionally unconscious in spite of the project of self-comprehension. Transcendental thought always promised a future consciousness that never occurred in its immediacy: "the near but withdrawn presence of the origin" (OT 362). Consciousness and representation are held apart in the "space of man," and this dissociation is definitive for the human sciences, just as it was for transcendental philosophy. "So the human sciences speak only within the element of the representable, but in accordance with a conscious/unconscious dimension, a dimension that becomes more and more marked as one attempts to bring the order of systems, rules, and norms to light" (OT 363). This dimension does not eliminate the importance of representation, but supplements and defines it. The problematic of the eighteenth-century episteme of representation remains in the internal division of man as the unconscious basis of conscious activity and is explained and elaborated by theories of the unconscious.

This entire development is constituted by "the general arrangement of the episteme that provides [the human sciences] with a site, summons them, and establishes them—thus enabling them to constitute man as their object" (OT 364). What does Foucault accomplish by this claim? He, too, thinks in this space that he characterizes as man's. He, too, is preoccupied by rules, norms, and systems. He, too, proliferates knowledges by his contingently connected genealogies. Yet man is neither the subject nor the object of his analysis. The space of man, the overlooked hiatus that marks the problem of man's knowledge, and the episteme that produces man are the subjects of Foucault's account. This space has formed Foucault's problematic, and it offers no possibility of solution, but rather only the continuation of dissolving the episteme that it defines. Such dissolution is the process one undergoes in reading *The Order of Things*. Historicist organicism, regional empiricism, preoccupation with the knower, the issues of universalization, the question of human nature, the relation of human being and nature, the status of the empirical: all these hallmarks of late modernity form Foucault's discourse in their conflicts and possibilities. None of these hallmarks, however, nor all of them together, establish Foucault's discourse. Rather, the rupture that problematizes them, moves them, and places them, functions in Foucault's genealogy as the moving force, not as something to be overcome, but as the discourse's continuing voice. As man passes away in this thought, Foucault's discourse finds its life and a future that it cannot desire to predict. This process, and not a group of values and goals outside of it, is Foucault's thought. It is the process of man's hiatus. In the space of that hiatus, something like a middle voice speaks.

The hiatus is not the same thing as finitude within the many versions of modern discourse. In that discourse *finitude* names the limits that appear in the interstices of self-relation: death, desire, and law. In psychoanalysis, for example, the relations of representation and finitude come into play as it shows the region of the unconscious "where representation remains in suspense, on the edge of itself, open, in a sense, to the closed boundary of finitude." The impossibility of man's being its own foundation or even constituting its own origins emerges as "the three figures by means of which life, with its functions and norms, attains its foundation in the mute repetition of Death, conflicts and rules their foundation in the naked opening of Desire, significations and systems their foundation in a language which is at the same time Law" (OT 374). Finitude in this instance emerges as the unfounded possibility of the goal of foundational certainty that in the several versions of modern knowledge proliferated and fractured man. Finitude underscores the slippage of self-representation and self-constitution, the *schiz* that makes impossible the projects of the modern episteme. But the meaning of finitude is found nonetheless within the boundaries of foundational thought and its epistemological and ethical motivations. It is found not in the hiatus, but within the boundaries marked by the disciplined exclusion of the hiatus from our orders of knowledge and action.

The disciplined and ordered exclusion of the hiatus is shown by the mirror of nineteenth- and twentieth-century madness, whose archetype is "schizophrenia," the divided mind (or the mind of division). This name for what is most foreign to our normalcy designates language that eludes signification, the wild state of desire, and the dominion of death over all psychological functions and the rules of rationality. We see "welling up that which is, perilously, nearest to us—as if, suddenly, the very hollowness of our existence is outlined in relief; the finitude upon the basis of which we are, and think, and know, is suddenly there before us: an existence at once real and impossible, thought that we cannot think, an object for our knowledge that always eludes it" (OT 375). Finitude stands outside our knowledge, permeating it at the same time, and in psychoanalysis (as well as ethnology) it makes questionable the man of knowledge who must found itself by its *own* activity of self-representation. Finitude is the wedge by which our knowledge's excluded limits began the splitting and ending of man. It is a phenomenon of modernity that is structured by the exclusion of the hiatus in a web of knowledge and action that cannot know its own divisions and remain true to itself.

Whereas psychoanalysis, as a practice, unfolds finitude into a knowledge by which an individual represents his or her being to him or herself as a creation of desire, death, and law, Foucault's genealogical knowledge works within the effects of their exclusion. In *The Order of Things* he can bring the question of the limits only this far: he can build a knowledge in which the intersection of unconscious discursive development and individual choice, which arises from the discourse in a given situation, are delineated in a language that is organized by the disordering elements of its own lineage (OT 380–81). A prominent word in this knowledge is *exposure*. It is a "counterscience," not a human science, that maximizes the disturbances that have shaken the structures of its own heritage, made doubtful the best inherited knowledge, and made possible the demise of the order that has held at bay its own divisive furies. Finitude also comes to an end in this exposing counterscience, because death, desire, and law no longer break in as abnormal things to be known with cautious and distant clarity; rather, they constitute the movement of thought and writing. We find even their names waning as the force of their exclusion weakens and no Same appears to provide a sustaining presence for finitude's interruptions. The language of finitude recoils on itself in Foucault's genealogy and springs away in a language without foundation and hence without finitude. Time without finitude? A different thought emerges.

In *The Order of Things* the fading of the knowledge of man and the lineage of that fading define the possibility of Foucault's own project. In contrast to modern ethnology, to studies of *ethea,* of different ways of knowing and living, his genealogy has no privileged basis for comparing and evaluating successes and failures relative to a higher and universalizable culture. He finds impossible a new self, now liberated from old restrictions and repressions, a self that would reconstitute itself in a fulfillment. Self-constitution as a form of self-representation is radically in doubt, not because Foucault wishes it so, but because the lineage of self-constitution makes it so. Exposures of the unconscious war on lack of unity and presence, on unhealable division and proliferation, on anomie and beginning without origin have put in relief, not evils, but the excluded limits of these formations out of which we have formed the thought and lives of selfhood and subjectivity.

By displaying the lineage of his own work, Foucault has placed his thought in the "hollowness" and gaps of his own time, thus giving place to an expectation of radical transformation from within his knowledge. By following the fissures in his lineage's search for broken unity, he has given a series of accounts in *The Order of Things* that recoil in their language back on the marginalized openings to absence of unity and presence; further, these accounts recoil away from structures and movements of knowledge and practice that tend toward the continuous reestablishment of unity and presence. Since all forms of self-representation have come into question in his discourse, the possibility for ethical thought and action has also come into question. Foucault's exposure of this question, which appears to be an unconscious characteristic of his heritage, raises the possibility of thought and action that are not based on representation in any form. This is a space for experimentation in the ending of man, a space of uncertainty and suspicion regarding our lineage's wisdom and goodness, and a space in which one cannot know who one is "meant" to be as one attempts to overcome the pain and suffering that individuals undergo in the destinies of their time.

5. Games of Truth, the Ethical Subject

Foucault's description of the relations among knowledges and power shows that what people know to be true and how they influence and control each other—the power that they exercise with regard to each other—are inseparably linked. When a system of knowledge/power closes on itself and functions to reestablish itself in a way that prevents thorough readjustment and transformation, totalization and domination result. In this context Foucault prefers a minimum of domination. This minimum does not mean an absence of power, but continuous readjustments within a culture of the rules of law, the techniques of management, the ethos by which individuals conduct themselves, "a sort of open strategic game, where things can be reversed" (EC 18). The openness of a culture is found in the changeableness of its hierarchies and the liberty that constitutes it and is ignored by the insistent stabilities of relationships and knowledges. When those who are subjected, for example, organize themselves and their relations so that governing principles arise with regard to *their* needs and not to those of the controlling groups, the values and customs change within the culture by means of needs and powers that are part, if usually an ignored part, of that culture. The peripheral values of the subgroup overcome those of dominant groups from within the society, and the society's openness is found in the dispersing and volatile factors that constitute and effect reversals within it.

Our study has shown that Foucault's own discourse embodies this process of self-overcoming in which the effects of traditional controlling forces follow processes of recoiling that not only reorganize our inherited values but also put in question the enduring validity of the principles by which the recoiling takes place. One consequence is that the idea and experience of self as a self-realizing basis of value is doubtful and that the project of self-constitution is put in question as its epistemic assumption of the founding quality of representation transposes into one of genealogical self-overcoming. The significance of minimizing domination is found in the language of self-overcoming in which the search for totalizing values loses its attraction.

Foucault's exposure of what is ignored in specific lineages is one of the moving forces of his work. Its effect is to show how rules of knowledge and relations of power have held in force certain kinds of suffering and, above all, certain limits of freedom that are catastrophic for groups of individuals. A society's investment in such suffering and limits is articulated in types of knowledge, situations of action, and character formations that are justified without regard to the dominance of their own interest or to their temporality. The critical dimension of Foucault's thought challenges these patterns of domination by exposing them. Another dimension encourages freedom from domination by the liberations incurred through exposure. And a third puts to work the process by which the liberty of self-overcoming governs the "games" of power and truth that have held people in check. In Foucault's work the language of exposure, as we have seen, is itself structured by self-overcoming recoils. Is self-overcoming a new discipline of self-relation? We have seen that his subject matter is not a self or subject, but combinations of texts, practices, and forces. The language of self-representation does not organize his thought.

Further, by developing his analysis of governmentality, Foucault intended to expand the area of investigation beyond the scope of individual rights and self-relation. *Governmentality* names "the totality of practices by which one can constitute, define, organize, instrumentalize the strategies which individuals in their liberty can have with regard to each other" (EC 19). Not self-constitution or self-formation, but a network of practices, knowledges, and techniques is the field within which people become subjects. By elaborating the lineage of various aspects of governmentality, such as population control and welfare for all citizens, Foucault continues to set aside both the priority of the self and the nineteenth-century thought of representation in his account of the formation of the subject. The heritage of the care of self is the aspect of governmentality that Foucault began to describe before his death. It is an account that speaks out of the question of ethics and that makes impossible a new ethic of self-constitution within the parameters of his discourse.

Foucault will not call processes of liberation from domination a work of the self upon the self. Such language has the danger of referring "to the idea that there does exist a nature or a human foundation which, as a result of a certain number of historical, social or economic processes, found itself concealed, alienated or imprisoned in and by some repressive mechanism" (EC 2). Rather, he defines his problem in terms of the interplay of truths and powers that congeal into seemingly unalterable structures of living and "prevent all reversibility" (EC 3). In this emphasis the priority of the subject is also reversed, and the subject is found to derive from games of truth and power. "I had to reject a certain a priori theory of the subject in order to make this analysis of the relationships which can exist between the constitution of the subject or different forms of the subject and games of truth, practices of power, and so forth" (EC 10). Rather than being identical with itself, the subject takes shape in those processes by which individual behavior is directed and truth is formed within specific patterns of knowledge and validation. Rather than providing an analysis of the contingency of the subject, for example, Foucault shows how relations of power and knowledge are both regionally definitive and ultimately unstable. Rather than contending that freedom is a characteristic of human subjectivity, he locates freedom in the reversibility, instability, and problematic formation of the relations of knowledge and power in patterns of direction and influence. Reversibility and instability characterize the processes by which we come to be who we are. This account of reversibility constitutes a reversal within the discourse of subjectivity that plays a major role in Foucault's inheritance, and, as we have seen, it is a reversal that arises from the discourse's own instability.

Games of truth are the interplay of rules, principles, and methods whereby people know themselves and other things. Games of power are constituted by the ways people direct and influence behaviors. Both types of games constitute the discourse whereby, in our tradition, the self worked upon itself to make a certain kind of being. Self-transformations arise from and perpetuate the complex interplays of knowledge and power by which, for example, people determine what are acceptable, pleasurable, and passionate relations with each other.

The formations of games of truth are continually emphasized in Foucault's work. According to *Madness and Civilization,* people *recognized* madness in themselves and others within specific structures of knowledge and practice, whether the 'game' be one in which the mad revealed God's grace or were instances of malformation that are correctable by medical intervention. Although *The Order of Things* does not underscore the power aspect of epistemes, it, too, shows that the empirical and human sciences are constituted by complex plays of rules and principles that are volatile (open to transformation in their instabilities) and traceable in their mutations. That study leads to Foucault's account of punitive practices in the seventeenth and eighteenth centuries in which the criminal and his or her correction are knowable within the given 'game' or episteme. These games of truth and error define both academic knowledge and popular social knowledge. People think of and experience themselves and others in them, develop institutions to advance truth and correct error within the game's domain, and create normal and deviant behaviors, as well as right and wrong bodies of knowledge, within the game's parameters. Games of truth make possible self-recognization and cultural recognization, forceful recognizations in which one knows, for example, that oneself or the other is mad or authoritative or normal.

In his trilogy on the history of sexuality, particularly in *The Use of Pleasure* and *The Care of the Self,* Foucault asks, "What were the games of truth by which human beings came to see themselves as desiring individuals?" (UP 7) How did people come to think of themselves and to experience themselves as subjects of desire? Human being came to be recognized by reference to desire, and the formation of this truth, of this game, was a heritage by which the self became the object of its dominant concern. In this game, the individual had to constitute itself as a kind of subject that occurs as self-relation. Self-constitution was the name of the game.

How is it that Foucault's thought is not itself a new kind of self-constitution? His studies, he says, are endeavors to find "to what extent the effort to think one's own history can free thought from what it silently thinks, and so enable it to think differently" (UP 9). Their value is found in a knowledge in which he "strays afield from himself." "There are times in life when the question of knowing if one can think differently than one thinks and perceive differently than one sees, is absolutely necessary if one is to go on looking and reflecting at all." This is a "game with oneself" (UP 8). Foucault appropriates the game aspect of truth and power that constitutes, if blindly, his tradition and allows the discourse of truth to overcome itself in his thinking: by finding itself a game of truth—finding its truth—the truth discourse recoils from its own conditions for being true, or such conditions as universality, continuing presence, self-founding, self-representation, and self-disclosure. But does this recoil demand nonetheless a new kind of selfhood? A new ethical subject?

Ascesis is the word Foucault uses to describe his philosophical thought: "Ascesis, an exercise of oneself in the activity of thought" (UP 9). Becoming free of what one silently thinks, from the subjectivization and behavioral effects of given ways of knowing and living that constitute one's identity, is the ascetic activity that Foucault has in mind. Transformation of one's mode of being is also the goal of the "practices of the self" that Foucault analyzes in his final trilogy. The emphasis in that discourse is on "the forms of relation with self, on the methods and techniques by which he works them out, on the exercises by which he makes of himself an object to be known, and on the practices that enable him to transform his own mode of being" (UP 30). One trains in order to gain self-mastery for the successful practice of virtue in relation to oneself as well as to others.

By careful training one becomes a moral subject and, in the history of this type of self-mastery, the individual becomes the object of training whereby his or her self is developed into a self-forming subject whose intention is to be good by the internalized, governing standards that tell the self who it is to become. In its full Western development, moral ascesis is articulated as a definitive representation of the self to itself, a representation which, when lived, is considered to be true freedom. Foucault, in naming his thought ascetic, ironizes his interplay with the tradition. In a Nietzschean move of self-overcoming he ascetically trains his knowledge to move through and beyond the self-mastery that formed the moral self. Moral self-mastery in this context recoils on itself and springs away from itself.

The knowledge that informs this experience of self-overcoming freedom constitutes a game of truth. It is made of rules and descriptions, regimes ruled by codes of behavior, prescriptions that put into practice certain formulas and beliefs regarding the self. But the liberty of individuals to develop all manner of codes and knowledges and to give them governing power by accounts of prescriptive origins and foundations—that liberty becomes a threat to the particular authorizing knowledge. This liberty is underwritten only by the limits and transgressions of knowledge, not by the substance of knowledge. It is found in the discontinuities and ruptures of discourses. The formation of the self as a self-representing subject is in question by virtue of its liberty not only because of the content of its knowledge but also because of its form. We saw in the last section that the form of self-representation emerged from the episteme of representation that could not deal adequately, on its own terms, with either its proliferation of knowledges or the relation between the knower and the known. In *The History of Sexuality* we find that the human subject emerges in Western thought as the subject of desire that finds itself within a lineage of caring for itself. How is it to use itself in its pleasures? How is it to regulate itself, form itself, *be* itself?

Self-relation is a structure that loses its power in Foucault's thought. His training, his ascesis, is one that recoils in the training that formed the ethical subject, a training which has been a silent presence in his tradition and his thought. Self-representation means subjectivation and inevitable denial of liberty. Foucault cannot propose another form of self-representation or self-constitution without returning to the formation that his work puts in question. His asceticism is found in a training that eliminates the ethical subject.

Further, liberty as he defines it cannot find its expression in a better ethical subject. It is articulated in a self-overcoming that blindly characterizes his lineage and that is exposed and appropriated by his thought. We have seen that *liberty* does not name a property of human nature, but the continuous reversibility and substitutability of things. The liberty of the subject, for example, is not found primarily as freedom of choice or as an anxious relation of subjectivity to an infinite other. It is found in part as the historical and optional development of self-constitution.

Self-constitution, Foucault shows in *The History of Sexuality,* is formed in a history of problematizations regarding human conduct. One conducts oneself according to prescriptive ensembles that various "mediating agencies" prescribe, such as family, educational institutions, and religious bodies. The emphasis on self-conduct that emerged in the West arose concurrently with the formation of an agency that constituted itself in accord with the prescriptions. In our early history, Foucault finds, individuals did not, strictly speaking, constitute themselves. They externally met external standards, and the question of being a moral self did not arise. One either did or did not do the prescribed thing. His genealogy of the transformation of our culture into an internally directed one, instead of one directed by the external authority of the ruler or custom, is also a genealogy of the formation of the self-constituting subject whereby the self represents itself to itself. Previously the ruling power was reflected back to itself by the conforming behavior of the ruled. Forming the self, however, became the dominant practice. Internal states of mind, internal transformation of desire, internal conformity to certain principles became the 'practice' for individuals. How the self related to itself defined the individual's identity. This massive cultural project of self-mastery, this program of training that Foucault calls ascetic, gives rise to the agency that defines itself by its self-regulation.

Foucault's work rises out of a self-constituting self as much as does our reading of him. How are we to understand this project of self-overcoming that takes place in a context of ethical subjectivity? What is the problem that allows the formation of a knowledge that puts in question the power and value of self-constitution? Although the specific context of Foucault's last work is that of sexual desire and the normativity that created moral perversion and the denial of many forms of erotic pleasure, the larger problem is that of the formation of knowledges and relations of power that created an agency which must and yet cannot give a complete account of itself: it is a problem of totalization and liberty.

The ideal of the episteme of self-representation, we saw, is full knowledge of the subject in representational activity. This project fails by the continuous escape of the subject from its own representation—always a representation and never the subject itself. The goal of total self-knowledge fails by virtue of the structure of knowledge that produces the goal. This failure, we saw, is informed by a Western preoccupation with completion and unity, a preoccupation that moved the epistemes that prevailed prior to the nineteenth century to an episteme of self-representation. We emphasize now that totalization is one of the continuing values in Western knowledge, whether it take the form of seeing fully into totality or of realizing a completely unified subject.

Self-constitution, as it developed into the Western ethical subject, is as much a part of that ideal as is the episteme of self-representation. Whereas the project of self-representation is full knowledge of the founding subject by the founding subject, such that this knowledge is a complete, founding order for things, the project of self-constitution is self-mastery by means of austere self-transformation. The "technology" that developed to care for the self involved making the self (not the city or the state) an object to itself such that it is the subject of its own mastery. If the self-constitution itself accorded to true principles and rules, it would itself *be* true. In that sense, although the self might or might not originate its regulations, it founded itself in its self-constituting activity. We see the totalization at work in a concomitant depreciation of proliferation and randomness. Mastery, superiority, domination, and subjectivization form together a major strand of self-constitution as Foucault traces it in volumes II and III of *The History of Sexuality*.

Liberty means in part the inevitable failure of all projects of mastery. Foucault does not argue that by pursuing mastery individuals deny an aspect of their being which is named *liberty*. Liberty, as we have seen, names the reversibility, mortality, transitional and mutational aspects, and arbitrariness of orders of knowledge and practice. The gaps among knowledges and practices do not open to an originary, teleological being, but to mere transgression at the limits of given structures, and to nothing other than our relations of power and games of truth. Foucault's response to liberty, as we have seen, is found in his desire to recognize the danger in all relations of power and forms of knowledge, including his own, and to develop an ethos of genealogy, which we have elaborated in its recoil and self-overcoming movements. The disciplines of genealogical knowledge are not found in an established mastery or in a method of mastery, but in transforming the desires for truth and totalization that move our traditional discourses. The problem that moves Foucault's work is the clash of totalization and liberty in the ethical subject as it has developed in Western history. That is the "problematization" that arouses his "vigilance."[16] His genealogy uncovers the strife that defines the limits of ethical subjectivity and that characterizes its dangers: its constitutive denial of the liberty of its lineage by its project of self-constitution in which self-mastery means in practice internalized domination of an individual by given rules and principles that support the interests of specific groups of people. This domination is elaborated socially by relationships of power in which mastery over others and controlled behavior are natural expressions of the ethical subject. Care of self has combined with games of truth and strategies of power to form an ethics that cannot prevent itself from maximizing domination in the name of values. The committed ethical subject is a microcosm of totalization that finds its expression in dominating others under the guise of taking care of them. The steps from ethical subjectivity to oppressive social practices is both small and inevitable.

We have examined the practice of liberty that Foucault values primarily with reference to his genealogy and the knowledge that it produces. In it we find an overcoming of ethical subjectivity, as the authoritative knowledge that is affiliated with it is put in question and as the movement of self-constitution is countermanded and sidestepped. Foucault's work is characterized by a concern for individuals, for their freedom from domination, for their pleasures, and for their specific thriving and pain. Yet this seemingly ethical concern has led to his appropriating the self-overcoming process that dissolves ethical subjectivity and the knowledge that is affiliated with it. This self-overcoming of the caring subject puts in question all that we can mean by *ethics* and maximizes the possibilities for reversal of traditional relations of power and knowledge.

The problem of totalization and its multiple forms of domination puts in question the subject that undergoes the problem. The practice of liberty mandates opening the field of social/individual life to self-overcoming without the hallmarks of ethical security, definitive origins and ideal goals. Is it possible that the kind of self-presence that at our best we want to realize and the goals that give us our best meanings arise from a heritage that makes inevitable our worst fears? Is it possible that as ethical subjects we are subject to a destiny of domination that we also want to avoid? That we are divided in our ethical subjectivity by an impossible totalitarian liberty, a conundrum of subjectivity, that makes doubtful the best that we can be and know? Is it possible that the *question* of ethics holds hope for a life without the ethical subject and without some of the suffering that we ethical subjects bring upon ourselves?

FOUR

The Question of Dasein's Most Proper Being

The ascetic ideal, which in Nietzsche's genealogy provides both the structure of resentment regarding human life and the disciplined strength that makes possible the self-sacrifice of self-overcoming, is not functional in our early history according to Foucault's genealogy. Instead, *ascetic* suggests a kind of training in the context of looking after one's behavior and taking care of pleasures and does not necessarily include an ideal of self-renunciation. It has that meaning only in the specific context of forming the moral subject for whom pleasure is an object of suspicion except when pleasure fits properly in a carefully regulated self. The *askésis* that includes suspicion of pleasure has its origin in the problematization of pleasures. Such training emerged as pleasures and their possibility created problems for the classical Greek individual, but became an integral part of the training for moral selfhood only when the formation of the ethical self developed as a major project for later Europeans. Whereas on Nietzsche's account the ascetic ideal is co-originary with priestly leadership and defines Western life-affirmation in a self-negating paradox, on Foucault's account that ideal is constitutive of ethical subjectivity and comes relatively late in our heritage. But Nietzsche's and Foucault's genealogies are in agreement that to be an ethical individual in our time is to be nonvoluntarily trained in subtle forms of renunciation and affirmation that are at odds with their own temporal processes of formation. Further, an *askésis* that is suspicious of the body, that negates the body in its ways of affirming it, and that produces ideals and values that we embody, constitutes the self in its moral/ethical self-constitution on both accounts. As this self-constituting training falls in question, the possibility of ethics falls in question.

One of the questions to which the following three chapters lead is that of the extent to which Heidegger's way of putting ethics in question articulates the ascetic ideal. We shall find in this chapter that ethical self-constitution is thoroughly in question in Heidegger's thought and that ethical thought and judgment are also in question. But does the question of ethics come into a torsion of counterforces as Heidegger makes ethics questionable? Does his thought have a quasi-ethical dimension that is problematic for his thought? In order to approach such questions we shall follow in this chapter Heidegger's destructuring of ethics in *Being and Time* and "On the Essence of Truth." Ethics is not eliminated but put in question, and the way in which the process of putting in question takes place provides a movement of thought that is able to think of and within the limits and origins of ethics.

The shift from Nietzsche and Foucault to Heidegger is sharp. The issue of power and the arrangements of power, the genealogies of basic epistemic and volitional capacities, the undertone of violence that marks their writing, their joyous play and irreverence, their witty departures from traditional seriousness, their continuous return to desiring bodies and to sensuous movement, their invocation of Dionysian intoxication and reverie, their hammerlike styling, their attention to perversion and animality: all of this separates Nietzsche and Foucault from Heidegger. The very element of Heidegger's thought appears to be ascetic when set in contrast to Nietzsche's and Foucault's thought. This difference is inscribed in part by the intimacy of Heidegger's writing with the piety and spirituality of both Protestantism and Roman Catholicism. His attractiveness to theologians and religious persons is not accidental. The ease with which philosophers, on first reading, have made Heidegger into a metaphysician, particularly by reference to his 'early' writings, appears to be influenced by Heidegger's use of quasi-religious terms and his style of thought. Heidegger seems to experience reverence where we traditionally expect it, while Nietzsche and Foucault play obscenely in the same space. We shall find a radicality in Heidegger's thought, however, in relation to his and our traditions of thought and action that is not exceeded in Foucault and Nietzsche.[1] He transgresses his lineage with a subtlety of effect that makes his and our reinscription of it always a question. Our tradition undergoes a dissemination by his pen that cannot be overstated in spite of a continuing obsession with unity on his part.

The genealogies of Nietzsche and Foucault show that our selves have developed in specific lineages and that the ability of our selves to be carries the history of self-formation. Nietzsche's genealogy of the human capacity for promising, for example, shows the affiliation of promising with retribution and pleasure in inflicting retaliative pain. Foucault's genealogy of modern self-regulation shows its affiliation, as a culturally developed capacity, with the decline of regency, the problem of population control, the fear of body, the division of soul and body in the dominant practices comprising the care of souls, and a persistent violence toward individuals embodied in the normal standards of goodness and propriety. Through both Foucault's and Nietzsche's genealogies we found that in the ascetic ideal, meaning overrides meaninglessness, presence marginalizes no presence, language drowns out mere silence, and positive values are textured with unconscious violence. Their own language and thought, by which they make their analyses, are part of the problems that they address. Their discourses give privilege to those abilities, types of people, attitudes, and ways of perceiving that have suffered from the limits and interests of the traditionally dominant values and practices. These differing 'infrastructures' delimit (in the sense that they show the terminations of) the capacities and values that control them. In the case of such capacities as promising, self-regulating, and self-constitution, Foucault's and Nietzsche's ways of recoiling in the functions of these capacities indicate how much a part of the tradition they are and how limited their discourses are, given their critique of these capacities.

In putting in question so thoroughly their own language and thought as they develop their genealogies, Foucault's and Nietzsche's discourses give rise to the suspicion that our best attempts to think, speak, and assess may advance suffering that we could wish to eliminate. Our clearest judgments may make obscure parts of our lineage. Our characteristic ways of observing, ordering, retaining, and freeing may well cover over, proliferate, repress, and confine with pathogenic blindness people, abilities, and possibilities. Do we know how to speak of our institutions? Of our inflictions and cures? Of ourselves? The self-overcoming discourses of Nietzsche and Foucault make uncertain the 'neutrality' and values by which we judge as well as our ability to judge and the security of the orders by which we know. Above all they put in doubt the certainties we have regarding subjectivity and selfhood. Far from the skepticism that argues that nothing is really knowable—the reversed side of positive, metaphysical knowledge—their genealogies embody a sense of the historical limits that define our capacities for knowing and believing. Things are known. But they are known in ways that have considerable social and cultural costs, and both the costs and the possibility of recognizing the costs are found within the lineages of modern use and knowledge.

As we turn to Heidegger we shall hold in mind that the question of ethics includes the question of whether we know how to think of our suffering as well as of our goods and bads. In this strand of thought both the processes and contents of judgment have fallen into question by the self-overcoming movements within the strand. We who are now thinking within it are not given confidence to believe that the clarity and objectivity by which we are led to what is right and true are unindicted by human suffering. 'Right' and 'true' constitute dangers for individuals. Their satisfactions may cause as well as incorporate suffering and distortion of which we are usually unaware. Although Heidegger's approach to Western philosophy—by means of the de-structuring of its language, thought, and certainties and by retrieving its forgotten elements—does not fit easily into a definition of genealogy, his work puts itself and our ability to think sharply in question. In it we meet one of the most persistent attempts in Western thought to confront the determination of patterns of thought by which we have established and maintained our ideals for living. We find in the center of his thought what is most disturbing, problematic, and painful for our lineage and what has traditionally been segregated, marginalized, and systematically forgotten.

1. Dasein's *Eigenste* Being

The second part of *Being and Time* shows that dasein is the unifying basis for its own self-disclosure and authenticity. In section 53, the last section of part II, chapter I, he sketches out what he will have to establish, namely that dasein's existential structure makes possible an individual's authentic *(eigentliche)* being to death. Because this possibility is dasein's own—is constitutive of dasein—it is said to be *eigentlich* or proper, true, and essential. The name of this condition for the possibility of an individual's proper, mortal way of being is the disclosiveness of situated understanding. *Disclosiveness* is to be read in Heidegger's sense of showing forth, opening up, or clearing; and *understanding,* in his sense of dasein's alert, projecting ability to be. Dasein's constitutive ability to be is a forecasting process of disclosure that manifests temporality as it projects forward, and in that sense understands, in its historical, social situation.

Heidegger interprets dasein's ability to be, in the language of possibility. In this context it is not a possibility for a future realization of something determinant, nor is it a possibility that takes place at a distance from dasein and can be known objectively by contemplation. Dasein's proper and true ability to be is mortal possibility, and is characterized as the possibility of the impossibility of existence: being to death. Dasein's world-openness, its clearing for the self-showing of beings, is an ability to be that is sheer, mortal possibility. Possibility *[Möglichkeit]*, Heidegger says, is disclosed *[unverhült]* as the impossibility *[Unmöglichkeit]* of existence. Being to death, then, is the meaning of dasein's ability to be, although we shall find that *meaning* is used in this context in a highly specific way. "Death, as possibility, gives dasein nothing to be 'actualized', nothing which dasein, as actual, could itself be." *Meaning* does not suggest any kind of supersensible world.

Vorlaufen, or 'running ahead', is, with *proper, possibility, understanding, and being to death,* the fifth organizing term of this section. It addresses this movement of being to death and possibility. "Being to death as running ahead in possibility first of all *makes possible* this possibility and makes it as such free." Dasein's ability to be discloses itself *[erschliesst sich]* in the running ahead of being to death. It is a movement in which the most extreme possibility of human being, its death, is brought forth and uncovered in its possibility. What is most dasein's own, its ability to be, is not *something* to be realized. Authenticity for Heidegger is not a matter of self's actualizing itself. There is no self there when dasein's ability to be is addressed. Its movement is one of running ahead to its impossibility in its mere ability to be. It is not, we shall see, a movement of self-constitution or of the unfolding of an essence that has a nature to unfold or of a truth that is to find its adequacy in an identity that is constituted on the basis of truth's form or content. The movement of dasein's proper and true possibility is mortal temporality in its difference from possible identities that we might become, the possible lives that we might lead, and the selfhood that we might achieve.

This movement is dasein's most essential *[eigenste]* possibility for interpreting its proper existence *[eigentlich Existenz]*. Existential understanding, in contrast to interpretation, is found in the projective aspect of dasein's temporal movement. Human being, in its care, continuously projects and designs *[Entwirft]* in the midst of its relations. Heidegger has shown in Section 31 that its projective character opens up *[erschliesst]* in and to the world as well as reveals the being of dasein as possibility of being. Projection is being possible. In the section at hand he indicates in a preliminary sketch that the temporality of understanding and its projective character *[Entwurf]* are revealed in its mortal running ahead. Heidegger's intention is to show how dasein "auf eigenstes Seinkönnen sich entwerfen kann"— how dasein can project itself on and by its most proper ability to be. Running ahead shows itself as the possibility for understanding the most proper, uttermost ability to be. If he can show this possibility *and* let it be shown in his account of it, he will have an interpretation that is designed after the temporal and mortal design of dasein's understanding. He will then be in a position to show how dasein might live in a way that, like the interpretation of *Being and Time,* opens to its being. Dasein's temporal and mortal movement, its *Vorlauf,* would then be the basis for the way we design our lives.

But this basis has no definitive or determinate nature. Dasein's most proper course of conduct takes place as it lets its disclosure disclose itself in whatever activity one undertakes. Heidegger says that his own work must uncover the structure of running ahead in death as dasein's truest possibility. If his writing succeeds and is proper to dasein, it will be responsive to its own *"vorlaufenden Erschliessen,"* to its own understanding *in* running ahead disclosively. That does not mean that the correctness of Heidegger's analysis will be guaranteed if he is true to the being of dasein. It means that an anxious desire for correctness will be experienced in the mortal possibility of dasein's being, which in its occurrence is not subject to correctness or incorrectness; and although Heidegger does not entirely face his own anxiety regarding unity, the impact of his account means that the book's project regarding unity is also in question by virtue of dasein's mortality of design. On the basis of dasein's movement, as Heidegger finds it, even the language of being, running ahead, and design do not escape the unfixing quality of dasein's truth. We shall see that its truth comes most clearly to bear as it puts itself in question in consequence of its own claims. Dasein's disclosive running ahead in mortal temporality and the ek-stasis that it constitutes undercut any predisposition to complete certainty, most particularly that predisposition that inclines one to canonize Heidegger's writings or to think on *their* basis rather than on the basis of their possibility for no possibility at all. Heidegger's interpretation of dasein is not the result of "staring at meaning" and coming up with the best reading of the meaning of life. It is designed, rather, to express dasein's ability to be in its disclosive being to death. It clears the way for dasein's world-openness as the temporal course of being to death. The account of Dasein's authenticity takes its departure from the finite, temporal movement that is the condition of possibility of both meaning and no meaning, that is, from the questionableness of meaning in being to death.

When dasein's *eigenste Möglichkeit* (most proper possibility) is named death (BT 263), the meaning of *most proper* or *ownmost* or *most essential* is thus interrupted. Dasein's *eigenste* ability to be, its truest can-be, is not something that properly can be said to be its own in the sense of a property at its disposal. Nor is its truest capacity to be self-relational in the sense that a subject relates to itself. The continuity of self-relation is ruptured by a course of coming to be that does not reflect or represent the self. It rather discloses human being as non-selflike possibility without identity or subjectivity. Dasein is clear *[offenbar]* not only in its difference from its everyday self-understanding but in its difference from selfhood. There is a wrenching *[entrissen]* quality in dasein's deathly openness. It lives out its existential understanding as it is torn from the meanings and values by which it makes its way in its society and as it is torn from its inherited interpretation of itself as self-founding. In this wrenching aspect dasein lives its disclosure of its being in the midst of its activities and connections. It stands out of—ek-sists—everything that it lives for. Dasein's deathly openness ek-sists its selfhood as well as its ethos.

Dasein in its most proper possibility is not finally defined by its linkage to people or things. This is not to say that it is not linked to people and things. It is found *only* in social, historical matrices. Human being occurs only in multiple human connections. But dasein is in excess of its definitive way of being. The human world's ability to be, its clearing for all beings, interrupts the matrix of connections, not in the active sense of doing something to the matrix, but in the sense of pervading and making possible the matrix without being identical to the matrix or having an existence independent of the matrix. Playing on *vorlaufen,* we can say that the world's ability to be courses through the connections of our lives as difference from connections and yields their fragility, their mortality, their disconnection in the midst of their connections. When Heidegger says that dasein's possibility runs forward as dasein's future, is dasein's ability to be, and is being to death, he means that dasein goes forward in this interruption: to go in its most proper being means that in moving into its future dasein never leaves its being to death, its possibility for no possibility. Its futural movement is being to death. "Es geht um sein eigenstes Sein" (It goes about its most proper being). One can see why interpreters have often mistaken this claim to mean that dasein is individually alone in its mortality and that Heidegger is a modern stoic who holds that humans must accept the fate of death with singular courage. But we also see that dasein, as an intrinsically social, worldly being, is a being marked by difference in its being from the totality of its relations and values. *In* its relations and values dasein is the opening *[erschliessen]* of its ownmost incapacity to own its being by affirming who in fact it is. It comes into its own by disowning its selfhood in the way it is a self.

How is this interruptive nonrelatedness to be lived? What is proper to it? The paradox in this part of Heidegger's analysis is found in his claim that by disowning the sufficiency of one's connections and identity vis-à-vis dasein, one owns not only his or her world but also one's being. Just as Nietzsche's self-overcoming in his account of the ascetic ideal echoes the theme of self-sacrifice, Heidegger's interpretation echoes the same thing. The individual individuates itself by discovering the singularity of its being to death and by living its connections with a sensibility informed by that singularity. One loves in the fragility of loving, not in the assumption of its founded meaning. One affirms values with the understanding that he or she and one's values are able not to be in the possibility of their affirmation. Nothing replaces the individual's life in its living. But rather than thinking in a connection between self-giving and universal principles, Heidegger thinks in the interruption of the meaning of our lives by the mortal *possibility* of living and finds in owning the being's interruption of our lives we may disown the theoretical and existential sufficiency of our selves for defining our being or our ability to be. Individuation means living responsively in the world with the *eigenstes Möglichkeit* of being to death, which interrupts one's historical and community identity and puts in question the meaning of life. This is saying something quite different from the statement that the individual must die his or her death alone. In owning one's being one owns no one, and that 'no one' is the truth of one's being. No one, no history, no community, no subjectivity authorizes the individual's life. The question is how we are to think of being without authority and meaning for life, without self-relational meaning. When Heidegger says that an individual is forced by the forward run [*Vorlaufen*] of existence to take over its most proper and true being in possibility, he is saying that the individual's world and life are decentered and ruptured by the individual's resolve. In this resolve the thought of selfhood, subjectivity, and self-constitution are set aside. In resolve one opens out in the world in the "understanding design" of dasein's mortal openness.

Dasein's situation is thus not one in which it constitutes itself and makes itself present primarily by means of realizing a given potential for selfhood. It intrinsically *[eigentlich]* lacks reality and is able to come into specific kinds of presence only by virtue of the historically formed world relations in which it finds itself. The 'wholeness' of its being is found in the stream of possibility—not a determinant possibility for a specific way of being that dasein may realize in more or less appropriate ways. Possibility is never surpassed, even momentarily, by some form of self-constitution. Rather, the very activity of self-constitution proliferates dasein and moves it away from its wholeness and unity, a wholeness that is found in its attunement "to the nothing of the possible impossibility of its existence." Dasein's true *[eigenste]* situation is found in an attunement that has neither subject nor object. It is the mood of sheer, mortal possibility: anxiety. The thought of whole and unity is pushed by Heidegger to a breaking point as he shows that human being finds its unity in nothing present or realizable. In speaking of this opening to dasein's whole ability to be, Heidegger uses a middle voice phrase: "Die Angst ängstet sich *um* das Seinkönnen des so bestimmten Seinden und erschliesst so die äussereste Möglichkeit" (Anxiety (is) anxious in the midst of the ability to be of the being that is so disposed and opens up the uttermost possibility). Anxiety discloses dasein's ability to be in a wholeness without substance and in the figuration of possible impossibility. Dasein is most true (that is, it is its own disclosure) in possibility that opens to all values and meanings and stands out from everything that makes an individual's life worth living. The thought of grounding thus falls away in the anxiety that grounds the thought.

Section 53 is entitled "Existenzialer Entwurf eines eigentlichen Seins zum Tode" (Existential Projection of an Authentic Being to Death). We have emphasized that *Entwurf* 'projected design' is closely associated with *Vorlauf* 'the running ahead of dasein's possibility as being to death'. This section appropriates dasein's proper Vorlauf in its Entwurf by developing an interpretation based on dasein's existential understanding of its mortal temporality, and in that process prepares to break the traditional thoughts of unity, wholeness, and ground. These thoughts are projected in the forward run of dasein's anxious possibility and can no longer suggest a transcendental grounding for value and meaning. Human being is uncovered in the process whereby the traditional and everyday sense of self and transcendence are ruptured by anxiety, which is the modal aspect of dasein's ungrounded mortality. The appropriateness of Heidegger's Entwurf, in this part of *Being and Time,* to dasein's possible impossibility, however, needs further elaboration. We must examine dasein's *Eigentlichkeit* 'its authenticity' vis-à-vis its *eigenste Möglichkeit* 'its most proper possibility', and the appropriation of its disclosiveness in its resolve to live responsively and alertly with its being.

2. A Recoiling Search for Authenticity

Since dasein does not provide a basis for a metaphysically founded ethics and since its being interrupts and ruptures meaning and values with sheer possibility and being to death, Heidegger investigates dasein's possibility of being a self that is appropriate to its being rather than a self defined by ethical norms. He uses the language of foundations and conditions for the possibility of selfhood in this discussion, as he does throughout *Being and Time*. Just as the language of wholeness and unity falls into question in the context of dasein's 'essential truth', this language, too, is broken by dasein's ability to be, its *Seinskönnen*. The term *eigentliche* now refers to specific ways in which an individual relates to its being. What is the proper way for dasein to live with regard to its being? How is it to constitute itself in its being, which interrupts the very meaning of self-constitution with its possibility of no self at all, a possibility that is dasein's and is most properly so? Whereas in the previous section Entwurf and Vorlauf interplayed to bring together the writing and the subject in question, in this section attestation *[Bezeugung]* will interplay with resoluteness *[Entschlossenheit]* around the themes of witness and own. Chapter 2 of *Time and Being* is entitled "Die daseinsmässige Bezeugung eines eigentlichen Seinskönnens und die Entschlossenheit" (Dasein's Attestation of an Authentic Potentiality-for-being and Resoluteness). Section 54 is "Das Problem der Bezeugung einer eigentlichen existenziellen Möglichkeit" (The Problem of Attesting to an Authentic Existentielle Possibility). Our issue is, how does Heidegger put ethics in question as he establishes dasein's proper way to be vis-à-vis its being?

Selfhood, on Heidegger's account, is a way of being. The struggle for proper selfhood puts the individual at odds with its normal world in which it has its possible roles and identities set for it. To be a proper, self-authenticating self, an individual must take its fundamental cues for living from its being, not from the standards of communal normalcy. There is a double rupture involved in this process. Dasein must break from the normal, ready-made certainties that have formed it from its earliest awareness. This involves the extremely difficult process of retrieving one's understanding and one's temporality, which is constitutive of dasein's being, and finding out how to be in accord with it as one lives in the patterns of life and meaning that have been developed in a trenchant, forceful ignorance of dasein's being. This direction of thought prepares us to expect some kind of natural knowledge of dasein's being, some basis for correcting our erring ways of life and for guiding us to a higher fulfillment of our human nature. But instead of an immanent knowledge of human nature, we have found a nonconceptual "understanding," an alertness that takes place in dasein's temporal projecting and one that attests to mortal possibility without the possibility of circumscribing itself. The first interruption takes place as an individual finds cultural and social assurances to be without ontological foundation, to be, rather, concerned reactions that have led our Western ethos away from its own being. Heidegger finds that traditional selfhood has been formed in this reaction, and his retrieval of the West's early thoughts and questions is an effort no less revolutionary than Nietzsche's to show that *who* we can be is invested in covering over the questionableness of the ability to be a 'who' at all. From the perspective of our traditional meanings and sense of presence, the lack of a selflike basis for the self and the lack of meaning in our meanings constitutes a dismal prospect, and although Heidegger does not invoke Nietzsche at this point, he indicates indirectly that, in agreement with Nietzsche's genealogy of the ascetic ideal, Western human beings feel that they could not live properly if their being were most properly merely the possibility of no possibility at all. The first appropriate interruption is thus one in which the assurances and sense of presence that constitute us are put in question by the *Vorlauf* of being to death. This mortal temporality, along with its refusal, are part of who we are. Our existence lives the interruption that Heidegger attempts to reinherit in his analysis of dasein in *Being and Time*.

Dasein's secular and religious rituals must thus be interrupted, and both its questions and answers must undergo the second rupture, that of dasein's truth, its disclosure, of being possibly impossible. The second interruption is like that of self-overcoming. The move natural for dasein, given its history, is to find a body of certainties to replace those that have proved to be inadequate. The certainty of Heidegger's 'strict' and careful description of dasein, for example, might give us assurance that we have our meaning in our temporality, or another account might be taken to prove that Heidegger is mistaken and to constitute more reliable analysis on the basis of which to conduct our lives. But there is a recoil at this point in Heidegger's thought. On the one hand, he is providing an account that he takes to be well founded and preferable to the metaphysical tradition from which it departs. On the other hand, his account leads him to the truth of dasein, its disclosive mortal temporality, which puts in question desire for certainty, the neutrality of accurate thought, and the ability of meaningful discourse to circumscribe and express dasein's being. *What* his analysis finds recoils on both the meaning and historical subjectivity of his finding and makes it doubtful that his grasp definitively holds the sheer possibility that it designates. Heidegger's thought in Part II of *Being and Time* expresses the meaning of dasein's being, which on its own account runs ahead and 'possibilizes' outside the circumscriptions of meaning.

As we proceed in the investigation of Heidegger's account of dasein's proper resolve and response to its own being, we are involved in a reflective movement that puts in question its own certainty, its structure of expression, its perceptive reach, and its prescriptive possibility. His word *Entschlossenheit,* which is translated as 'resoluteness', also has the normal meaning of decisiveness or of bringing something to a conclusion or end. The *Ent,* however, can have both an intensifying function or one of opposition; for example, *entkommen* means to escape, *entschlüsseln* means to decode or open up. When the *ent* of *entschliessen* is taken as intensifying, as it usually is, dasein resolves and decides for its being; it makes up its mind. But the ambiguity of *ent* allows Heidegger, in the context of his account of *Being and Time,* to say in effect that dasein unlocks or opens itself to its being, to *erschliessen* or disclose its being, and to be opened to its continuous closing, its mortal temporality. To be resolved in one's being to death provides no ground for concluding anything with certainty and puts in question the appropriateness of the kind of thinking that expects human existence to find its fulfillment on the basis of structures like those of good and evil that are decided by human being or human nature. Although *Being and Time* cannot be read as proposing a historicist position, neither can it be read as finding an enclosed universal basis for normative ethical judgment. Resolution, by opening to dasein's disclosive mortality, interrupts the enclosing structures necessary for traditional systems concepts and universal principles. The priority of both judgment and universality is in question by virtue of the mortal temporality that constitutes dasein, its language and its conceptuality.

The tension that we thus have to work with in *Being and Time,* when we consider dasein's propriety regarding itself, its authenticity, is found in Heidegger's emphasis on dasein's ontological structure as the unifying origin, in the sense of condition for the possibility, of all relative, ontic ways of existing, and his showing that this ontological structure and its account are in question by virtue of dasein's own disclosure. Dasein's ontological structure provides the basis for raising the question of being, for interpreting its historicity, and for showing how it might exist appropriately with regard to its being. But the basis is more like abyss than like anything that can be properly called normative. Given our inherited senses of ultimate meaning for reality and the intrinsic value of human existence, this discovery appears at first nihilistic. If we have no solid reference to support the values of individual lives, then anything can be justified. But anything *has* been justified in our history by appeal to universal values and meanings, including the most severe repressions, torture, extreme cruelty, wars, and the morbid enslaving and destructive segregation of vast groups of people. The proliferation of 'universal' norms whereby we justify certain values and contend against other values mirrors our fear of what the world would be like if we lacked an adequate basis for justifying our values and realizing the best possibilities of ourselves. The tension in Heidegger's thought between the search for a normative basis for thought and the discovery of a 'basis' that puts that search in question arises directly out of the fear to which our tradition responds by supporting its ideals and highest hopes with a combination of axioms, authorizing disclosure and careful judgment, be that disclosure God's, reason's, nature's, or humanity's.

The tension in Heidegger's thought, we shall see, puts in question the combination of axioms, authorizing disclosure and judgment, as well as the belief that with a proper normative basis for our values we can hope to overcome the destructive proliferation of violently opposing ways of life. The question we are approaching is whether people can find options to grounded normativity as the basis on which they come to be who they "should" be. Do options to the traditionally ethical ones arise for our language and thought when the tension between ontological grounding and being that cannot be a ground, but is like an *Ab-grund,* defines the space for thought? Does Heidegger's account of the basis for authenticity twist free of its ethical desire for grounding presence?[2]

Heidegger uses *self* to refer to 'who' dasein is. The term is meant to suggest not universality but the relative activity of a socialized, acculturated individual making its way in life. The self is a mediating agency who ordinarily chooses on the basis of something other than itself. Even if it chooses itself it chooses an agency that has been constituted in a history by language and customs that are not selves or like selves. Usually the 'something' that functions normatively is the vague, general, and pervasive image of normalcy that Heidegger calls 'das Man'. It functions as the general, anonymous agency by which we desire, decide, and constitute ourselves within a range of options that define proper identity in our broad culture and specific society. Only if we make our decisions on the basis of our being, Heidegger says, are we who we are as I myself *(ich selbst).* Being an authentic self is a modification of our normal, quasi-anonymous identity, a modification that takes place when our way of life makes manifest and in that sense is based on our being, not primarily on selfhood. The self twists free of its inherited way of being by coming to attend to its being, its disclosiveness. As we have seen, *this* movement of twisting free is not incidental to the authorship of *Being and Time* or to Heidegger's account of resoluteness. One characteristic of our everyday identity is a quality of certainty that seeks universalization in our daily personal and professional disciplines. Most things are already decided and known by virtue of the rules and standards, the assignments of values, the sense of relative urgency and range of applicability that structure and provide meaning and significance in our environment. We are relatively at ease in our communities of value even with regard to what shocks and horrifies us or inspires us unless something occurs to interrupt or to unavoidably challenge the shared values of our lives. When our ethos is threatened we naturally bristle and become hostile and resistant.

Heidegger's analysis suggests that our 'natural' identities are formed within complex histories and communities that structure our identities as though the inherited values were absolute. It further suggests that their conceptual structure is based on the assumptions that being is continuing presence and is simple, that time is linear and quantifiable, that death is the end point of life, and that human being has a kind of nature that is available to objective discovery. Our everyday, "fallen" lives are thus the basis of traditional metaphysical thought and the manner of evaluating that accompanies it in the name of ethics. He further shows that dasein's ability to be, its ungraspable running ahead in the possibility of no possibility at all, is not only not a clear part of everyday identities, but that our sensibility is formed in a traceable movement away from our being. Analogously to Nietzsche's making plain that philosophical thought as such, given its lineage, invokes the ascetic ideal, Heidegger shows that to be who we normally are and to think as we normally think is to live out a history that is adversative to the being that we are.[3] And, analogous to Nietzsche's account of the ascetic priest's giving hope to desperate people by relieving them of the burden of meaninglessness is Heidegger's account of normal selfhood as providing the benefit of relieving people of the burden of confronting themselves with regard to their being. The middle voice of dasein's being is silenced for all practical purposes in the structures and processes of normal living, and the perplexity of being without reality in the midst of everything that we experience as real and of being abysmal in the ground of our being is relieved.

The normal is thus improper, not true, not essential [uneigentlich] and lost [verloren]. When we hold in mind that the possibility of ethical thought and action is found in traditional 'normalcy' and its history, we see the cutting edge of Heidegger's thought concerning dasein's resolve: as we turn to the possibility of Eigentlichkeit 'authenticity', we are turning away from ethics as we know it. This turning away is nothing less than a twisting free of a body of selfhood that is given in its investment in not knowing its being or its propriety vis-à-vis its being. Heidegger's position is far stronger than one that provides only a formal basis for determining what our normative values should be. We shall see that the metaphysical strategy of formal-positive determination is changed by his thought. The question is whether we are able in our normalcy to recognize our suffering and pleasure or the meaning of the institutions and disciplines by which and in which we become who we are.

The "voice" of dasein's possibility "calls" in the midst of our involvements. Heidegger uses the experience of conscience, not its contents, as his phenomenal field. In his account, we undergo a calling away from our identities and selves to the possibility of our being. This call is corrupted by religions and moralities that make it seem as though it were calling to a specific way of life or ethos and as though it were initiated by specific violations that arouse guilt in a given individual. But the call itself discloses not the power of an ethos but the difference of human being, in its being, from its traditional ways of life. One undergoes, in the disclosiveness of dasein, a continuous "call" to its propriety, its eigenste Selbstseinkönnen, its most appropriate ability to be itself. Dasein's call to itself is like a voice that comes to dasein in the midst of its traditional life, like an appeal or summons to undergo the difference, in its being, from its self: "It gives dasein to understand" that its being is found in the disclosiveness of its ability to be the possibility of no possibility at all, not to be its values or the objects of religious and philosophical projections. The voice of conscience as the disclosure of dasein's being in the midst of its everyday values and standards functions to make those values and standards uncertain and to "call" dasein to its difference from who it is in its efforts to be someone recognizable in its culture.[4]

The wrenching away from dasein's self and the interruption (Heidegger says breaking into) of our identities by the call of conscience are constitutive movements of dasein that put it in touch with itself. Dasein's self, Heidegger says in Section 57, is clearly not in the call of conscience which presents neither a person nor a definitive and definite way of life. Nothing familiar is encountered. In our experience of ourselves we ordinarily say that we are lost when we find no landmarks or customs to which we can relate with familiarity. But on Heidegger's account we begin to find ourselves when we are dislocated and displaced by the disclosure of our being that has no 'stand', no name or heritage in our environment. The wrenching movement and displacement are aspects of the disclosure of being in our everyday world. In this "call" we began to hear the "understanding" that constitutes the *Vorlaufen* of our finitude. There is no observer, no judge, no clear definitions or standards. But instead of being lost, we are homing in on our being. In the context of *Being and Time,* this wrenching movement means that we are being freed from our "lostness" in the familiar world of our cultural inheritance and from the surveillance of the identities that make us who we are. To be *eigentlich*—proper to our being—and attuned to our being in our everyday lives, we have to overcome the monopolizing power of the valences and exigencies that define who we are.

Heidegger's account of the call of conscience provides for his interpretation the possibility of this overcoming, this twisting free. It further establishes the difference that constitutes our lives and shows that in this difference we, as culturally determined identities, have access to the being whose erasure is part of who we are traditionally to be. To trust our meanings and values by giving them axiomatic status, to stake our lives on them, and to know ourselves in their mediation is to forget our being and the possibility of living appropriately as the being that we are. Only by the severity of the wrenching, recoiling, twisting movement out of the surveillance and authority of our normalcy and identity can dasein come into its own.

If the being of dasein were determinate and if it provided immediately a nature to be realized by individual action, it would not put ethics in question. We could in principle find out what our nature is and how to meet its standards. But since dasein, in being called to itself, is called to a being whose meaning is mortal temporality and thus has no intrinsic, determinate meaning at all, the structure of ethics as such is in question. To be in question does not mean that we may hope for a time when ethics will be abolished and we will live a higher life, unstressed by the difference between our being and our cultural lives. The "lostness" of everyday life is itself not to be lost, on Heidegger's account. It does mean that as we follow unquestioningly the patterns of our best ideals and values in a state of mind that knows, at least in principle, what is genuinely and universally good and bad, we are lost to our being and to our mortal indeterminacy. Whereas in the traditional thought of subjectivity one expects some type of self-realization consequent to conformity to the reality of the subject, whatever the subject might be, in the instance of *Being and Time* authenticity means the disclosure of human-being-in-question without the possibility of resolving the question or the problems that follow it. Is it possible that our systems of self-realization and self-sacrifice for higher values make inevitable a maiming of human life that is recognizable only when our best ways of being are profoundly disturbed by the non-presence of our being? Do our axiomatic values at their best constitute a blindness to who we are and what we do? Does the disclosure of our being and its appropriation, along with the pain and disruption that constitute it and follow it, make possible a profound and thoroughgoing uncertainty that itself reveals the limits of ethics?

The question of ethics in the context of *Being and Time* is a way of being that is concerned in the world and with other people. Heidegger's analysis in Part I of *Being and Time* has made clear that dasein is constituted in world relations. Dasein is not a simple thing existing with other single things to which it may or may not relate. Solipsism is an ontological impossibility for dasein since dasein occurs only in disclosive relations. It happens in language and practice and comes to itself as an individual who is already constituted by such relations. The difference between being and everyday existence takes place only in world relations, hence the emphasis on continuously twisting free of cultural domination *in* cultural life, never outside of it. The terminus is not a life that is withdrawn from culture and history, nor is it projected experiences that are ahistorical and purged of secular corruption. The aim involves an individual's being with others in a specific environment and history, attuned in its relations to the Vorlaufen of its being without presence. The "perversion" that inevitably occurs in our standards for living is found in their insensitivity to mortal temporality.

Heidegger articulates his interpretation in the traditional language of being as presence. Existential understanding is "given." Being "presents itself." Dasein "comes to itself." His interpretation is no less involved in the wrenching, twisting recoils than in dasein's authentic movements. In association with this articulation, Heidegger shows that as being presents itself, no subject or substance or nature come forth. The possibility of no possibility at all comes forth. Mortal disclosure takes place. As dasein comes to itself, no specific course of action is indicated. The given existential understanding—dasein's *Verstehen*—has neither a subject nor an object. Dasein's being does not name anything present, but names rather mortal, temporal disclosure that forecasts itself as temporal possibility rather than as a standing nature. The language of presence in this text is thus in a process of twisting free from its own inevitability in the tradition in which it occurs and in which Heidegger thinks. This movement in *Being and Time* articulates dasein's recoiling movement toward the possibility of propriety regarding its being.

The issue of dasein coming to itself is thus one of dasein allowing its difference in its being vis-à-vis the status of its life. If an individual can allow and affirm its mortal temporality, in contrast to the invested obfuscation of mortal temporality, and can allow also the *question* of the meaning of being in its historical identity, if it can want the 'address' of its being in spite of wanting a sense of continuous and meaningful presence, it can, perhaps, come to appropriate the difference of its own being as it decides its daily issues. This alertness is like a person's affirming or loving another person with a full sense of mortality in the relationship.[5] Or it is like experiencing the validity of a system of values without a sense of certainty or universality. Nothing specific is there to will in dasein's owning its being, hence the anxiety to which Heidegger gives attention. Allowing its being, dasein allows the "calling forth" of its continuous need to take care, given its primordial lack of stasis. This allowing, given the constitution of its identity, is like dasein unburdening itself of traditional resistances and opening itself to the inevitability of being without foundations. Resoluteness thus cannot be conceived in terms of self-constitution. Rather, self-constitution requires a basis for validation, and authentic experience itself falls into question as dasein comes into its own through resoluteness.

The middle voice is particularly important to Heidegger's account of authenticity. His claim that dasein's wanting to have conscience, its affirmation of the difference of its being and the dislocation that this difference makes in its life, is a self-understanding *[Sich-verstehen]* in its most proper *[eigensten]* ability to be. Affirming conscience includes allowing a self-understanding that is "a manner *(Weise)* of dasein's disclosure." If, however, self-understanding is taken as a reflexive state or as a self-constituting state, his claim is missed. Understanding and dasein's disclosiveness determine willing to have conscience. We might say that they stand out of the circumscription of action and of will. Self-understanding is to be read as understanding understands (itself) in dasein's ability to be; that is, dasein's ability to be is at once mortal, temporal awareness which, in understanding itself, is unmediated and beyond willing. Further, affirming conscience is not circumscribed by an individual's action. Affirming conscience is conscience-in-act and the (self-)understanding of dasein's ability to be is determinate with it. Although an individual may incline to hear the call of conscience *in* conscience's call, understanding is neither active nor passive on this account. The call of conscience is an occurrence that is constitutive of dasein and that is neither active nor passive in the context of an individual's action. And the occurrence of dasein's ability to be is neither active nor passive. The call of conscience and the ability to be refer to themselves in their occurrence without the mediation of a subject. The middle voice gives articulation to dasein's ability to be, its understanding, and its wanting to have conscience, each of which constitutes a manner or *Weise* of disclosiveness [*Erschlossenheit*] that also is not a subject or object with regard to an action. We are in a position to see that in resoluteness [*Entschlossenheit*] and authenticity [*Eigentlichkeit*] disclosure discloses and time times, that Heidegger's emphasis is not on self-constituting action or intentional action, but is on the (self-)disclosure of dasein's disclosiveness. In opening to its being and allowing its being, dasein does not constitute itself. It stands outside the possibility for self-constitution and finds itself in question in all of its reach and stretch. Dasein's disclosiveness is its being. It is being to death, the possibility of no possibility, the Vorlaufen of no continuing presence that disrupts dasein's presence. Dasein's being is *its* difference from the finite continuity of its identity and its being in the world. In its most proper being, no 'I' controls. Rather, the I is interrupted and something other than a self takes place.

'I' is always situated in a locality of specific determinants. It does not enjoy the benefits of an ontologically founded ideal that can guide it to right decisions. Decisions are made in the power of the values and possibilities for action that are allowed by the situation. This is not a version of historical relativism, however, since the ontological indeterminacy of the specific situation is made inevitable by dasein's being, not by the control of history. This inevitability is the possibility of no possibility that is heard in dasein's being. The proliferation of values and meanings that characterize our history has its meaning in dasein's being, in its situated ability to be, as we have seen. The I that resolves properly opens to its being in its situation, twists free from the control of predominant standards of judgment by attending resolutely to its being, and makes its judgments and commitments in the loosening of the bonds of the everyday by virtue of concerned and open attunement to its being. Insofar as the I, as it judges and chooses, is always in the heritage and culture that is invested in turning away from its being, Heidegger's and Foucault's positions are similar in this respect: every decision and involvement is dangerous because of its inevitable everyday drift toward universalization and totalization in defiance of its temporality. Their interpretations of time are different, but both see that distortions of time are distortions of human being and that time does not tell people which specific decisions are right or wrong. The silence of being/time, in Heidegger's terms, regarding how we are to take our stand in life, is a part of dasein's mortality and the close distance of being in our lives. Hearing in this silence is finding oneself in the question of ethics. It is like acting without knowing the necessity of the action. It is like having to be without resolving the question of being. As dasein lets itself be called forth in its most proper being, the I is modified by the non-I of its being. It becomes strange to itself in its clarity of purpose and certainty, and it acts forthrightly in understanding the collapse of clarity in its being. No less situated, no less concerned or committed, the individual's attunements and expectations, its perceptiveness, satisfactions, and priorities are conditioned by, as it were, an open door to mortal time that lets in an element different from the presence and totality of value. It acts, but now it acts in the questionableness of the possibility of its actions and in the transgressions of being that mark its living. To be this way is to be resolved, and to be resolved is to attest to the difference of being in the value-laden situation that one lives in and through. Hearing this difference might well include a pause, an interruption, a standing out of the law of rightness. What can be heard in such a pause? I am persuaded that what can be heard is not predictable by the law of rightness, that an other to rightness and wrongness may be heard, and that in such hearing an obsessiveness regarding both right and justification, an obsessiveness that determines who we are, is given pause in an indeterminacy to which we belong and that is other to us. We stand out in the questionableness of our ethos, knowing less who we are and who we are to be, in silence before the decisions that we have to make. In *Being and Time* this silence is proper to dasein's being, and it makes dangerous the values by which we give ourselves common lives and establish the rules within which we are constituted and become clear to ourselves.

3. The Question of Suffering

We all know what suffering is when we experience it: starvation, intense and unchosen pain, enforced and radical restriction on movements that are natural for a conscious being, the many forms of paranoia regarding others, despair and depression, schizophrenic dissociation from oneself and an incapacity to intend with continuity, oppressed human life without dignity or value. The question of ethics as we are thinking of it puts in question the 'we' that knows what suffering is. Heidegger's account of authenticity as well as Nietzsche's genealogy of good and evil and Foucault's genealogy of institutions and self-constitution give us pause in our judgments. The question is not whether the suffering we know is suffering. It is whether the 'we' that knows is constituted by suffering that is difficult or traditionally impossible to identify.

Nietzsche made it evident that the ascetic ideal institutes multiple forms of suffering by dividing body and soul and blinding us to the pain of the division. Foucault showed that the close yet obscured link between punishment and social-intellectual discipline, as well as the association of curing and radical alienation, and that of sexuality and the marginalization of the body's pleasures suggest a high degree of blind suffering in our culture that is systematically (rationally) excluded from recognition. Heidegger's account of traditional living means that within that living we are unable to perceive or think of profound distortions in our existence as long as we are ill-attuned to our being. These accounts differ significantly in their context, but they have a common suspicion: that what we ordinarily take to be satisfaction and the good conceal suffering that we have an investment in maintaining because of who we have come to be.

Temporality and continuing presence are two of the foci for these accounts. A systematic loss of the meaning of our temporality, that is, a covering over of the experience of thoroughgoing mortality by the ways in which we have objectified mortality, and a systematic loss of experiences of the limits of meaning are major aspects in all of these accounts. Experiences of thoroughgoing mortality and the limits of meaning are in our heritage and are accompanied by the erasure of our knowledge and values. Continuing presence and meaningful time have occupied the space of these experiences. The result is a proliferation of human life that is at odds with its own conditions. The 'at odds' names the condition and movement of possible suffering. This thought draws heavily from the inherited notion that a human's deepest suffering is constituted by its alienation from itself or from its creator. But as we have seen, this idea recoils on itself in the three accounts that show that the individual does not have a being that is selflike. To know oneself is to experience oneself in a historical proliferation of meanings and events that reveals nothing to fall from or to fulfill. In Heidegger's language, dasein's most proper being makes the self questionable; dasein's proper existence takes place in affirmed questionableness and not in fundamental accomplishments of personal virtue or community practices. When human existence is at odds with its own conditions of being, it lives as though there were a nature or an essence to fulfill. The question of suffering arises with urgency, since, if suffering is present and optional, 'we' want to eliminate it.

The question is vexing because we who ask it are the we who are in question. We have found that the subject who investigates and knows undergoes a measure of recoiling transformation in the writings of Nietzsche, Foucault, and Heidegger. All three think from, in, and toward transformation and delimitation of the organizing authorities of their language, thought, and discursive identities. The very thought of question in the context of the question of ethics arises from the transformations that are figured and resisted in our heritage. The strategy is to intensify the question and to hold at bay the answers that press themselves on us—as well as the predisposition to definitive answers—out of the form and content of the inheritance that constitutes us. We attempt to hold in play the recoils that make the questions and that are alien to the tradition in which they occur. The range of our suffering thus will not be clear. We can experiment with options and partial insights, with styles of thought and writing that recast the hierarchies and capacities by which we know and feel, and with the formulations that have defined our problems and solutions. Nietzsche, for example, experiments with universals, Foucault with mainstreaming marginal voices, identities, and values, and Heidegger with retrieving thought that has been lost to the philosophical canon. If we do not maintain the recoiling, transformative movement of thought that puts in question our concepts, systems of meaning, and values, we can be reasonably sure that the habitual patterns will dominate and that we will be involved in a spiral not unlike that of the obsessive person who becomes obsessive over the strategies and behaviors that are supposed to relieve the obsession. With these cautions in mind we shall consider a type of suffering that is related to the ontological difference of temporality and appears to be a part of our normal ideals and satisfactions. If we do undergo blind suffering in the patterns of our lives, we shall want to be alert to the possibility that this unrecognized suffering contributes to or even generates suffering that we can easily recognize in our everyday lives.

Does the everyday, metaphysical experience of time as linear and countable occasion human suffering that is unique to this experience of time? For Heidegger this experience is forecast and given definitive expression in Aristotle's concept of time. In his *Basic Problems of Phenomenology*, Part II, Heidegger introduces his analysis of Aristotle's concept of time with a reminder that is not incidental to the question of suffering: our understanding "must be based in temporality." He turns to Aristotle and the Aristotelian interpretation of time in order to show the concept of time that is "basic" for dasein in its everyday life and in its philosophical heritage, and hence the concept of time that is basic in his own thought. He turns to Aristotle in order to destructure and put in question the temporality that characterizes dasein in its everyday way of existing and that will necessarily involve a destructuring movement in his own experience of time.

Further, Heidegger's turn to Aristotle indicates the historical contingency of dasein's experience of time. He carries out his destructuring process in reference to a traditional way of living, not in reference to a continuously present 'Time'. The mortality of 'Time' is forecast in this move: constituted as they are by this 'concept' of time, our life, as well as his life and thought, are to be implicated in his destructuring analysis. This *use* of Aristotle to develop his own interpretation of existence suggests not only that Heidegger's interpretation of dasein is thoroughly historical, but that dasein, that being that is formed historically and linguistically, is in its structures a factical network of finite meanings. These structures of dasein constitute an historical, inherited lived interpretation of time that is made in part by Aristotle's lineage, both by the interpretation of time in this lineage and by its suppressions and quandaries regarding mortal temporality.[6]

According to Aristotle, *now* is both countable (it is a particular being) and "a continuum of the flux of time" (it is not a particular being, but the ground for the particularity of the countable *now*) (BP 249). *Now* is countable as continuity in transition with moving beings. It is in some sense always the same while it is also always different in each instance. The stretching out of time thus cannot be understood solely by reference to a series of ontic now-points. A "basis" must be found for time in its function as a conditioning dimension of all moving beings. If time as numbered is not bound either to an intrinsic content or to a mode of being, if the *now* is "intrinsically transition," and yet can be counted as different points, how is one to think of time fundamentally? Some notion of ontological difference is called for, but is not explicitly conceived, in Aristotle's interpretation. This call for ontological difference and its obfuscation is one of the constituents of everyday dasein. We shall say more about the ontological difference in a later section.

Further, Aristotle's claims that our access to time is "the counting perception of motion as motion" is "at the same time the perception of *what* is counted as time" (BP 257). This perception of the counted *what* has led to an emphasis on perception without alertness to the temporal basis of perception. According to Heidegger, this leads to "inadequately founded methods of interpreting time," and this seemingly abstract problem in turn leads to the dominant Western experience of time in which time is something we can count and something we are in.

Aristotle's experience of time calls for the ontological difference between temporality and countable time and puts in question the priority of perception regarding time, a priority that it nevertheless also establishes. It raises the issues of how the *now* demands a temporality that is a continuous, transitional stretch beyond the circumscription of any *now* or group of *nows,* a stretch that is also not conceivable within the given limits of this thought. We can see that there is in the ordinary experience a quandary that tears through the apparent coherence of the experience.

We can see the tearing effect in Heidegger's account of Aristotle's concept of time. Although Heidegger uses the language of a priori structures when he speaks of founding the concept of time in temporality, in effect he also shows that the continuous now that is implied by the idea of a priori structures is a part of the tradition that he puts in question. Heidegger's thought of a priori structures is founded not in a transhistorical being, but in the broad Aristotelian tradition. Our normal philosophical confidence in such words as *original, sufficiently clear, fixed, unity, wholeness,* and *systematic order,* the very words that punctuate Heidegger's introduction to his discussion of Aristotle, is equally in doubt. Given his reading of Aristotle, the use of these terms seems to arise from a common interpretation of time that has stated temporality's status in terms of a timeless transcendence in relation to changing beings. As Heidegger develops his claims that "original time" is founded in dasein's expecting, retaining, and preventing, a claim that his own thought brings to articulation in a horizon of interpretation markedly different from Aristotle's, he shows also that his thought of time is buried in Aristotle's concept of time. He also shows in contrast to Aristotle that the movement of time carries away each moment of time in a strange removing or remotion *[entrücken]* and opens each movement "out to openness" in temporal overturning *[Umschlag]*. This account of temporality recoils on itself in the sense that it, too, must include remotion and overturning. The movement of Heidegger's thought away from Aristotle's, and its opening out to a horizon that it cannot comprehend and that tears away from his own experience—this movement becomes, in the course of the essay, the issue at the forefront of Heidegger's thought. As the recoiling, removing, opening process addresses his own "method," a "temporal ecstasis" takes place, his thought comprehends that it does not comprehend time, and the philosophical technique that Heidegger sought to develop fails before the horizon that it has opened up.

Outside Heidegger's thought and its tradition, this tearing effect appears to be insignificant. He claims, however, that in this rift we find not only the "obsolescence" of his "method" (BP 328), but the suppression of aspects fundamental to Western temporality. This suppression is a definitive part of our normal experience of time, and it includes closure to the ecstasis, the remotion, and "opening out to openness" that are fundamental for our temporality. The opening beyond his thought removes the authority that defined his thought and invokes a considerable transition in his thinking: dying away, loss, discovery of illusion, removal of the focus of his passion for many years—and the exhilaration of an opening that he was able to welcome. Within the context of his thought, this marks a transformation of dasein as he lives it, a radical, if momentary, shift in the structure of his everyday world, and a repeated experience of the fissured temporality of dasein that is never without its costs and passions as it opens to its own *Umschlag*, its own overturning and transformation.

Loss of "animation and vibrancy" *[Schwung, Schwingung]* in beings accompanies the everyday experience of time. This vibrancy, on the other hand, is intimately connected to the nothing, the nonpresence, of temporality and its difference from our everyday experience of time. The loss is lived in a flattening of things and people into their usefulness, their roles, their "fit" in a circumscription of meaning in a given setting. The dimension of being other than their traditional significance is lost—on occasion Heidegger uses *annihilated*. Their being is ensnared by their value and cultural meaning. Beings are conservable, arrangeable, cultivatable, disposable—in the broadest sense, humanly usable. But they are not known in their excess of meaning, nor is the activity of knowing experienced in its excess of meaning. Their lack of cultural meaning, their standing out from meaning and value in their mortal temporality, their transgression of value and the recoil in their being from accountability threaten the structure of our everyday experience of them. The direct connection between our dominant experience of time and the priority of disposability of beings signals not only the danger of radical objectification that was found by 'existential' thought but also the danger of well-intentioned institutional and governmental disposition of people, which Foucault recounts, and the danger of environmental destruction, which is now so apparent. The danger arises according to Heidegger's thought from the obliteration of time's meaningless excess and transgression of the possible presence of all things.

Suffering in this structure of life arises not only through the policies of use that it makes natural, but in the closure to beings that it makes inevitable. The welcoming of temporality and being that Heidegger notes in *Being and Time* as well as in his 'later' writings can be interpreted in the language of meditative serenity. It can also be interpreted in Nietzsche's language of Dionysian creativity, in which types of ordinary suffering—isolation and alienation, intense and destabilizing uncertainty, self-rejection, and psychosomatic sicknesses that are analogous to the trauma induced by earthquakes: these painful symptoms of radical, cultural change—are the "benefit" of overcoming the lived distortion of improper, normal temporality in which dimensions of creativity, joy, and life-affirmation are thoroughly blocked by the meaningful fabric of our daily lives. Controlling the blockage, managing the stress of living in blind resistance to mortal temporality, intuitively forcing the senses of continuous presence, proliferating systems of value by totalizing gestures and strategies, the warping effect, the unconscious hostility, the aggravation, competition, acquisitiveness, and belligerence among individuals and groups bred of fighting both time and its meaningless difference in our lives: all of this constitutes a depth of suffering that traditionally we are pleased to overlay with symbols of transcendent meaning and with values that hide their anxiety and their incalculable temporality. This suffering takes the form, initially addressed by Nietzsche, of making a virtue of its ignorance by means of anxious beliefs and affirmations that hide their dread of time. Communities find their bonding in repeated assurances of the absence of meaningless temporality, in rituals of spiritual and intellectual pleasure that create devitalizing designs of normalcy and everyday complacency. The expenditure of energy in this *contratempo* produces a metabolism that denies its own movement and institutes an invisible cruelty in which life fights itself to its infinite satisfaction. This account, however, assumes a form of thought in which the conditions of human life are countermanded by the way that life is lived: a traditional form of thought taken by an ethics of self-realization or obedience to God. It suggests that propriety of life can be found if the contradiction is properly addressed. Impropriety and suffering are aligned. On the basis of this study we must thus assume that the suffering we are approaching is also in our approach to it and that the implied ideal of proper life will in all probability advance the stress that it addresses. 'Proper' and 'authentic' fall further into question as they appear in this context of hidden and manifest suffering.

We are clear about many types of suffering in our world. We have reason to believe that temporality is distorted in our traditional lives. And we find in our noun-dominated account of the possibility of hidden suffering that we seem to perpetuate the hiddenness that we wish to expose. Have we repeated a spiral of suffering, or have we found an opening that shuts almost as quickly as it appears? A trace of suffering that we found inexpressible? A quest that misleads as it leads? A psychological anxiety is manifest in this discussion of suffering, not the anxiety that is the mood of mortal temporality which Heidegger describes in *Being and Time,* but a specific and pervasive unease that arises in the question of suffering. This mood points toward resolution and arises out of an area of uncertainty with high stakes. The *question* of suffering seems aesthetic, like a theoretical luxury, in the presence of 'real' suffering. And yet the implication is that we can become absorbed by our everyday suffering, that another obscure suffering can be advanced, and this second kind of suffering might indicate a historically perpetuated context that makes our everyday suffering unavoidable, even by virtue of the measures that we take to eliminate it. We find reason to believe that our ethical and sensitive response to suffering may be a part of our traditional normalcy which makes the certainty of suffering a manifestation of another kind of suffering that in our everyday perspective seems trivial and abstract.

We are anxiously familiar with the frequent situation in which an alignment of well-intentioned actions boomerang to consequences that are opposite to the projected result: the peace treaties that make war inevitable, political actions that fall prey to subtle intrigue and serve the interests of the opponent, kindness that leads to cruel consequences, types of alleviation that allow pathogenic conditions to remain in force and flourish. We know that in certain people unconscious hostility and malevolence pervert their apparently constructive and supportive action into subtle undercutting. They set the others up for failure or present them with situations that make impossible demands on them or deprive them of the possibility for robust assertiveness and self-confidence. Now we face the possibility that our culture and its forms of evaluation are constituted by human suffering that it not only cannot know without fundamental transformation but that the culture is structured to overlook as it perpetuates the suffering. We discover that our effort to face this possibility is also a part of the issue and that we confront the necessity of putting ourselves further in question even as we make our initial attempt at putting ourselves in question. The reality and moment of suffering seem to fade in this process of multiple recoils. We are anxious in the process as we appear to lose the possibility of grasping the issue of suffering, as the *presence* of suffering falls apart yet proliferates. But do we in the anxious process become more alert to suffering in its proliferation and its difference vis-à-vis everyday pain?

Is our *understanding* of suffering part of the issue? Heidegger's account of anxiety in *Being and Time* as the disclosure of dasein's indefinite being shows that ontologically, as distinct from psychologically, anxiety manifests the nonstatus of dasein's being, its being nothing and nowhere within the circumscription of our traditional ways of being present and meaningful. It is the mood immediate in dasein's ability to be, its possibility for no possibility at all, and its possibility of propriety with regard to its being. Anxiety is evident in dasein's everyday, normal concern over use, control, denotation, management, and techniques for purposeful action. Dasein's energy is fundamentally directed toward making things definite enough to allow for survival and flourishing in the midst of a world that guarantees nothing. It, as an energy, 'understands' that it must care for everything that is to play a continuing role in dasein's environment. Otherwise the presence of things, in the absence of careful structure, passes as though in the night, being no things at all outside of dasein's world of care and concern. Dasein's being gives things their worldly continuity by virtue of its taking care of them in social and cultural structures. The continuing presence of things thus arises in an 'understanding' of nonpresence in the fabric of the human world and in the nonpresence of being that is manifest in ontological anxiety.

To affirm dasein's being is to allow, not to resist or to cover over, ontological anxiety. Anxiety is proper to dasein's being. To live properly with ontological anxiety, in the terms of *Being and Time,* is to find beings and the world generally, as well as oneself, in their ungraspable, that is, nonconceptual, nonobjectifiable, mortal temporality. Our psychological anxiety in the question of suffering arises, at least in part, as suffering puts in question the assurance of our lives. In the midst of the best that we know to do, suffering occurs. It appears not only to elude our technology, but to characterize it. It can be like a tear in our environment's fabric, shocking us by its mere facticity and obliviousness to our ideals. We are now focusing on the possibility that suffering may also transgress our ideals and the procedures that are customary in our society for establishing our general welfare as well as assuring our survival. Suffering and its possibility put in question the symbol of an adequately caring community or of a community on the road to ideal human fulfillment. In it is manifest the unquenchable anxiety of dasein's being, which puts in question the ideal of human welfare achieved by proper values and selected technologies.

Concern for suffering in suffering's transgression of our certainties does not need to include an expectation of its elimination by ways of life that are right and proper. Because, in the language of *Being and Time,* anxiety and mortality both constitute the movement of our lives and are, in their indefiniteness, primordially different from our standing in life, human existence, with all of its satisfactions, involves suffering. Human existence is torn by the difference of mortal temporality, and to care for mortal temporality is to care for suffering in its excess of meaning. In more traditional terms, this thought bears the threat of indifference. Can we care for suffering without the expectation of meaningful alleviation? Can we avoid despair if we know that our alleviation of suffering would also reinscribe it? Do we take precautions against another holocaust only to advance other suffering, perhaps less apparent, but no less pernicious and beyond our definitive grasp? Do we hear the ascetic priest in these questions, in the traditional sense that we can survive only if we believe in ideals that deny our being?

The strangeness of suffering, its *Unheimlichkeit* or alienness in the language of *Being and Time,* is its affiliation with human being. The question we face with regard to suffering is whether we can care for it without the hope of curing it. Can we work with passion to eliminate torture, to feed and clothe those who suffer deprivation, to recognize and respond to suffering as we find it every day, and yet not domesticate it and thereby proliferate it blindly in a system of meaning and virtue? Can we live in the perpetual mourning that is here prescribed without becoming morbid and ineffectual? These are issues directly related to the question of authenticity in which we face the issue of living properly with our being in the alien, meaningless, and ungraspable difference that we undergo vis-à-vis our being. Our "most proper" living is found not in the rightness of our values or of our ethos but in a demanding alertness that intensifies our sense of suffering in the absence of its resolution or removal.

This account recoils on itself, of course. The psychological anxiety that we confront can make us available to mortal suffering in the failure of our thought before it. The asceticism of this language, its distance as it confronts its subject, its *suffering* this distance and turning again to the magnitude that dwarfs it, drive it away from itself and make it appear in its paltry dimensions. The satisfaction in this recognition of its paltry dimensions, its invocation in spite of itself of the virtue of humility and self-honesty—does it not, in its failure, also reveal the trace of suffering that it cannot capture? Is it an opening that clears for a moment a dimension that loses its syntax, which itself is a syntax of suffering, one that slips through the fingers of its own grasp?

Heidegger's thoughts of temporality, ontological difference, everydayness, mortality, and ecstasis, when followed in his discourse, open out to experiences of suffering and alertness to suffering that are inseparable from his thinking. They are also part of his diagnosis of our heritage and part of the transformation of human existence that takes place in the movement of his thought. We are finding this transformation hesitant—painful, I would say—and demanding. It involves far more passion than one finds on first reading. We shall find that the transitory remotion and transformation in Heidegger's thought put him at odds with himself, remind him repeatedly that he does not own either his language or his thinking, make his otherwise conservative instincts anxious and uncertain. Viewed in cosmic terms, it is a small event. But viewed in its microcosm this process is one of radical human transformation that finds itself and its heritage in question and finds in seemingly abstract texts a body of suffering that can be written very large with enormous consequences for institutions, personal lives, and world events. The claims are that the suffering of time in our heritage is not yet understood and that, until it is, what we actually call suffering is closer to mystery than to certainty.

4. Ecstasis

Heidegger uses middle-voice phrases to speak of temporality in Section 65 of *Being and Time:* for example, *Zeitlichkeit zeitigt*, 'temporality times'. In this instance the middle voice intensifies the ecstatic meaning of *Zeitlichkeit*, which he makes clear is not a being and cannot properly be said to exist. Rather than something called 'temporality' existing, *Zeitlichkeit*, which is not something, *zeitigt*. No entity at all refers to itself in temporality's timing. The quandary posed by this expression arises in the context of the traditional aporia that time must be something and cannot be something. The thought of 'something' problematizes the traditional concept of time. Heidegger begins a process of working through and beyond this aporia by the thought that temporality is "outside itself" in its timing and that being outside itself is its "essence." We shall see that Heidegger's thought on the ecstasis of time is itself ecstatic in the sense that he finds thinking opening out in a "horizon" that divides his thought from the tradition in which it formed and took its "stand"; the horizon overturns his thought in the manner we addressed in the previous section. The essence in temporality is the "unity" of future (dasein's being ahead of itself), past (or having passed, dasein's having been), and present (dasein's being alongside beings). This unity is more like a "Zuspiel," as Heidegger will later say, more like an interplay than an entity. We thus begin this discussion of ecstasis by noting that the unity and meaning of dasein is not a being. Rather, 'it' 'is' a nonactive, nonpassive occurrence, one most appropriately expressed in the middle voice, one that cannot be grasped by a framing structure of concepts. Further, that 'outside itself' or ecstasis is the thought that projects our thoughts toward temporality as not a being. As Heidegger's thought undergoes an ecstatic movement of time, temporality comes to thought.

Dasein's resolve *[Entschlossenheit]* opens to mortal temporality as it closes in on its own possibility of being. Mortal temporality is the "essence" of dasein and the ontological possibility of resolve. But mortal temporality is outside itself. It temporalizes in the interplay of being ahead of itself, being already in, and being alongside. None of these 'ecstases' of time derives from the others. Dasein happens as coming toward itself in being possible and is never whole in its presence. It comes back to itself in its given having-been. And it is always by or in the presence of beings. Each ecstasis releases itself from the others in its intimate relation with the others. The 'outside itself' names the absence of a single defining nature in temporality. Mortal temporality is always outside any given stand or status. The future withholds the completion of presence, and the past denies priority to presence. As dasein 'resolves' its temporality by opening to it, uncovering it in its existence with beings, the ecstatic occurrence of temporality is uncovered [*erschliesst*] in dasein's resolve. Resoluteness is thus not a way of living that is defined by a system of normative values. It is found in a process of disclosive and owned temporality. An individual will adopt values and customs and will find its identity in them. But in its proper resolve, it stands out from its communal identity as well as from its (everyday) having been, coming to be, and present moment. Its proper "unity" is the ecstatic interplay of mortal temporality, the temporalizing of temporality.

The ambiguity of dasein's coming to its ending by *Entschlossenheit* does not mean that *ending* is a conclusion in a moment. It means that ending is an ecstatic interplay of delimitations, on which we shall elaborate later by using the metaphor of horizon. Present, past, and future delimit each other in their interplay. In being in the presence of beings, for example, dasein's presence is delimited by having been and coming to be, which cannot be present. Ending is thus not a question of conclusion, but of delimitation and termination *within* the interplay of time. Resolve is an occurrence of ecstatic temporality, and *its* occurrence must be interpreted in the horizon of mortal temporality. It is not like a commitment that causes one to stand firm in a set character or virtue, but it is like being alert, undefended, and accepting with regard to one's finitude. The ending flow of time comes to alertness in resolve, not in the metaphor of a subject's coming to self-consciousness, but in the metaphor of alert, clearing openness. We shall return to this metaphor. For the moment I emphasize that resolve is of the temporality to which it is available. It is not a formation of character or the opposite of character formation. It is dasein's explicit availability to its own (and proper) temporality, which sets dasein beyond the reach of the power of traditional life over its thought and emotions. 'Set beyond', however, is not like an accomplishment that makes one otherworldly. It is not virtue, but is like a flowing awareness that is not defined by any particular form of life. It is more like frustration than serenity. It is ecstatic in the recoiling sense that it stands out from its own definitions and is, as we shall see, more like a moment than a personality.

The decisiveness indicated by *resolve* is itself thus put in question by its broken, interrupted unity. An individual's resolve will be traumatic to the extent that the individual is fixed on its identity or expects to find the proper continuity of its existence in who it fundamentally is. In this context, *Entschlossenheit* opens up—breaks open—rather than intensifies the identity of the resolving subject. Rather than constituting itself by relating to a deeper, defining essential self, the deciding subject is de-constituted by constituting itself in alert openness to its temporality. It is not only delimited in relation to temporality. It finds its ecstatic delimitation in mortal temporality, in the very possibility of its being. The dissolution of normal self-identity and traditional thought concerning time, self, and will is, in proper resolve, the disclosure *[erschliessen]* of dasein's being.

In Section 68 Heidegger shows that proper or authentic understanding, the appropriate way of being alert in dasein's running ahead in its ability to be, is ecstatic in the sense that it is freed from the dominance of everyday concerns and is able to transpose those concerns in a momentary prospect of temporality *[Augenblick]*. The proper *[eigentliche]* moment of presence is not, for Heidegger, one of firm standing, nor a moment of integrated confidence, but a moment of remove from the firmness of an ordinary life-world. This remotion *[Entrückung]* is integral to resolve and is consonant with the ecstases of temporality: dasein 'understands' its ecstatic temporality in its removal from the continuities of daily life and in this proper movement gives voice to its being. Dasein is then able to concern itself with beings out of the care of its being. Its concern for beings occurs in the remotion of time, in dasein's ecstatic remove within its continuing and constituting relations with beings. It does not stand and care for its being, like a shepherd looking after sheep, but is caring for being in its open availability to mortal temporality. Temporality temporalizing in the temporal openness of dasein is care of being.

If one emphasizes the metaphorical meaning of *entrücken,* which is 'to enrapture or entrance', Heidegger's proximity to one strand of traditional spirituality is clear. By loving God in God's disclosure one is able to live with all things in God's spirit. One can be transported in God's love beyond the fallenness of human existence by means of God's disclosure, which makes possible something like what Heidegger means by *resolve,* but in relation to God instead of human being. Human division from God (original sin) is overcome in God's self-presentation, and so on. A glimpse into eternity through worship, prayer, or meditation, or a movement of grace by which one knows oneself to be touched by God, will not last in a continuous experience of divine immediacy. But in such moments the meaning of one's finitude is nonetheless revealed in the eternal love of God, and one may live in light of this meaning by a continuing openness in and to God's love, which can transform one's life. God, who cannot be grasped or known in its meaning by categories, is the meaning of this life.

Probably this worrisome proximity moved Heidegger to emphasize in Section 65 that the ideas and experiences of infinity and eternity are derived from mortal temporality and give expression to a "vulgar" time-consciousness that is closed to its own mortal temporality. In such experiences one projects an active status onto time that is conceived and experienced without its mortal ecstatic quality. This projection produces a kind of ecstasis on the basis of time that is lost to its mortal interplay. Eternity and infinity, conceived in terms of rapture and ecstasy, are thus profound perversions of temporality. The transformation of "spirituality" that takes place in *Being and Time* is one in which dasein undergoes its own 'proper' remotion and frees itself, if momentarily, from the experiences that are dominated and organized by countable, entitylike time. In this transformation it discovers its mortal temporality, and in its resolve it allows the hold of traditional time to break open to the open play of mortality, which is dasein's "truth" and "essence." The ground drops away for an individual in this moment as dasein's mortality occurs in alert remotion. One is left shaken, given the temporal ecstasis, and perhaps experiences even fear of remaining available to it. This movement of remotion, which takes place in *Being and Time* as it undergoes, in the course of its study, the overturning of its domination by traditional time, is an instance of temporal ecstasis. By this movement the traditional experiences of religious ecstasy and rapture are undercut and their authority for human existence is overcome. A temporal ecstasis in resolve takes place in *Being and Time* and constitutes a movement of thought that is definitive of the book as a whole and that creates a horizon of possibility that is transformative of the heritage in which the book is conceived. The question of ethics, with its implications for 'spiritual' life, occurs in this movement.

What am *I* to do in this resolve? How am I to constitute myself in open, ecstatic temporality? Clearly, no prescriptions are given. If one clears the way for others to find access to their being, if the world no longer appears in the traditional powers of ownership and disposability, if one is sensitized to suffering human life and to the unconscious depression and resentment that are found in our satisfactions, if one is attuned to beings in their being—*their* ungraspable ecstasis—and if one is careful, alert, and resolved vis-à-vis being, one will still be unguided regarding specific decisions. The possibility of institutional guidance, whether it entails external or internal regulation, appears condemned to misadventure by its very fixations. The danger of totalization and the inevitability of violent entrapment of ecstatic time by the best of social intentions discourages one from making either a policy or a morality of this most proper event of dasein. The morbidity of knowing just what to do or of feeling what is clearly right threatens the possibility of human action.

Or rather, does it indicate the futility of finding human community on the basis of *self* and *I*? Does it suggest the depth of our malaise in our traditional efforts to take care of ourselves? A companion to ecstasis in this case is depression in our experiences of cultural inevitability over which we have little effective power—the depression of existing in the attraction of our highest satisfactions *and* their danger and violence, the depression of wanting what is right to such an extent that right seems to become timeless and then is experienced in violation of its limits and contradictions.

Being and Time suggests that dasein's recall of its being is through, not around, this kind of depression and discouragement. Dasein must pass through multiple terminations intrinsic to its existence, if temporality in its propriety is to be thought and intimately known. The overturning of our traditional 'highs' and our deep sense of peace, our inherited ecstases, is part of the process of coming to the thought of time that is proper to dasein and that emerges on the horizon of our culture. The question of ethics takes place in the depth and intimacy of this overturning. The criteria and force of profoundly human 'spirituality' that are based on the projections of our traditional experiences of time are uprooted by dasein's propriety. This question addresses our deepest emotions as well as our concepts, and until the impact of *Being and Time* is felt in the regions of our obligation and worship, in our nonvoluntary reactions to suffering, disease, and death, it does not, as a work on and in the question of being, have the possibility of coming to thought. Temporality temporalizes; and what is true comes to pass. This 'movement' leaves no place outside itself for neutrality and objectivity, for the comforts of unquestioned observations and strict knowledge, or for belief and commitment without question. Dasein as a whole is involved, and its wholeness is found in the broken, ending ecstasis of nonobjectifiable mortal time.

One indication of the horizon of time and the overturn that it occasions, as well as an instance of Heidegger's effort to respond to it, is found in the lectures that he gave a year after *Being and Time* was published. We turn now to those lectures.

5. Overturning in *The Basic Problems of Phenomenology*

In the first two paragraphs of Part Two of *The Basic Problems of Phenomenology,* Heidegger states that we must see thematically "in a clear and methodologically secure way the like of being in distinction from beings" if we are to carry out philosophy "as a science." "Being and its distinction from beings can be fixed only if we get a proper hold on the understanding of being as such." But before we can "fix" being in its distinction from beings in a "sufficiently clear" and "secure" way, we must understand the ontological constitution of dasein. The understanding of being belongs to the ontological constitution of dasein. We must "bring to light the ground of the basic structures of dasein in their unity and wholeness."

We are thus led to expect that by a strict and disciplined study of temporality we will have laid the basis for a clear differentiation between being and beings. Rigorous, scientific, methodologically secure thought is called for. Our goal is "to fix the ground of the ontological difference." Then we will be in a position genuinely to raise the question of being without confusing being with a being.

Heidegger turns to Aristotle and the Aristotelian interpretation of time in order to de-structure and overcome the temporality that characterizes dasein in its dominant and everyday way of existing. Heidegger's *use* of Aristotle, as we have seen, also uncovers the incomplete and open character of his own account of temporality, and the methodological strictness of his account brings him to the point of showing, by reference to horizon and ecstasis, that a different view of thinking from that forecast at the beginning of Part Two is necessary as a consequence of working through and beyond the Aristotelian concept of time. Dasein's structures of existence constitute an historical, inherited understanding of time that is made in part by Aristotle's lineage, both by the positive interpretation of time in this lineage and by its suppressions and inadequacies regarding mortal temporality. Heidegger's own dasein-analysis is *in* this understanding as it moves beyond it. Dasein is made of language and history, of Western traditions, that cover over how dasein comes temporally to be in its traditions.

The *history* of the problem of ontological difference and temporality is not a secondary aspect of the problem of temporality and ontological difference. That history is partially uncovered in a de-structuring reading of Aristotle, as we shall see. But just as phenomenology promises a careful way of thinking that shows the limits and concealments of the Aristotelian tradition, the Aristotelian tradition also shows the limits in the phenomenological approach. As he uncovers the issues and inadequacies in Aristotle's interpretation of time, Heidegger also shows that the phenomenological method is partially founded in these inadequacies. Phenomenology is limited by the history in which and out of which it develops. This is a peculiarity that we shall think more about: the *history of the problem* of ontological difference and temporality, as it is uncovered by Heidegger's de-structuring reading of his own tradition, and *the temporal structures of dasein,* which are ontologically different from dasein's factical, historical situation, are in tension in Heidegger's thought, and this tension between the historical-factical and the ontological in part constitutes the problem of ontological difference. This tension also opens toward a way of thinking that is neither Aristotelian nor phenomenological, one that we shall see opened up in Heidegger's thought on the ecstatic, horizonal aspect of temporality.

Heidegger understands Aristotle to be the major contributor to "the traditional concept of time" (BP 231), which Heidegger also calls "the common understanding of time" and "the natural concept of time" (BP 232). So, when we begin with Aristotle, we are beginning with the history of the ordinary, everyday, often intelligent, always metaphysical interpretation of time. Aristotle's interpretation of time is based on "the phenomenon of time" in the sense that he "forced inquiry back to the phenomena, to the seen, and [he] mistrusted from the ground up all wild and windy speculations" (BP 232). Aristotle was rigorous and also engaged in a nascent version of de-structuring the inherited interpretations of time. By his work an epoch-forming horizon becomes manifest. As we look for a rigorous interpretation of time by de-structuring Aristotle's lineage, we are engaged in a process that, like the idea of ontological difference, is to be found nascently in Aristotle. Heidegger's own phenomenological work also shows a horizon different from Aristotle's, but one that emerges from Aristotle's horizon.

The context of Heidegger's interpretation of Aristotle in *Basic Problems* is the problem of ontological difference, a problem that is *in* Aristotle's thought, but one that Aristotle and his followers were not able to bring to thematic development. That problem is in some way related to the problematic of temporality, and the problematic of temporality as Heidegger conceives it is also nonthematically a part of Aristotle's thought. The aim of Heidegger's reading of Aristotle is to bring out the problem of ontological difference in the problematic of temporality; that is, he intends to thematize aspects of Aristotle's thought that could not come to speech and interpretation within the horizons of Aristotle's thought. As we follow his account we can also say that the horizons of Heidegger's thought are themselves a transformation of Aristotle's thought, which opens in a different present onto different futures and pasts. This turnabout, or *Umschlag*, takes place as aspects of Aristotle's thought that could not play an open, formative role in the process of his thinking come now into a different process, a different *Vollzug*, a different stretch of history and thought, and facilitate a transformation toward a very different interpretation of time and way of thinking, one that includes a tearing movement within Heidegger's thinking.

Further, while the phenomenon of time is always in Heidegger's sight, *Aristotle's interpretation* of the phenomenon of time is the subject of Heidegger's inquiry in Section 19 of *Basic Problems*. His interpretation of Aristotle is the important point of departure for his account of the problem of ontological difference. Aristotle's interpretation orients our everyday understanding of time. By uncovering Aristotle's account of time and at the same time interpreting it with emphasis on transition and difference, Heidegger prepares for a phenomenological account of dasein's everydayness. The historical account of Aristotle shows the extent to which traditional processes and thoughts give content and factual orientation to what we can and cannot think. Our *ability* to think time and ontological difference, that is, our *understanding* of time and ontological difference, occurs in the future-giving, present-forming horizon of the Aristotelian tradition. A peculiarity of this tradition that we shall consider further is that it is within a horizon that is increasingly remote from our own time, although this remoteness is a part of the movement of our time.

This is a puzzling combination. The phenomenon of time is interpreted in order "to put ourselves in a position to grasp the distinction between being and beings . . . to fix the ground of the ontological difference" (BP 228), and our orienting access to this phenomenon is a given, factual, historically formed interpretation of time in which the phenomenon of time is so conceived as to make extremely difficult a clear understanding of the ontological difference between being and beings.

In this section of *Basic Problems*, Heidegger says, we grant that any interpretation of time presupposes the *Zeitlichkeit* or temporality of dasein, that the basic structures of temporality are of "dasein's original constitution." In other words, we assume the accomplishment of *Being and Time*. Temporality is "the ontological condition of the possibility of the understanding of being." How time is understood implies an understanding of being. But dasein's "original constitution" continues to be *the* question partially because it is founded in and constituted by the Aristotelian tradition. Heidegger shows that something approximating the ontological difference between being and beings is found in Aristotle's interpretation of time and, thus, in the interpretation that structures a significant portion of our everyday lives. By this demonstration he shows that an inchoate understanding of ontological difference is historically constitutive of dasein. For Aristotle, as we have seen, 'now' is both countable (it is a particular being) and "a continuum of the flux of time" (it is not a particular being, but the ground for the particularity of the countable now) (BP 249). How are we to think of time fundamentally if the now is "intrinsically transition" (BP 249), and yet can be counted? As Heidegger interprets Aristotle, we find that the ontological difference embedded in Aristotle's account of time as numbered motion is secreted and obscured, because the relation of number, in its difference from the now, to fundamental temporality is not clear. Yet a fundamental temporality is indicated by the continuing countability of time.

Further, we find that until the very basis for temporal transition is grasped, this obscurity about temporality will be part of the flow of Aristotelian thought. In the language of the first paragraph of Part Two, we need to "fix" *[fixiern]* the understanding of being "in our grasp" *[in den Griff]*. The grounding of time in dasein's "basic constitution" is the important, perhaps necessary first step, and this is because our tradition's interpretation of time, and Aristotle's interpretation in particular, points to the soul as the foundation of time without clearly showing how time is of the soul or clearly showing how time and soul establish an ontological difference between the countability of time and the continuity of time. Dasein is constituted partially by this drive to understand its own temporality and by deep uncertainty and confusion over its own temporality. And in its history dasein is prone to think of difference in relation to beings rather than in relation to the ontological difference between being and beings. Heidegger's move to Aristotle is a move in and to Dasein's own confusion over time and ontological difference, but it is a move also within a changing horizon in which temporal dasein, not soul, shows itself to be the region within which the difference between being and beings can be thought.

Aristotle's access to time is "the counting perception of motion as motion." This counting perception "is at the same time the perception of *what* is counted as time" (BP 257). As we noted above, perception of the counted 'what' is associated with an emphasis on perception without alertness or attunement to the temporal basis of perception; this means that the ontological difference *in relation to time* that is built into Aristotle's interpretation has been overlooked. Hence, "it leads to inadequately founded methods of interpreting time." Aristotle's approach, says Heidegger, is an "initial one," but his approach has become basic in the fabric of Western experience, thought, and speech. What in fact invests our lives and our institutions in the West is an initial and inadequate understanding of time, one that has not appropriated the difference between temporal continuity and what is counted and one that could not, in its time, account for its own temporality. The Aristotelian interpretation does not think the finite moving fullness of its own time, time's *Vollzug*, its continuous, finite stretch beyond anything conceivable as 'now'. *Our* living heritage, in its life, in turn fails in its everyday pursuit of life to give way to the ontological difference of temporality that Aristotle foresaw in an epoch-forming, albeit inadequate, beginning. This interpretation could not appropriate either the ontological difference that invests it or the temporality about which it spoke. In its rigorous failure and in ours regarding time we will probably find indications of a difference whose shadow follows us in all our lives like a dark fissure in the light of which everything appears.

Heidegger also grants in Part Two of *Basic Problems* that everydayness is a basic aspect of dasein. In our tradition we can *easily* say that everydayness is an a priori structure of dasein, that *our* everydayness is ontically characterized by Aristotle's tradition-forming understanding of time, and that another dasein is characterized by some other understanding that has given direction to some other tradition. But our confidence in this language of a priori structures is now less sure. We realize that the language of a priori structures, with its sense of a continuous now, fits nicely into the everyday intelligence of our heritage. Does this thought of everydayness as a priori, like the traditional interpretation of time, also hide some difference, one that is hardly thinkable, but that is built into the ideas of 'a priori' and 'transcendence'?

If the inherited understanding of time, in Aristotle's wake, is tradition making and is in that sense everyday, the temporality of foundations, unity, and systematic order is in question. The possibility emerges for thinking that temporality is finite and that thinking, to be disciplined, must be founded in its own finitude, that is, it must be founded in the *Umschlag* of its own tradition as well as within it. The confident beginning of Part Two is shaken, although Heidegger did not clearly intend to challenge his goal of "a clear and methodologically secure way" of thinking, because the very basis of the confidence comes into question only in the course of carrying out his confidence in the most rigorous possible way. He intended nonetheless to show that the clouded thought of ontological difference in relation to temporality simultaneously clouds our interpretation of being. There is a striking simultaneity here. Time and being are simultaneously obscured as ontological difference is obscured. The 'now', the *Umschlag*, the transformation, of the *obscurity* of time and being is not at all clear: the history of that obscurity and its horizon and present constitution are obscure. How are we to think the ontological difference of time as *continuity* in the lives of beings in the simultaneous obscurity of time and being, an obscurity that occurs in the *disclosure* of our language and thought? Are 'foundation' and 'a priori' part of the obscurity? The question of being that emerges with the obscurity of time and being puts in question the very basis for a strict method for interpreting the ontological difference of being and beings. We will return to this issue when we look at what Heidegger says about the ecstatic structure of temporality.

Our confidence in the possibility of a highly disciplined account of temporality, a confident hope that we can find access to time, is not destroyed, however. Consider the following paragraph:

> What Aristotle presents as time *corresponds to the common prescientific understanding of time. By its own phenomenological content* common time points to an original time, *temporality.* This implies however, that Aristotle's definition of time is only the *initial approach* to the interpretation of time. The characteristic traits of time as commonly understood must become intelligible by way of original time. If we set this task for ourselves it means that we have to make clear how the now qua now has *transitionary character;* how time as *now, then, and at-the-time embraces beings* and as such an embrace of extant things is still more objective and more extant than everything else (intratemporality); how time is *essentially counted* and how it is pertinent to time that it is *always unveiled.* (BP 257)

In this subsection, 19b, we find Heidegger moving beyond the Aristotelian heritage by giving an account of "reading time from a clock" and by leading us, by means of his account, to characteristics of dasein that point toward "original time," specifically, toward expecting, retaining, and presenting. This subsection elaborates and expands the Aristotelian interpretation of the now and of motion, as the very horizon for interpreting time expands and transforms: the stretching out of the now is given a dasein-oriented account that shows the "inner coherence" of time in terms of the structures of dasein. We can feel the progress of this account in the sense that we seem to be working on the same phenomenon that Aristotle worked on, something original and already there, independent of Aristotle and of us, too. It is as though by turning to dasein we were looking through a gate that opens to a unified, finite, original time and shows the ontological difference between being and beings.

We know, however, that this section is an elaboration within a tradition, a tradition that is being subtly de-structured. Heidegger interprets the 'now' in terms of overturning and passage and by elaborating transition and passage as disclosive stretching out beyond the measure of counting or number. *Overturning, we find, occurs within a temporal horizon.* Within a horizon, time stretches out, but not as a series of now-points. It stretches out ecstatically. Having been, going to, and presenting—each, Heidegger says, carries away *[entrücken]* from itself toward each other within a horizon of given, presenting, enabling possibilities. The horizon, like a space of vanishing and appearing, opens out to openness: this 'opening out to openness' elaborates both the 'now' as overturning [the *Umschlag*] and the carrying away or remotion of time. Temporality, original time, is the unity of dasein and is thus historical, metabolic remotion into openness. Our language is stretched beyond the reach of the Aristotelian horizon. Another horizon becomes manifest. Something is vanishing, removing another kind of region. Our language has begun to stand out from the Aristotelian stance. The standing-out itself is becoming a problem for thinking.

We also know that our language is in the debt of Aristotle, that our horizon of interpretation occurs in the remove of Aristotle's horizon, and that our debt to Aristotle is being paid not only in what we can say, but in what we cannot say in our increasingly deferential regard for ontological difference. We understand that the play of saying and not being able to say in some obscure way implicates the stretching out of time in dasein's understanding of being. How can *we* think the phenomenon of time in a given horizon that has beyond it nothing to be counted or disciplined into any kind of enumeration? Must we think of time as a phenomenon that is available to all human beings, one that moves in and beyond the motions of daily life, a phenomenon that is beyond and at the basis of all traditions? Can we, in fact, think at so far a distance from our everyday, structuring, enabling concept of time that the stretching out of time itself comes to thought? What makes the difference for thought in the face of the power of our inherited concept of time?

Heidegger's account of Aristotle suggests that now, in the turnabout, the *Umschlag,* of the Aristotelian horizon, something original for thinking takes place. It takes place—shall we say—in the blend, the fusion, the fission, the simultaneity of the horizon of Aristotle's thought and a horizon that opens out in Aristotle's remove. The remoteness of ontological difference in Aristotle's tradition now becomes transformed into an originating remoteness, one that moves people to think again of time and temporality in their uncertainty and their ubiquity. This transformation in relation to original time appears to occur like a foundation. But the very idea of 'foundation' seems to grow remote in this procession of thinking.

We turn to two paragraphs on the ecstatic aspect of temporality. They are poised within a discussion of original time, which is founded in dasein and consequently in the history of Aristotle's account of time as well as in dasein's ecstatic temporality. The discussion is disciplined by a recognition of its own closeness to and distance from Aristotle. The distance from Aristotle originates in part in the dimensions of Aristotle's own thought that were problematic and remote for him. These two paragraphs combine the Aristotelian problematic of time and ontological difference with the dasein-oriented phenomenological account of temporality. We are now thinking through our history as we think about it. Heidegger's account also shows that the problems and obscurities of time and temporality are in the language by which we attempt to fix the problems in a unified, disciplined way. This account shows that temporality is a problem in its historical and horizonal presence and that, *as a problem* in our language and thought, temporality is not to be conceived as a timeless being. As a problem and not as a fixed being, temporality has motivated and driven in our language all attempts to give it articulation. The *continuity* of temporality is not thinglike, but is, let us say experimentally in the context of ontological difference, *ecstatic*. In Heidegger's account of the ecstatic, horizonal character of temporality, the *problem* of temporality unfixes our fixations on transitory units of time and unfixes our emphasis on the division between temporal and nontemporal beings. This account releases, like a differentiating horizon, the problem of ontological difference in the problem of temporality. The language of ecstasis, in other words, is a horizonal language. Here Aristotle's horizon fades into a different opening of thought.

As we think through the language of temporal ecstasis, the problem of ontological difference takes place in our language and thought. Something remote on the tradition's horizon—the problem of ontological difference—removes itself and stands out upon a different horizon. It brings with it the horizonal opening. The very basis of our conceptual grasp loses its steady possibility for self-awareness. In that occurrence the confidence of Heidegger's lectures in the structural unity of dasein as a sufficient, rigorous answer to the problem of ontological difference is broken: the difference of temporality, in its horizonal ecstasis, from beings and from timeless certainty makes way for something other than what these remarkable lectures can say. The *language* of this account, its own grounding efforts, its relation to its own history, and its own temporal analysis of dasein come into question. Both the certainties of everyday time on the Aristotelian horizon and the remoteness of the openness of temporality on the horizon of this thought are unfixed and brought to problematic speech in Heidegger's account of original time, which is not a being but which stands outside itself and perhaps even outside the horizon of its history. If the horizon of the ecstasis of temporality "is the open expanse toward which remotion as such is outside itself" (BP 267), how are we to rethink this language in the remotion of its own history?[7]

Consider this paragraph:

> Within itself, original time is outside itself; that is the nature of its temporalizing. It is this outside-itself itself. That is to say, it is not something that might first be extant as a thing and thereafter outside itself, so that it would be leaving itself behind itself. Instead, within its own self, intrinsically, it is nothing but the outside-itself pure and simple. As this ecstatic character is distinctive of temporality, each ecstasis, which temporalizes only in temporalizing unity with the others, contains within its own nature a *carrying-away toward something* in a formal sense. Every such remotion is intrinsically open. A peculiar *openness,* which is given with the outside-itself, belongs

to ecstasis. That toward which each ecstasis is intrinsically open in a specific way we call the *horizon of the ecstasis*. The horizon is the *open expanse* toward which remotion as such is outside itself. *The carrying-off opens up this horizon and keeps it open*. As ecstatic unity of future, past, and present, temporality has a horizon determined by the ecstases. Temporality, as the original unity of future, past, and present, is *ecstatically-horizonal* intrinsically. "Horizonal" means "characterized by a horizon given with the ecstasis itself." Ecstatic-horizonal temporality makes possible not only the constitution of the Dasein's being, but also the temporalizing of the only time of which the common understanding of time is aware and which we designate generally as the irreversible sequence of nows. (BP 267)

We have seen that Aristotle's interpretation of time opens out in its temporality to the ontological difference between being and beings, a difference that Aristotle's interpretation of time could not think. We may say that the thought of ontological difference is on the horizon of Aristotle's thought. His thought is carried away toward it. The temporality of his interpretation of time is found in an ecstasis that removes his thought from its own stasis. This remotion is a part of the de-struction of Aristotle's concept of time in the unfolding thought of ontological difference. Heidegger 'founds' dasein in a horizonal-ecstatic temporality: "Ecstatic-horizonal temporality makes possible . . . the constitution of dasein's being." It is not a thing. "Within its own self, intrinsically, it is nothing but the outside-itself pure and simple." Temporality in its occurrence temporizes any moment, carries away a moment, opens it out. Aristotle's concept of time is opened out beyond what he could say. And the discipline by which we have come to think this overcoming of Aristotle's concept is also under the sway of ecstatic openness, an openness that will not be grasped by the discipline of its discovery.

Heidegger appears to be addressing an ecstatic remotion in his own thinking in the concluding pages of *The Basic Problems*. He notes that "*the method of ontology* is nothing but the sequence of the steps involved in the approach to being as such and the elaboration of its structures. We call this method of ontology phenomenology" (BP 328). "But," he adds, "what is most essential is first of all to have traversed the whole path once, so as, for one thing, to learn to wonder scientifically about the mystery of things and, for another, to banish all illusions, which settle down and nest with particular stubbornness precisely in philosophy." Then he addresses a distinctive ecstasis in his own thought. He had begun Part Two of this book with a call for a strict phenomenological method, one that would "methodically secure" the ontological difference between being and beings (BP 227). Now, after finding the ecstasis of Aristotle's concept of time, he says:

There is no such thing as *the one* phenomenology, and if there could be such a thing it would never become anything like a philosophical technique. For implicit in the essential nature of all genuine method as a path toward the disclosure of objects is the tendency to order itself always toward that which it itself discloses. When a method is genuine and provides access to the objects, it is precisely then that the progress made by following it and the growing originality of the disclosure will cause the very method that was used to become necessarily obsolete. The only thing that is truly new in science and in philosophy is the genuine questioning and struggle with things which is at the service of this questioning. (BP 328)

We are now prepared, through these lectures, for experimentation in thinking that finds its origin in both the *Umschlag* of the Aristotelian heritage and the *Umschlag* of the method that has provided access to original temporality. We will retrace this process again and again. But, having "traversed the whole path," we come to the disclosure of temporality and find again the method in its originality to have moved beyond itself in its original moment. Its temporality has opened it out beyond itself. Thinking begins again and recoils in this overturning. The ontological difference of temporality might have become thinkable in the temporalizing of Aristotle's interpretation of the *now* and of our approach to his interpretation. Temporality, not a being, appears thinkable, but not graspable. How is being without grasp to be thought? How can being be thought in the ecstasis of temporality when temporality is found to be not a being at all?

When the transformation of these lectures is interpreted by the concepts of horizon and ontological difference, we find the thought of mortal temporality taking place in the *Umschlag,* the overturning and transition that characterizes Heidegger's thought. In it dasein is made insecure. Not only Heidegger's account of dasein, but the basis for feeling and thinking is shaken in this thinking by the transformation that takes place in it. As always, Heidegger's abstractness, which we shall confront in the final chapter, makes the tearing effect appear at first gentle and 'philosophical'. But when we draw closer to it and undergo it without the control of our traditional protections, it appears more like suffering than philosophical discourse. The basis for original thought recoils on itself and puts itself in question. That means, in the context of Heidegger's writing, that the circumscription of our lives is solicited by a remotion that leaves nothing secure in the mortality of its ecstatic temporalization.

The horizonal aspect of this thought also incorporates the possibility of exhilaration and the feeling of going forward. The reverse side of the depression that we discussed, which is both a part of our heritage and a part of dasein, is found in the expansive feelings that accompany dasein's opening out to the finite openness of its being, to its "truth." The question of ethics is no less a part of dasein's truth than it is a part of dasein's open resolve.

6. The Truth of Ecstasis

Ecstasis means, in the context of the question of ethics, that the 'essence' of human being is not susceptible to conceptual grasp and hence not to definitive judgments concerning it. Dasein's mortal temporality might be 'thought' in movements of transformation in which the structure and methods of a tradition come into question and are overcome in their axiomatic certainty by elements that are in the tradition but are not clear to it or are lost to its values and rationality. Mortal temporality, we found, is such an 'element'. *Ecstasis* further means that human being is riven, in a certain sense broken, by the difference of its being vis-à-vis its existence. We have found that the certainty of Heidegger's own disciplined phenomenological account of dasein recoils on itself and away from itself by virtue of what it uncovers as its own primordial condition of possibility. It is no less subject to mortal temporality than is dasein in its general bearing. "We have not *shaken off* the tradition," Heidegger says in his discussion of truth in *Being and Time* (Section 44.B). "But," he continues, "we have *appropriated* it primordially" [die ursprüngliche *Aneignung*].[8] The claim of appropriation is justified if he can show how the ordinary idea of truth is based in a more primordial phenomenon of truth. The process of appropriation generally is one of turning again to the tradition, as we have seen, and turning over or recoiling in that turn to a new horizon and thought. It is a process that implicates and involves dasein's life and one in which an individual may open to the disclosive openness of dasein's being. In this process of turning Heidegger finds that dasein's mortal temporality comes to thought. Thinking takes place, as the universal validity of what is thought falls more and more into question.

Ecstasis also means that dasein's existence, the context for valuation and action, is characterized by a loss of a sense of what is proper to dasein's being. 'Propriety' is contaminated in its specific expressions. Its appropriation is more like the blink of an eye [*Augenblick*] or a side glance than it is like ownership. In open resolve an individual is maximally alert to this ontological situation. One relates to things and to oneself in an alert acceptance of one's inevitable impropriety. All of dasein's values and actions, all of its forms of power, are in question in the open, proper side glance of resolve. No possibility is offered of avoiding the impropriety of losing touch with the being of people and things and degrading them even in our respect and commitment. In resolve, Heidegger says, we may come to accept this inevitability. This means a continuous reopening of our relations, a continuous destructuring of our defining structures, analogous to Heidegger's retrieving and rethinking his philosophical heritage.

The reopening of all relations to the disclosiveness of mortal temporality, not the establishment of true and sufficient, that is, 'proper', guidelines and values, is the emphasis of Heidegger's thought. When we remember that his process has nothing to do with destroying values or suggesting a way of life without values, we see that ecstasis in daily life indicates relations that are attuned to the limits, to the ending of values *in their value,* and not a depreciation of the importance of values. Heidegger's attention is on human bearing *[Verhalten] with* values in open resolve regarding mortal temporality. A continuous transvaluation of values appears to be one of the consequences of this bearing. We can evaluate properly a specific process of transvaluation only when we come to think in the ecstasis proper to dasein's being.

What kind of freedom is that of ecstasis? Although Heidegger discusses freedom in *Being and Time* in relation to a number of topics—dasein's ability to be, its project, being ahead of itself, anxiety, and resolve—he does not raise the question of freedom in his section on truth. He has shown that dasein is free in its being for its own propriety. It is free in its being for the freedom to choose and to avail itself of itself; that is, it is free for open resolve and in that sense it is free in its disclosure for its proper truth (Section 40). Dasein is free to be true to itself. Dasein's being true to itself is, as we have seen, its free openness in and with its own disclosiveness, its ecstatic mortal temporality. Freedom is thus closely associated with ecstasis, and this association leads us to his essay "On the Essence of Truth." In this description of freedom and truth we shall find a turning, a metamorphosis developing in Heidegger's thought. Various descriptions in *Being and Time* are advanced, turned by another approach, placed in a different context, or rethought. Heidegger retrieves his own thought in some instances and transforms it in the retrieval. We shall follow in particular what happens to *ecstasis* and *resolve* in order to determine how the question of ethics was developing in his thought in the early 1930s (and throughout that decade as Heidegger reworked the essay before it was published in 1943) as we prepare to consider his Rector's Address of 1933.

When Heidegger turns to freedom in the fourth section of "On the Essence of Truth," he uses in his first sentence the word *erschüttern,* which means to shake violently, like a tree in an earthquake, or to convulse. The English translation appropriately uses *uproot.* Traditional preconceptions about truth are shaken and uprooted when they are seen in their proper connection with freedom, if, Heidegger adds, one is prepared for a transformation *[Wandlung]* of one's thinking. Uprooting and transformation are part of the 'thought' of freedom. Freedom comes to pass *[west]* properly, in its essence, as the traditional conceptions of correctness and accuracy are found to be rooted in freedom, which is not subject, as the 'origin' of correctness and accuracy, to their categories and proper rationality. Calling to mind in a disciplined way this connection between freedom and truth closely associates us with *Entschlossenheit,* dasein's "concealed essential ground" (Section 4). We are poised for an "experience" that is strange to us, in which the ground of our being is disclosed as concealed.

This experience, Heidegger says, removes us from the suasion of our inherited convictions and displaces *[versetzen]* us in regard to ourselves and our culture. *Uproot, transformation, displaced*—these words are associated with the experience of the concealed ground of human existence and "the essential domain of truth." The *possibility* for correctness, when we are available to it and are able to let it come to pass in our awareness, has a strong effect on our lives. The embodiment of a proper investigation into freedom and truth is like a convulsive metamorphosis. A tradition and an individual are shaken and left very much in question. Further, the possible correctness of Heidegger's account of freedom and truth is based on freedom, which has the effect, in its coming to mind *[Besinnung]*, of uprooting the 'correct' way of thinking about truth and of displacing the individual who now, presumably, has a correct account of freedom and truth. The ecstasis of freedom means an uprooting of Heidegger's own careful account.

Freedom "reveals itself as letting beings be," and "to let be is to engage oneself with beings" (Section 4). But this engagement is not a matter of managing or disposing or of any other kind of power or valence (value). "To let be—this is to let beings be as the beings which they are—means to engage oneself with the open region and its openness into which every being comes to stand, being that openness, as it were, along with itself." The side glance *[Augenblick]* that we discussed earlier in this section means in part that letting beings be properly means attentiveness to the disclosure, or unconcealment, of beings. Their disclosure is not something that comes to stand before us in an experience or by mentation. It is not subject to direct encounter. It is "uncomprehended" and concealed as it comes to pass. But our struggle to let be the unconcealment of beings disengages us from those preoccupations in which we are dominated by the issue of what to do with beings or how to treat them: "To engage oneself with the disclosiveness of beings is not to lose oneself in them; rather such engagement withdraws in the face of beings in order that they might reveal themselves with respect to what and how they are and in order that presentative correspondence might take its standard from them." The proper freedom of beings is found in their unconcealment, their disclosure, and dasein's proper freedom takes place as the individual admits *[einlassen]* and gives way to the unconcealment that he or she cannot comprehend. Freedom is not a matter of recognizing beings for *what* they are or relating to *them* correctly. It is a question of letting beings come to pass so that they *can be* taken for what they are. In this sense they are engaged properly when they are allowed in their unconcealment. As this letting be comes to pass, freedom reveals itself.

Freedom, then, is "ex-posing" and "ek-sistent." Its ecstasis is double: letting beings be *ex*poses or displaces a discourse or an individual in relation to its usual place with things in the disclosure of beings; and, second, this account of freedom *ex*poses a freedom that is thoroughly obscured in our heritage. In both cases the individual and its heritage are transposed vis-à-vis subjectivity and singularity. The priority of all relations of force, including the 'good' valences, is displaced, and freedom is manifest in the displacement that shows an incomprehensible unconcealment. A proper bearing with beings gives way to their disclosiveness.

The energy and intensity of this account, its passion for propriety, are focused on a bearing *[Verhalten]* that makes valuation and recognition possible, one that can pervade all relations but is not structured by values. Its incomprehensibility is absorbing. The movement is one of recoiling back again and again on the incomprehensible trace of being that marks Heidegger's tradition but eludes its grasp. The movement of his thought springs forward out of these recoils by the energy of the displacement that it has occasioned. Nothing in everyday life is trustworthy in this turning. Heidegger's thought turns out from the reliabilities of his life and is turned by this passage to something that will not quite come to thought. Far from an abstract formalism regarding value, Heidegger's thought is a passionate engagement with freedom in which freedom is accorded great value and yet cannot be valuable—a conundrum that is not uniquely his, but one that belongs to his cultural inheritance as he finds it. The ecstasis of his account is found partly in his breaking free from the patterns of thought that organized his heritage, by virtue of the fault that traverses it. In the case at hand, the ecstasis is found in the cleft of freedom that comes to pass as dasein's stance is transposed by the disclosure of freedom's concealment. This is a movement that recoils ecstatically on its correctness and abandons issues of correct everyday life as well as the priority of correctness. For Heidegger, something momentous is taking place: the sway of a tradition is metamorphosing into something like a process that is unavoidable and unthinkable. It is a process that appears to Heidegger to hold clues to the deepest questions of human deprivation and tragedy. Yet it resounds strangely from a distance and depth that he cannot fathom and that betrays a single-minded obsession to hear within its concealing and unreachable disclosure.

In this strange element Heidegger finds something preserved for human life whereby the ecstasis can take place. It is not a rich inheritance of valuables or a buried nature that will fulfill a human self in its realization. The possibility for a human's standing out of fixation with beings is found in the preservation of a question, an uncertainty that pervades our inheritance (Section 4). *Our* history of ek-sistence is initiated by the question that began to loosen the grip on individuals by specific things and communal bonding: What are beings? By this question the unconcealment of beings comes to be an issue. By asking this question, people in our lineage "for the first time experienced" beings, not primarily in the beings' thingly quality, but in their emerging presence *(aufgehendes Anwesen)* with regard to their (non-thinglike) emerging presence. The emerging presence of beings referred to itself in this experience. Again a double movement: beings are set apart from their everydayness by their emerging presence, and people are set apart from their everydayness by questioning the emerging presence of beings. Unconcealment provides a sense of wholeness that is strange to the thought of a totality of individual things. Unconcealment (is) whole, but it is not a being or a "sphere of beings." This experience "conserves" beings in their unconcealment, brings things back to their truth, that is, to their disclosiveness, and sets in motion the possibility of being with beings in a way that does not diminish them to the status of their use, identity, and knowledge. They stand outside their status, and the one who experiences them in this way is transposed to a relation that is outside the inherited region of usage, identity, and knowledge. The possibility of ecstasis is thus preserved in the experienced question, What are beings?

The emergence and loss of the question in relation to beings and un-concealment is the proper history of Heidegger's thought, the experienced and largely forgotten question that festers in the organizing thoughts and values of Western culture. "History begins only when beings themselves are expressly drawn up into their unconcealment and conserved in it, only when this conservation is conceived on the basis of questioning regarding beings as such" (Section 4). The possibility is opened up for attending to "the open region for every measure," and thus finding our bearing with beings without the complex and pervasive mediation of all forms of measurement. The momentous quality of this possibility is still to be appropriated. It suggests the diminishing force, in at least certain aspects of our lives, of measuring people and other beings, whether the measure be by means of race, beliefs, family, heritage, professional expertise, quality of mind, or simple 'spiritual' depth. We are approaching the possibility of bringing to mind the unconcealment of beings, but we remain for the most part locked in a mindset of valuation, disposal, management, and objectification in our care for our lives, a mindset whose overpowering force hems us in throughout our everyday world, confuses freedom with the condition of possibility for certain types of subjectivity, and gives priority to correctness and measurement in matters of truth.

"The rare and the simple decisions of history arise from the way the original essence of truth essentially unfolds" (Section 4). If we said that history unfolds according to the way we *use our* freedom, we would exemplify the loss that Heidegger finds in our history. The assumptions that freedom can be used and that it belongs to human beings are parts of the problem of our cultural inheritance. We concern ourselves with the proper use of freedom. *Use* organizes our concern, and we, the subjects of freedom, are taken to be the agents who determine its propriety. In our commitments we find ways to make ourselves present to each other by reference to values that commonly identify us and have proven trustworthy for our survival and well-being. But the context for *trustworthy* is a history of thought and practice in which engagement in the disclosure of beings is thoroughly overlooked and excluded from thought. We tend to calculate freedom's use by intensity of commitment and a degree of responsibility to given standards. The exclusion in our thought of freedom in its dimension of disclosive ecstasis is compounded by the experiences of trust and survival. The question of beings and their disclosiveness is distorted. Their disclosiveness is found in their identifiability, their use, or, in the case of other people, their ability to be answerable to standards, to themselves, or to God. The disclosiveness of beings is thus distorted into their presence and their quality of will regarding other beings. In this sense, distortion expresses ecstasis: the way in which human beings give voice to ek-sistent freedom mistakes and misplaces freedom by making it a property of selves. This distortion constitutes our history of relations with each other and with other beings and both puts in question the authority of our communities of value and yet holds the trace of disclosure, the ek-sistence of beings, in the initiation of the question, what are beings? "The rare and simple decisions" of our history arise from the distortion. They have happened in giving definitive power to derivatives of disclosive openness, for example, in defining the truth of beings by reference to a determinant essence, interpreting time by primary reference to count-ability in presence, interpreting human being by primary reference to will, and interpreting truth as the adequation of intellect to things. These deci-sions cover up beings and constitute a history in which the semblance of freedom rather than the disclosure of freedom as letting beings be is the controlling power. The original essence of truth has thus unfolded in our culture by means of semblance and distortion.

Heidegger poses the beginning of an option to the entrapment of beings by the dominance of volition, identity, and valuation. "Every mode of open comportment flourishes in letting beings be" (Section 5). In contrast to contemplative activity, Heidegger makes reference to the specific ways in which people relate to specific beings, to the ways in which we use, identify, evaluate, or address. This issue continues to be one of ek-sistence. There is no question of eliminating usage or valuation. It is rather a question of engaging beings with alertness to their and our ek-sistent, disclosive freedom, the disclosiveness that is not for use, identification, evaluation, or management of any kind. Withdrawal from the world of concern is foreign to Heidegger's thought. It is an issue of undergoing the strain and uncertainty of engaging beings in such a way that they are allowed their disclosiveness which transgresses their familiarity. Their familiarity ends in their disclosiveness, and our familiarity with ourselves undergoes a simi-lar ending. In this case, we are not confronting being-to-death or the *Vorlaufen* of the future. The thought of human finitude does not quite fit. Nor is it an ending that marks an entrance of eternity into finite life. It is rather an ending that is marked by nothing identifiable by the categories and experiences of familiarity. We encounter the limits of our thinking and experience in the ek-sistence of letting beings be in their disclosiveness. Heidegger refers descriptively in this context to *flourishing:* "Jedes offenständige Verhalten *schwingt*" (Every mode of open comportment *flourishes*) (Section 5; emphasis added). *Schwingen* has a connotation of soaring and exhilaration. In accord with freedom in our dealings with beings, this open comportment, this *offenständige Verhalten*, flourishes and composes a rising anticipation of itself in all situations. Heidegger does not say that the self flourishes or that the community flourishes. Letting beings be and the way of being that stands openly in this freedom flourish.

The entire situation of flourishing appears to be strange "from the point of view of everyday calculations and preoccupations" (Section 5). Heidegger's emphasis is not on dasein's coming properly to itself, but is on the disclosiveness of beings. Disclosiveness is not a being. It does not privilege any being or any status; no particular being provides special access to it. "Being as a whole" is indicated by disclosiveness, not by dasein, and Heidegger's 'option' intensifies the question of being rather than indicating a suggested or prescribed way of life. Intensifying the question of being, its incomprehensibility in our ways of life and thought, is the 'aim' of the option. Our accord with the disclosiveness of beings comes to pass in the questionableness of being, the questionableness of letting beings be. This is an accord marked no less by uncertainty than by dasein's resolve with regard to its finite temporality.

The history that Heidegger highlights is thus characterized by the question of being and beings in the context of emerging presence and disclosiveness, a pervasive and damaging loss of both the question and the unconcealment of beings, a pervasive normalization of this loss, and the faint indication of an option to this normalization. This history is also characterized by a *Verbergung*, the concealment of truth, in distinction to the *Unverborgenheit*, the unconcealment of truth. The loss of the question of being and beings and the normalization of this loss in our culture hides rather than preserves the letting be of beings. The distortion that we have noted twists the disclosiveness of beings into a culture of usage and valuation, and this distortion constitutes the "unfolding" of truth in our heritage.

Concealment, on the other hand, "preserves what is most proper *[das Eigenste]* to *aletheia* as its own *[als Eigentum]*" (Section 5). The word "points to the still unexperienced domain of the truth of being (not primarily of beings)" into which dasein ek-sists. Dasein's ecstasis in being is freedom, which is concealed in the heritage that constitutes dasein. It is freedom, the letting be of beings, that is "the resolutely open bearing that does not close up in itself." Open resolve, with strong emphasis on the unlocking and opening-out sense of *Entschlossenheit*, as the word is used in this essay, is the opening in which dasein ek-sists and which conceals and preserves what is most proper to truth, a propriety that is lost to dasein in its history. The returning step to the open freedom of letting beings be that is part of Heidegger's 'option' is one of allowing the concealment. An opposite to this comportment is "clinging to what is readily available and controllable" and taking "directives from the sphere of readily available intentions and needs." In this opposite case, a person takes his or her bearings from the values and meanings that structure the familiar life-world and is closed to the concealment that marks the end of familiarity and meaning. One bypasses the ecstasis of dasein and intrinsically, although involuntarily, resists the concealment—Heidegger also calls it the mystery— of disclosiveness. People are "left in the sphere of what is readily available to [them]." They are left to their own resources, which is a needy state that is sharply contrasted, particularly in the instance of value satisfaction, to "flourishing." We propose and plan "on the basis of the latest needs and aims" and manage our lives with attention directed exclusively to what we can accomplish under the immediate circumstances of our lives. Rather than the flourishing of beings, we have a deeply obsessive attachment to beings and to circumstances whereby everything gets used up in the management of our lives. The boundary of our environment in the disclosiveness of beings is thoroughly obscured. We now find that the concealment of being and not only the finite temporality of *our* being marks the ecstasis of being.

This concealment means for Heidegger that his own view of concealment and the clarity of his thought are "essentially misleading." He uses these last two words at the end of Section 7, in which he says the following: dasein is constituted by obsessive entanglements with beings and by the consequent inevitable loss of the disclosiveness of beings; dasein *is* a continuous turning away from being—it "is a turning into need." Dasein's turning away is also dasein's own disclosure; that is, dasein occurs in its being as the possibility of transposition *[Versetzung]* out of absorbing involvements, a transposition effected by its ecstatic ending in the total unfamiliarity of disclosiveness. Dasein is tossed about in its being by the simultaneity of disclosure and concealing. It occurs questionably. Its view *[Ausblick]* of the open region of disclosure "is a question"; such questioning takes the form of the question of the being of beings; that is, one asks the kind of questions that take shape in Heidegger's work as he elaborates the questions of his philosophical heritage; and the question of the being of beings "is essentially misleading." The *question* recoils on itself in questionableness. Dasein's proper turning into need, *its* disclosure, turns in its questioning. It enjoys no transexistential neutrality or perspective from which to sufficiently define its propriety. Rather, its propriety takes place as its own thinking and questioning transform metaphysical thought and become questionable in the process. When one recognizes the concealment of concealment by virtue of dasein's "perpetual turning to and fro" in its ek-static existence, one enters reflectively into the proper, true essence of human being only to find that *this* turning also comes to question.

The same tension that we noted in *The Basic Problems of Phenomenology,* Part II, is found in "On the Essence of Truth." On the one hand, Heidegger proposes a strictness of conceptualization and method that will enable a movement through and beyond the metaphysical tradition. This movement is appropriate to dasein's horizonal and ecstatic way of being. Heidegger also finds that his own strictness of approach and his desire for definitive clarity, as well as his formulations, are put in question by the issue under investigation. Dasein *is* questionable, and Heidegger's thought is an instance of the overturning that dasein inevitably undergoes. Danger invests his thought as much as it invests the valuation and philosophy that he works through. On his terms, nothing commonsensical, philosophical, or political can properly avoid the questioning recoil that is made inevitable by dasein's errancy and ecstasis.

7. Ethos/Ecstasis

Heidegger's troubling division of ethos and ecstasis raises, and is designed to raise, doubt within the certainty that characterizes the values of our culture. Even though we are clear that ecstasis occurs in our daily lives and in our heritage, and even though we are aware that doubts arise in our habits of mind and heart that were formed in bypassing and suppressing the disclosiveness of beings, the questions that are basic to our survival and welfare do not appear to be addressed by Heidegger. He puts off, even foreswears, dealing with the values, maxims, and principles that give us hope of avoiding, or at least judging, the savagery and the wrongs that constantly threaten our lives. The question of being and the question of ethics appear anemic or luxurious when they are held up to the starvation, torture, war, and oppression that systematically result from our ways of organizing ourselves and maintaining power. Our measures of wrong and right are not to be lost, not even to the measureless mystery of being. We cannot believe that our recognition of wrong, our commitment to right, our worship of God, our love of just laws, and our respect for human beings have as part of their fabric the inevitability of what we most abhor. We are certainly not prepared to believe that the loss of the question of being and the failure to maintain the question of ethics constitute grave weaknesses in the structure of our culture at its best. We are rather more inclined to expect that the deepest meanings of our religion and ethics will come to light again as Heidegger peels away the veneer of superficiality from which we and they suffer. A profound reinheritance of divinity or a renewed reverence for life as we find it or the emergence of an almost Eastern, specifically Buddhist piety could give a constructive edge to Heidegger's destructuring of Western thought. Or, at worst, the absence of such redeeming qualities might be taken to explain his behavior in the early years of the Third Reich. In the absence of a reemergence of the values and beliefs most prized by us, we are driven to believe that the difference between ethos and ecstasis marks a questionable division in Heidegger's thought, particularly when the question of ethics is under discussion. The issue, however, is whether or not (1) our values are thoroughly in question as we make these judgments, (2) valuing as such is genuinely dangerous, and (3) we have undergone the question that moves Heidegger's writing and defines what is most proper to us in maintaining such questions. The relations among *ethos, nómos* (law), and *nomós* (field) can help us to address this issue, to find questionable again our hopes and assurances, and to provide another look at the division between ethos and ecstasis.

The word *éthea* in Homer was used to name the places where animals belong. The animal's *éthos* is the place to which it returns, its dwelling place. If the animal cannot return to its *éthos,* a violation of its particular order occurs, as when a wild horse is hobbled in a stall and cannot return to its own environment. In the *Iliad* (6.506–11) Homer says: "As when a stabled horse, having been fed at a manger, breaks his bonds and runs galloping over the plain, since he is accustomed to bathe in the flowing river, glorying. He holds his head high, and his mane leaps on his shoulders on both sides. His knees swiftly bear him, trusting his splendor, through the *éthea* and pastures *(nomós)* of horses."[9] In the *Odyssey,* Homer speaks of *éthea* to which pigs, specifically sows, return after grazing. In both uses of *éthea* one finds the connotation of appropriateness for particular animals. In the instance of the horse running free back to his *éthea* and *nomós,* he has not been successfully habituated to the stall, and he is returning to his site of eating and bathing. The *éthea* of animals are associated by Herodotus with the *éthea* of barbarians and names the places to which the various non-Greeks belong. These places resist Greek civilization. The theme of belonging to a place that is not fully human and that resists civilized transformation also runs through Hesiod's and Theognis's uses of the word. *Éthea,* prior to the fourth century, are also distinct from *nomós:* the *nomós* is a specific field for grazing, the *éthea* are specific environments that are associated with patterns of actions peculiar to the animal.

The association of *nomós* 'pasture' and *nómos* 'law' links the word for law to *éthos* in the following way. *Nomós* is associated with the nomad. It is associated with wandering, with random search for pasturage. The *nomádes* were pastoral, nomadic tribes. The word *nomás* meant division and distribution, such as the distribution of an inheritance, which at one time probably consisted primarily of land. The word could also mean possession or regular usage, and *nomós* could mean district, province, or sphere of command. The verb *nomízo* meant to use regularly, to own, to acknowledge. In its passive form it meant to be esteemed or held in honor. This remarkable association in the word of nomadic, pasture, division, possession, regularity, accustomed, and honored is, as we shall see, echoed in *éthos.* In the latter word, there are the associations of accustomed, familiar, custom, foreignness, separation, belonging, and different. In both words habitual practice—the primary meaning for *nómos,* which means both law and melody—struggles with nomadic, uncivilized separation. This

is a fateful struggle. In it the limiting principles of order and random movement without limiting principles unsettle each other. To overcome randomness, principles of order must be applied beyond the locale to give order
to the distances and differences of locales. And to maintain the distance
and difference involved in the many ways of belonging and being well
placed, one must resist the use of principles of order to overcome the
randomness and to order differences in a dominant way.

As *éthea* increasingly gained usage in the singular, Hesiod and Theognis
used *éthos* to refer to a locale of characteristics and to the hidden but
characteristic part of a person—the place, as it were, to which one returned
when one was really him- or herself. It was the aspect of a person that
came to light over a period of time and in a variety of circumstances.
Theognis says that he once praised a man before he "knew [his] *éthos*
thoroughly" and that he had lived to regret confusing the man's appearances with his *éthos,* which "time shows forth" (*Op.* 963.70). Isocrates,
Demosthenes, and Plato used *soul* to name the locale of *éthos.* As a part
of soul, *éthos* continued to have an habituated and resistant quality and
to exist separately from the *nómos* of the soul. An *éthos* can be ordered
by reason, but its variant structures are not the same as rational logos.

The words *éthea* and *éthos* had the connotation of recalcitrance. Both
barbarians and animals, once they became accustomed to places and ways
of life, were hard to change, even in the direction of civilized happiness.
The *éthos* of a person or a group of people was often hidden from view.
One was wise to be cautious in relating to the *éthos*-reality that could
be hidden by appearances, language, and behavior. And because of its
difference from the seeming and appearing, it showed itself through time
as something that lay behind or within what appeared. To know a creature's
éthos, one had to see where the animal went to be at home, as it were,
or where it went when threatened, or where it went to die. One needed
to experience a person in good times and bad to discover where he or
she really lived. Something like real character only came to view circum-
stantially.

Éthea also were places and regions. The specificity of *éthea,* the places
of belonging for these sows or those Trojans, allowed the word to give
emphasis to differences and to resistance respecting claims and laws that
sought to overrule the specific places and ways of belonging. The horse
broke loose from the stall and manger and also from his caretakers and
returned to *his* place. His return was not an act of reason, any more
than the Trojans' reception of Helen was rational according to Aeschylus
(in *Agamemnon,* 717–36). The power of an *éthos* is in its peculiarity, its
regional characteristics, its quality of belonging, and its resistance to outside
influences. We recall that the Indo-European root of *éthos* (*Swedh*) meant
"one's own." *Éthos* names how one is properly one's own or how we
are of our own. Once people have grown up in the *éthos,* they are unlikely
to adopt another way of being. The regional aspect of *éthea* and *éthos*

indicates resistance to expropriation by a different *éthos* or by the authority of laws and principles that would blur its difference and its arbitrariness, its ownness. The differences of an *éthos* are deeply associated with its ordering, identity-giving, and nurturing force. Recalcitrance and separation are combined with identity and nurturance. The difference of an *éthos* also means its identity. To attempt to overcome its difference is to attempt to overcome its own reality.

Most likely the conflicts of various *éthea* and the range wars for pastures, the suffering of those conflicts, and the hopelessness occasioned by their continual renewal contributed greatly to the attraction of rules and laws that overrode the hostile, recalcitrant aspect of *éthea* and the nomadic quality of *nómos*. There is also the self-destructiveness that appears to inhabit humans within the same *éthos,* our killing self-contradictions and our stubborn refusals to make those adjustments and changes of character that would provide a greater measure of peace and happiness to ourselves and to those whose lives we affirm. If *éthea* become evident through time and extremities, sometimes to the shock even of the individual whose *éthos* shows itself, if the element of *éthos* is contingency and differentiation, do we not need a limited field of nurturance, a kind of *nomós,* a structure that shows itself differently, that shows itself to be outside time and outside ethnic suspicions and conservative provinciality? Or if manifestation outside time is asking too much, perhaps we need a kind of *nómos,* a field of laws and principles, that brings with it, into time, indications, more than hints, but patterns that point to a transtemporal circumscription of the writhing, belligerent interplay of *éthea*. Yet the belligerent play of *éthea* is closely associated with their nurturing and protective power, and this hopeful goal of peace through unification suggests the establishment of an encompassing *éthos* at the expense of the difference and singularity of the encompassed *éthea*.

These issues have more than historical interest. We are now in a time when we cannot avoid thinking of laws and principles for thought and action as regional, as a group of claims characteristic of one cultural and historical segment. Who can doubt the contingency of all claims to transtemporal authority and being? The classical resolution of the problems created by the diversity and unruliness of *éthea* and their many rules and ways—a direction of thought that has enormous forming power in our history—was the hypothesis of forming powers that were unconditioned by time. Their timeless universality suggested superiority over all time-generated, contingent powers. The relations among the different organizations of life are perhaps governed by laws that are not nomadic and by an organization that is not regional and temporal. The distances and differences that separated *éthea* and partially defined their belligerence were taken to be under the governance of a reality that, when known and appropriated, would make possible a proper ordering of the temporal differences. The hypothesis of eternal realities filled in, as it were, the distance and disconnection that pervaded the free-flowing life-organizations, none of which could dominate the others without violence and destruction.

The denial of mere and ungrounded difference by the idea of eternal connections has its many and sometimes terrible consequences as it prompts the imposition of goods, rights, and orders that now appear to us to be as ethnic as the expropriated regions, whether geographical or soulish, upon which the regions of 'eternal realities' did their work. Ethnic valence took a new turn. It involved the repeated application of the meaning of timeless realities to specific states by those especially privileged by their access to these realities. Meaning founded in the hypothesis of eternity and access to unconditioned beings struggled to overcome the distances among *éthea* and *nómoi*.

The present study suggests the possibility that our desire for universal laws and values and a changeless basis for them arises out of human's clinging to security and familiarity in the face of displacing and threatening differences, in combination with inattention to the mere difference that separates beings, constitutes them, and conditions their lives together. Until the ecstasis of difference and its concealment are thinkable, our desire for universal commonality and either an overwhelming tendency to look for a noncontingent basis for the desire or an insistence on the repetition of some value unaccompanied by the question of ethics will rule like a *nómos* that divides and possesses even as it functions to unite and set free.

I doubt that the viability of Heidegger's thought in the context of the question of ethics can be felt if our largely unconscious desire for definitive unity is not experienced as a question. This desire is apparent throughout Heidegger's writing as he makes wholeness and unity the apparent goals of his retrieval of the question of being. But that question and the abysmal quality of disclosedness, its thoroughgoing unmanageableness and lack of quantified repeatability, turn the desire for unity toward an ecstasis that limits judgment and challenges the presumptions of this desire. Perhaps the exhilaration of the recoiling process, in excess of its trauma and depression, occasions the possibility for the turning of desire toward a "flourishing" that is not measured primarily by the identities of individuals or communities, one that feels no need of transcendental unity, the love of God, the sustenance of enduring being, but that releases people in a direction outside the limits of inspired imagination and spiritual conquest.

This direction, as we have seen, is both tenuously marked and largely erased in our heritage. It is a direction articulated in such distortions as we find in the concepts of the freedom of the will or of presence-dominated temporality. But it appears nonetheless to be one that can attract as well as repel in a process of thought like Heidegger's when we stay within his discourse and share his passion, mourning, and exhilaration. What comes to language in it recoils in the countervalences of our culture and finds in the recoils an opening for thought that in its violation of the familiar is strangely telling, like an ecstasis during an ordinary day. In the ecstasis vis-à-vis our *éthos,* the tendency of the *éthos* to intensify itself without question, to make itself authoritative and encompassing as a nurturing defense: these tendencies of a healthy cultural environment to insist on itself are not eliminated but complemented by an excess that limits the *éthos,* marks its boundaries as an *éthos,* and lets something unspeakable and unmeasurable in the *éthos* emerge strangely and questionably on the horizon of its region.

When our inherited desire for universality and noncontingent grounding is experienced in its questionableness, and probably only then, the relation among the question of being, the question of ethics, and the terrible suffering that encroaches on the order of our lives can also be experienced. The possibility emerges that many types of suffering are produced not only by orders that preserve certain interests at the expense of others, but also by orders that are preoccupied with beings and to which the dis-closedness of being is concealed. In such order we could be blind, by overlooking the inevitability of being's concealment, to human being's way of coming to pass and to the propriety of beings in the *éthos;* we could be blocked to our own temporality and truths as well as to that of most beings; we could form massive, uncritical structures of defense against mortal disclosiveness; and we could propagate suffering—radical nonflourishing—under the guise of cultural satisfactions. In the weakening of the insistent desires that are definitive of our *éthos,* ethnic familiarity becomes questionable, its limits echo at least slightly in its structure, and it is experienced as shaken in its unity. Its contingent difference may stand out momentarily, and questions deeply embedded in its heritage may take a tentative shape in the wake of the ecstatic shaking of ethnic confidence.

Such thoughts and questions as these—rather than, what ought I to do? who ought I to be?—emerge in the *question* of ethics, because the laws governing the thought and desire of our *éthos* are themselves in question and in their questionableness have opened the way for a different discourse. In this discourse the stakes appear to be too high not to maintain the questionableness of these laws in the recoils of *éthos* and ecstasis.

FIVE

These Violent Passions

The Rector's Address

The division between ethos and ecstasis constitutes a major problem for Heidegger's rectorial address of 1933. In the address he attempts to apply his interpretation of human existence and the loss of the question of being to the formation of the German university in the context of the new and, for many at that time, exhilarating political changes taking place under German National Socialist rule. Because it is an ethical writing, the address has a singular importance of Heidegger's relation to the question of ethics. We shall work on it by paragraphs, indicating at the beginning of our own paragraphs which paragraph in Heidegger's text we are reading. We will also examine both the relation of this work to those that we considered in Chapter 4 and the role, or absence, of the question of ethics in it.

The title of the address, "Die Selbstbehauptung der Deutschen Universität," can be translated "The Self-Assertion," "The Self-Maintenance," "The Self-Affirmation," or, in this context, "The Self-Governance of the German University." According to his 1945 reflections on the address, Heidegger had in mind the importance of the word *Haupt* 'head' in the word *Behauptung*.[1] He contrasts, for example, what he means by *Selbstbehauptung* with self-decapitation.[2] How the university is 'headed' is a preoccupation of the address. The role of the Rector is noted at the beginning in the context of essence, and not primarily from a practical, institutional point of view. The *Wesen* or 'essence' of the German university heads it, provides the continuing reference for its direction and struggle. The Rector is to follow the university's *Wesen* in molding the institution. The word *Selbstbehauptung* thus raises the question of how the university is to head itself with regard to both internal institutional structures and outside political pressures. It indicates that the political, social, and cultural functions of the university are to be delimited by the essence of the German university. But the essence is also to guide the Rector in his leadership of the university. In addition to an ecstasis that breaks into and radically conditions a people's history, we find a function of heading the German university given to essence. It is to imprint, form, lead, and delimit the institution. It is to provide direction for a determined institutional identity. Heidegger has before him the task of both speaking in the *"Aufbruch"* of essence and of speaking out of his rectorial chair. How will the essence of the German university head Heidegger's language? Will it lead him to put in question his own relation to it? Will it have the effect of casting doubt on his determined program for the university? Or will it confirm his rectorial authority and provide in addition an authority for his language that confirms the right of his intentions for the German people?

(1) The Rector is to be led in his intellectual leadership of the university by the unremitting task of spirited *[geistige]* mentation, a task that is defined and constrained by the imprint *[Gepräge]* of the history of the German people.[3] The dispensation, destiny, and fortune *[Schicksal]* of the German people is to be found in the constraint of this imprint. Likewise, the fortune and flourishing of teachers and students alike come to pass by rootage in the essence of the German university, and this essence finds specific authority, clarity, and power when the Rector and other authorities lead by following the obligations imposed on them by the history of the German people. The entree to the issue of the university's self-maintenance and self-affirmation is the authority of the Rector's office and the definition of that authority by reference to the history of the German people. *Essence* at this early point in the address appears to refer to the history of a people. It is an ontic or regional essence, one that appears to have played too small a role heretofore in the development of the German university. Heidegger's initial appeal does not lead us to expect an invocation of being, ontological difference, ecstasis, or truth. We look rather to the conformity of an institution to a history. This history has only the relative transcendence of a history vis-à-vis a present aspect of it. But we are initially unsure of the significance of this transcendence. It suggests ethnic self-conformity and can be given authority, clarity, and power. It can be established. Will it also address the question of being and truth?

Heidegger begins his address, as he so often begins his treatises, with an appeal to strictness, exactness, and unbending criteria for discipline. The personal convictions and values of the university's administrators are secondary to the essence of the university. The Rector, for example, is to attend to this essence, follow it, and bring it to expression in the form and content of his administration. His office is to describe the essence in the sense that the office gives the contours and direction of the institution by reference to the contour and direction of the essence. The question before us is whether this beginning will lead to a process of destructuring that will put in question the ontic and almost technological emphasis on criteria, their fulfillment, and strictness of approach.

(2) The first question raised by Heidegger is whether the teaching staff and the student body are truly and mutually rooted in the essence of the German university. By using *Hohen Schule,* which can be read in this context as either a school of higher learning or a school that is high

in the sense of elevated or lofty, Heidegger suggests that the essence of the German university elevates its participants and sets them apart from the rest of society. The university has a mandate in its essence which may or may not be known, but which in any case must set the agenda for the university, must imprint, by inspiring the staff and students. Even if they do not understand the university's essence, they must make it the focus of their will. We may assume at this point that something is to be overcome and something is to move with force toward an essence-centered university. It can *imprint*—not just form or suggest directions for, but powerfully stamp—the university only if faculty and staff will "this essence fundamentally" *[von Grund aus]*. Heidegger asks, who can doubt this mediational relation of will to essence? Intensity of will is essential for the operative establishment of the German university's essence. It must mold our existence, our dasein, in a determined way. But first we must see that the university's self-government is grounded commonly and primarily not in a legislated independence from other authorities but in its essence, and the task of university people is to adhere to this essence through the Rector's leadership even if they cannot say what that essence is. We note Heidegger's reach to his hearers—this man alone at the podium—in the name of commonality. He indicates a sense of commonality, that will be hard to find, one that apparently is shared in German civilization, but that can be retrieved only by strenuous exertion of will. On the one hand, the faculty and students must mold their passion to essence. On the other hand, essence must be approachable by powerful, willful exertion.

Heidegger's emphasis at this point has a double edge. It eliminates a liberal democratic interpretation of the university's independence, on the one hand, and, on the other, claims authority for the university by appeal to *its* essence, not to a state authority. The autonomy *[Selbstverwaltung]* of the university is not to be founded in its constituted identity or in the state government, but in an essence, yet to be described, that is found in the history of the German people. Its mission is said to be higher and other than that prescribed for it by any office or governmental body. In principle, all acts regarding the university are to be taken as subject to appeal to the university's essence, not to a party, ideology, or state government.

(3) The university's autonomy means that the body of teachers and students can set their own duties and procedures and can determine how to bring to realization the task that they find before them. But the *Selbst* 'self' of *Selbstverwaltung* 'autonomy' is a question. Heidegger himself is unclear about the identity of the university's constituents as a body, and he doubts that there is an adequate understanding of this identity in the university as a whole or on the part of its individuals. He can hardly know what their autonomy means without continuous and unsparing attention to the question of who they are as the constituted body of the university. Their ability *[Können]* to know themselves and to be properly autonomous

depends on their attentiveness *[Besinnung]*. They must retrieve themselves from the uncritical habitual assumptions that govern them if they are to find the meaning of autonomy; that is, the essence is to occasion, in a way still to be specified, the autonomous individuality of university citizens.

This early move of destructuring the sense of identity that pervades the university community, a move that puts in question the meaning of autonomy, is an opening move on Heidegger's part to initiate a struggle by which the being of the German faculty and student body can come into the open and by which the unknown essence of the German university can become manifest. It is a move toward interpreting the *Haupt,* which is the essence of the German university, and it makes questionable the function of the Rector as much as it makes questionable the identity of the German university. Rather than an assertion of rights and privileges, *Selbstbesinnung*—self-attentiveness, self-reflection, and self-recollection— names the activity that opens the academy to itself. This attentiveness is prefaced by uncertainty and unclarity, the acceptance of which makes possible initial steps toward the openness that Heidegger says is necessary for a proper exposure of truth. In this case he is addressing the ontic truth of the university's being. The elevation of the university can come to sight by means of this *Selbstbesinnung.* The affiliation of *Selbstbesinnung* and elevation of the educational enterprise will continue to play a major role in the address. I find an incongruence between the spiritedness of the imagery of elevation and the inward, deepening overtones of the *Besinnung.* The inflaming, rising, and consuming dimension of Western spirit and spirituality about which Derrida has written eloquently, the rising movement that leaves behind the ashes of its consumption, is not fully in accord with that meditative attentiveness that lets something come out in *its* disclosiveness and in the full flavor of its difference and distinctness.[4] But Heidegger clearly does not find such an incongruence in this address and links closely spirited mentation and attentiveness to self and history. Between these two kinds of movements a new university is to rise, rooted in the history of the German people which has been disastrously misappropriated.

(4) Knowledge of the contemporary situation of the university thus does not constitute an adequate basis for the required self-attentiveness. Nor can the academics count on acquaintance with the received histories. Something more is needed to care for and give refuge to the essence in question. They must first delimit this essence, find the region of its future coming *[die Zukunft umgrenzen]*. In this effort they will it. They do not make it an object of desire or pinpoint it as something just outside of their present reach. They exert themselves and constitute themselves in self-delimitation *[Selbstbegrenzung]* as they find the region of the essence's coming: *this* is their activity of willing, and *this* is their effort to find their 'head' to which the Rector and the university community are subservient. Their single-minded search and self-delimitation constitute their self-

assertion, their governing themselves in the light of the essence they know they do not know. The destructuring move on Heidegger's part is thus advanced a step. He is showing that the German university must maintain itself in the question of its essence and thereby hold in question the received knowledge of what the German university is.

(5) The first four paragraphs thus establish that the assertion of the German university is found in maintaining the question of the essence of the German university. The proper autonomy of its faculty and students occurs in retrieving the essence that is lost to view. The university takes charge of itself—heads itself—and finds its future in this activity. It finds its 'head' by the discipline of holding itself in question, by knowing that its essence is not manifest in its current self-understanding or institutional identity. We are not led to believe that the essence is something to be known at the end of a search. The essence, rather, appears to take place as the university community holds itself in question in *Selbstbesinnung*, in attentiveness to itself, recollection of itself, and self-reflection. The attentiveness that Heidegger emphasizes appears to occasion displacement of the university's identity vis-à-vis an essence different from the identity in which the university holds itself. "Autonomy comes to stand only on the ground of self-attentiveness," and this attentiveness can turn the university to its essence when the university heads itself. Heidegger is invoking both a mentation that he finds rare in the university and a culture's history that can return the academy to its originary mission. At this point we can say that the essence does not constitute the university's identity. Its identity is constituted by searching for and returning to its essence. The question is whether and how the university will assert and find itself.

(6) The *will* to the essence of the German university is closely affiliated with the will to disciplined knowledge *[Wissenschaft]*. In *Selbstbesinnung* the mission of the German people and the self-affirmation of the university come together under the heading of the essence of the university. The disciplined knowledge of the university's faculties educates and cultivates "the leaders and guardians of the fortune of the German people." Hence, the future leaders and guardians are followers of the knowledge and culture that the university maintains, advances, and teaches. The German people knows itself in its state, Heidegger says, so the education of the leaders of the state in Germany's universities brings together the people's self-understanding, disciplined knowledge, the future and destiny of the German people, and the will to the essence of the German university. The university community must combine its disciplines with the university's essence and stand firm with German destiny "in its most extreme need."

Whatever this need might be, it will be addressed by the elusive essence of the university and the disciplines, at least three of which—history, sociology, and political science—have indirectly been called into question in the preceding paragraphs. The disciplines must be formed and presumably transformed by this essence. Already the essence of the German university, for which we have as yet no name or definitive interpretation, is heading up the organization of Heidegger's address. We can imagine at this point in the lecture that both university disciplines and the fortune of the German people are, on Heidegger's terms, being addressed—headed—by the form and movement of his remarks. The turn to essence is being made. Heidegger is also laying the groundwork whereby the German university provides a unifying force for all national culture and for the evaluation of good and ill fortune in the state. The German university is to be the leader of German culture when it is organized in self-attentiveness by its historical essence. The turn to essence is to unify national culture.

(7, 8) The newly developed and up-to-date disciplines, or their critique, will not help with Heidegger's question about the essence of the university and the disciplines. They function with virtually no careful contact with their history nor with critical evaluations of the assumptions that pervade them. They lack the range of reference and the persistence of self-criticism to put us in touch with the question of essence, even when we engage these disciplines critically. No *Selbstbesinnung* there. Given the drift of the disciplines toward mere superficiality—a motley cacophony of academic talk without substance—his hearers must decide whether to allow this disciplinary drift and the rapid demise of discipline in any serious sense of the word. Heidegger leaves hanging the question of how to attempt to restore traditional disciplinary knowledge to serious knowledge and thought and turns to the question of what the necessary conditions are for the disciplines to exist and be "*for* us and *through* us," that is, what the disciplines would become if they were developed in *Selbstbesinnung* with attention to the essence of the German university. The *us* seems to refer to those who are now engaged in the de-struction and questioning that clears the way for the appearance of the essence of the German university, to those who in the process of this address constitute the assertion of the German university.

(9) The necessary move, if Heidegger's colleagues are genuinely to find themselves in their state, is to return to the beginning of their heritage, to the time of departure that brings them to the situation of their intellectual and mental existence *[Dasein]*. In Greek philosophy the West experienced its awakening in its interrupting departure from the national and cultural characteristics that had held intellection in provincial bondage. This is a move on Heidegger's part that will play a significant role in the remainder of his address and in our understanding of it. Greek philosophy rises above the Greek *Volkstum*, that is, above the Greek national, ontic, and ethnic character. The move beyond its ethnic character is important in the context of Heidegger's claims: he is arguing that the German university should not be restrained or defined by its present cultural situation. His move here is analogous to that in *Being and Time* in which he shows that proper selfhood must be formed by reference to its interrupting being, not to itself. The German university must rise up to its essence, beyond the

hold of current opinion and knowledge. This move to the *Aufbruch* of essence is an ontic ecstasis that occurs solely within the historical dispensation of the Greek-German heritage. On the other hand, Heidegger is arguing that the German university, by virtue of this ontic ecstasis, should mold and form the German state. That claim, as we shall see, is an ethical one, and our question is whether it falls into question in this address. At this point Heidegger directs his hearers to the Greek heritage of the German people and indicates that the Greek philosophical move beyond the *Volkstum* is a decisive and continuing aspect of their German heritage. This is a movement in the Greek language, one that we can expect to indwell the German language, and one that the mission of the German university is to bring to prominence in its institution and its knowledge. Greek philosophy breaks free of the bonds of its popular situation by questioning and conceiving the totality of beings according to its being. This is the revolutionary inauguration of thought that is not under the sway of things in their unquestioned significance and thoughtless impact on the lives of the people. Heidegger's questioning the essence of the German university is in the direct lineage of this ecstasis, while the present state of German disciplinary knowledge is in the lineage of popular domination by unquestioned, inchoate beliefs and preconceptions. So he must persuade his hearers that what they believe in their commonality actually is separate from their common essence and that the essence that is foreign to them gives them a commonality that now is strange to them. He is very much alone at the podium. But disciplinary knowledge is also structured by the heritage of philosophy: Heidegger, in fact, says that all disciplinary knowledge is philosophy and is bound to its commencement, from which disciplinary knowledge draws the vigor of its essence as long as it grows and develops in the opening that marks its philosophical beginning. The power *[Macht]* of this beginning, which we already know is brought to bear in essential *Selbstbesinnung* and which is to imprint the entire German culture, can be reinstated in the culture and intelligence of the German people, but only at the cost of breaking inherited bonds and transforming what occurs in the process of coming to know the world. The clear implication is that a transformation of language *[Sprache]* must take place as a condition of this inheritance and that such a transformation will have revolutionary consequences for the university disciplines.

(10–13) The Greek experience of breaking the hold of everyday knowledge and belief gives knowledge an essence and bearing that originated in the West. A continuing and leading departure from the everyday is a characteristic that German scholars and thinkers can regain for their dasein. *Regain* in this context means a transformation of people's existence by reappropriating an originary aspect that indwells their language and tradition but is lost to the knowledges that characterize German culture. Heidegger's emphasis on the intrinsic relation of dasein and knowledge is pronounced as he turns to the Greek heritage in German language and thought. To "win back" the Greek essence of disciplined knowledge is to redress the German way of being.

Aeschylus's Prometheus says that "'knowing, however, is far weaker than necessity.' This is to say: All knowing about things remains previously delivered over to the overpowering destiny and fails before it." Heidegger translates *techne* as knowledge *[Wissen]* and anticipates the claims that knowing, disciplinary knowledge, and philosophy are all characterized by departure from essence and that they are not themselves essential or *wesentlich*. The weakness of knowing, we shall find, is its 'distance' from the revealing and concealing of being, a distance that is in part measured by its defiance. The further implication of translating *techne* by *Wissen* is that as knowledge finds its mission and telos in essence, its productions disclose essence, although they do not constitute a thought of essence. The essence of the German university then delimits knowledge, and knowledge gives expression to this delimitation. Within this delimitation disciplinary knowledge recognizes its subservience to a surging event that makes knowledge as we know it possible. Such knowledge allows a confrontation of its present state—dominated, we may surmise, by technology and subjectivity as well as by a complacent forgetfulness of everything essential—with essence that is traced in but overlooked for most of its history. Knowledge is thus derived from a destiny-giving dispensation, from a *Wesen*, that is not to be circumscribed by knowledge, but which may come in the German university to its own disclosure by the attention of disciplinary knowledge to its questionableness and origin. Knowing can be a *techne* that knows how to bring itself to its essence and how to imprint both the process of willing the essence and the meaning of the process on German life. But as *techne* it will not be the thought of being. In this sense, Heidegger intends his address to constitute a process of knowing in the sense of *techne*. Only if it disrupts itself before the disclosure of *Wesen*—only if it puts itself in question—will this address escape the bonds of the technological age that circumscribes it and its values and makes possible a way of thinking that is not knowledge.

In order to fail properly, knowledge must develop "its most extreme resistance," for only then does "the full power *[Macht]* of hiddenness rise up." The discipline of knowledge taken by itself exists in spite of destiny. People attempt to counteract the implacable flow of events; that is, they interrupt the flow by the intervention of knowing and appear to challenge the unmitigable process of destiny by the power of their knowing. As knowledge becomes more disciplined and thorough, the concealing of things, their imperceptibility and withdrawal from the grasp of knowledge, is all the more unavoidable. Knowing genuinely fails before the "unfathomable unalterability of beings." In the language of *Being and Time* we could say that this failure is proper to knowledge. In this failure beings are opened up in their unfathomable unalterability. They are disclosed to knowing in their dimension of unknowability and hiddenness. The defiance of knowing fails in its own intractability and finds, by owning its failure, its truth—the openness of beings in their concealment. In contrast to every-day knowledge and certainty, this knowledge finds its essence as its defiant will against destiny collapses before the unrelenting concealment of the beings that it knows, and in this process the originary Greek experience again emerges.

We readily see that knowing, by virtue of its effort to overcome the world's, and particularly human, destiny, is predisposed to rely on itself, to separate itself from the force of inevitability, and to forget its own destiny, that is, to forget its inescapable impotence. In that case, knowledge would play a blind role in the concealment of beings, oblivious to its own fate of concealing and revealing. Knowing then would not be able to speak of its destiny in its destiny, but would conceal the concealment of beings in its language and thought. It would be a mere technology instead of a *techne,* that in its resistance to destiny and the everyday comes up against its limits and finds that disclosedness that both defines its destiny and offers it its fortune.[5] Far from understanding *theoria* as distant and pure observation and reflection that enacts itself for its own sake, the Greeks experienced in theoretical activity a passionate closeness to beings in their travail. They struggled to conceive and to carry out a way of thinking that, in its troubled closeness with beings, is always like a question and is the highest measure of *energeia. Theoria* is the highest and most genuine *praxis.* For the purposes of Heidegger's address, the primary point is that thinking and disciplined knowledge are not just cultural values for the Greeks, but are "the innermost invoking center of the entire national-political dasein." They constitute a power that encompasses dasein and keeps it well focused, because the Greeks know and think with regard to the failure of knowledge before destiny. Heidegger is giving emphasis to an involvement with beings that continuously (that is, originarily) experi-ences the rift of beings vis-à-vis the stubborn certainty whereby people establish the semblance of their own destinies in their communal and social lives. He is further showing that the center of German culture is not only, at its best, a highly disciplined knowing, but one that knows itself to be without power before its disclosing and concealing destiny. Whether this "impotence" shapes the cultural power of knowledge in Heidegger's address is a question we shall hold in mind.

To be well focused, dasein is thus in its passion to be held close to beings in their perplexing, troubled, and fateful concealment. People attach, as it were, to their destiny when the limits of their knowing are appropriated in the impact of the concealment of beings. Their "defiance" of destiny, when properly centered, allows the disclosure of immeasurable destiny that will not be captured in the language of disciplined knowledge. In this context a people's self-determination is put in question by the indetermi-nate reach of beings in their concealment. A considerable rift occurs in the cultural fabric, a break from the certainties of organized, institutionalized, ritualized ways of living, and when this rift is appropriated in trained and careful knowledge, such knowledge 'centers' and focuses human being. A 'decentering center' heads up genuine knowledge and reveals the indeterminate, nonteleological destiny of a people. "Disciplined knowledge," Heidegger says by way of summary, "is the questioning resistance [to destiny] in the midst of the ever self-concealing totality of beings. This negotiating perseverance knows as it preserves and negotiates its impotence before destiny." This impotence focuses and disciplines the power of knowing as the power of knowing forms and leads people in the entirety of their culture. One could expect at this point a severe critique of German political culture, and why such a critique is not forthcoming focuses our own questions about Heidegger's address. Does he replace the impotence of *his* disciplined knowledge with a power of cultural formation that, true to his ethnic tradition, is unquestioningly exuberant in its sense of essence and destiny?

(14–16) Heidegger uses a virtually marching cadence as he speaks of the beginning of the essence of disciplined knowledge and its "irruption" in the future. His language throughout this rectorial address appeals to power and often has a strident, elevated, and spirited quality in spite of its theme that the essence of academic knowledge and of the academy's leadership is beyond the power and skill of academics and politicians alike. As he makes the transition to discuss the situation of the disciplines, he notes the roles of Christian theological interpretation and mathematical-technical thought in distancing the beginning of the essence of disciplinary knowledge. He underscores the nonnarrative character of this beginning— its coming to the Germans from the future—and names the beginning "the greatest," which cannot be overcome by the perversions that have let it lapse into obscurity as they have given it expression. Only if the German academics join themselves in a fitting way—release themselves—to this beginning, with its fateful decree for knowledge, will knowledge become the innermost necessity of their dasein. Their situation, their being, and its structure of necessity will join appropriately to disciplinary inquiry and its Greek-pronounced destiny in a future that reinherits a lost fortune. So if they are to be fitting to the originary enunciation of their beginning, the disciplines must both be appropriate to their essence and become fundamental for the intellectual and political occurrence of German existence *[Dasein]*. The greatness that Heidegger celebrates gives hope for overturning technological predominance and democratic slackness of discipline. A new beginning for German culture is under way.

Heidegger's play in the last two paragraphs on *fügen*—fit together, join, unite, dispose, decree, accommodate to, be fitted, suited or proper—and *Verfügung*—decree, disposition, enactment, arrangement—indicates that the German intellectuals are to *arrange* their way of being in a way *fitting* to the beginning of the essence of their disciplines, which has *bestowed* on those disciplines, as though by *decree,* a *disposition ordered* by it.

The italicized words mark this play. The further implication in the context of the rectorial address is that the German university is to carry out the 'decree' of the beginning of the essence of disciplined knowledge in the organization of its disciplines, knowledges, and education. But such organization is founded in the rupture of the ordinary orders of life by the question of the being of beings. Hence, Heidegger says that the fitting connections to the beginning are to be found in disciplined self-attentiveness, fundamental questions, developed uncertainties, severe self-critique, the maintenance of the question of being, and that way of thought that eventuates in these endeavors—all of which disrupts what we ordinarily consider traditional knowledge and proper institutionalization.

(17) If it is true that ours is a heritage in which we are without ballast and are bereft in the midst of things, if *that* is *our* situation of extreme need, if it is true that in our usual search for knowledge the very essence of knowledge is lost, a claim that is analogous to Nietzsche's discovery in his search for God that God is dead, and if it is true that our very own and most proper [eigenstes] dasein confronts a great metamorphosis, then what is the situation of disciplinary knowledge? The modern situation is quite other than it would be if dasein's most proper being were welcomed in our disciplines.[6]

(18) Since we are in no position to know what is, having lost the language and manner of thought necessary to this knowledge, having lost even the passion proper to the endeavor, we are relegated to cultivating questions. "Questioning becomes the highest form of knowing." The purpose of the questioning is heralded in the Greek persistence in holding out without reserve and with wonder before the way things are. But we find ourselves now, given the change of fortune in our heritage, vulnerably exposed to the hidden and uncertain, that is, to the questionable. Questioning is the highest configuration of knowing. It "unfolds its most proper strength in unlocking what is essential in all things." It leads to utter simplicity regarding what is inevitable and, in the context of this address, regarding what is specifically inevitable in the heritage of Germany. The interruption of ordinary life in Greek culture now interrupts German culture, and properly so, given the heritage-forming impact of this interruption. It calls for questioning in the absence of language and thought appropriate to both the being of things and the ecstasis that the being of things occasions for thought. It calls for a simplicity of focus that is not imaginable within the current state of committed scholarship. The lost transformation of the question of being recoils on itself and becomes transformation of certain knowledge into a discipline of questioning. Ironically, this discipline is to lead the German university in its self-assertion.

(19) Heidegger emphasizes the power of questioning to *interrupt* the common certainties, which are divided in the academy into distinct, segregated bodies of knowledge, and to *initiate* a *unifying* force among these disciplines. This combination of interruption and unification controls a

major strand of thought in the remainder of the address. His language becomes more strident and willful as he condemns the encapsulation of disciplinary knowledge and as he insists on a way to bring unity to them by the discipline of questioning. On the one hand, he shows that the distribution of knowledges is uncentered and lacks a unifying essence. On the other, the interruptive essence of knowledge will radically disturb the divisions of knowledges and bring them to a focused and centralizing power.

When we hold in mind that the essence of the disciplines is indeterminate and thoroughly questionable, that it breaks certainty and unsettles working assumptions from the ground up, that it is not yet thinkable or knowable, and that it is defined by an essential impotence of disciplined knowledge, the confidence of Heidegger's own assertions appear all the more questionable. What accounts for this counterflow, this clash of assertion and unassertability? He wants to transform the German university and German culture. He wants to imprint the essence of the German university by a far-reaching metamorphosis of learning and teaching. His address constitutes a pressing insistence on heading the German university by a leadership that adheres to the call of the obscured essence. He has insisted on the German university's freedom from the defining authority of the state, the society, or the institution's infrastructure. His appeal to the autonomy of the university in its complex heritage outside of the present cultural and political regime is unmistakable. He reflects the stubbornness of his own appeal in the resistance that he notes as a characteristic of Western knowing, a resistance that allows the unknowableness of beings to stand out in relief. He *knows* the direction that the German university is to take, and he draws this cord of knowledge tightly around the degraded and, we may assume, nihilistic state of German learning and culture. He clearly gives his Freiburg audience and German academia their marching orders with a heightened and spirited sense of vocation. Instead of a starved and depleted dispersion of information- and profession-dominated fields, he invokes the "fertility and blessing of all world-shaking powers" that will nourish human existence in the plenitude of their history. These powers include nature, history, language, thought, fate, disease, madness, and technology. With persistent and questioning attention to the essence of knowing, Heidegger says, with certainty of knowledge, their knowledge will lead people back to a wholeness and unity that is presently beyond dream. The discipline of questioning will galvanize the German people in a unified endeavor of mind and draw them together with their lost inheritance into a new and productive community. He foresees a *praxis*—and he attempts such a *praxis* in his rectorial address—that will eventuate in a renewed encounter with beings in their unfathomable questionableness. He is applying his thoughtful obsession with being to the shaping of a new world. His ethnic hope and its agenda have led him into ethical thought.

(20) The tension between questioning and certainty indwells the essence of disciplinary knowledge when this essence is taken in the sense of "resist-

ing in a questioning and vulnerable way in the midst of the uncertainty of beings as a whole." *Questioning, vulnerable [ungedeckt],* and *uncertainty* could be taken to caution against an all-out assault on the question of essence, and Heidegger will give priority to resistance, struggle, and revolution because of the vulnerability of essence. But when the German people will the essence of disciplinary knowledge, theirs is an essential will, a *Wesenswille,* that "creates for our people a world of the innermost and most extreme danger, that is, its world of true mentation and remembrance" [seine wahrhaft *geistige* Welt].

Is the most extreme danger reflected in Heidegger's call? Is the vulnerability and uncertainty of the resisting firmness *[Standhalten]* of knowledge heeded in Heidegger's words? Is the danger recognized in the cadence of his address? One could well expect Heidegger to step back from a headlong will to essence, whereas his assertion here is in a volition and for a volition that is based in certainty concerning uncertainty. There is no recoil in a questioning uncertainty before its perception and situational meaning. The march to essence is not in question. A direction for committed action controls Heidegger's ethical agenda.

Further, no specter of uncertainty appears to haunt Heidegger's appeal to *"Geist,"* which he defines as "originary, attuned, knowing, resolved openness *[Entschlossenheit]* regarding the essence *[Wesen]* of being." And the *"Geist"* of these paragraphs? Heidegger is firm; his *Standhalten* is not in question. *"Geist"* is neither cleverness nor worldly reason nor argumentation, he says. It does not properly lead to the artificial divisions in the disciplines or to self-enclosed methodologies. It leads to danger in the life of the mind that grips and shakes one to the core. He uses the word specifically to reinstate the priority of *Entschlossenheit* and the question of being in relation to the university disciplines. But the strident shaping power of openness to being and the power of the will to follow it overrides the vulnerability of open resolve and leads one to a sense of aggressive spiritedness that one otherwise might assume Heidegger would wish to avoid by his typical avoidance of a positive use of a *Geist.* His appeal invokes a sureness of dedication that recalls the spirit of ethical discourse. *This* spirit, in fact, is a haunting element in his address that he ignores. As he transforms the word to his own purposes, an incautious, ethically centered optimism nevertheless overrides the question of ethics, and the creations of the *Wesenswille* appear to track a course that is without question true, no matter how ill-advised the specific efforts along the way might be.

If we read Heidegger to be using the new hopefulness and exuberance characteristic of many Germans at the time of his address, using them as an entree to a far more cautious and meditative endeavor, if his cadences and invocations constitute a strategy, we could say that Heidegger is leading his hearers to a way of knowing and thinking that will recoil on the incautious loftiness of spirit and transform it into a different kind of reticent thoughtfulness. He does speak of a knowing that finds its disposition in open resolve, and we expect that kind of knowing to be one of reserve and uncertainty. But even as a strategy, in the context of the self-assertion of the German university, his thought is overwhelmed by the ideas and ideals of unity, which are firmly associated with the Führer principle and by the German ethos of which he is a part. The complexity of the rectorial address is found in its affirmation of an unknowable essence of beings, which eventuates in a certain stubbornness of mind (one of the connotations of his use of *Standhalten*) before the unfathomable uncertainty of beings as a whole, in combination with an unquestioning affirmation of this stubbornness of mind as he applies his thought to the shaping of German culture and the German university. In this application, in the ethical move, the priority of the question fails in Heidegger's assertion of it. We can expect that the processes of thought and inquiry idealized by Heidegger are to result in a discipline of questioning. But the affiliation of his thought with the exuberant sense of new life and hope that accompanied National Socialism for many people, this ethnic and ontic exuberance, his attaching his thought to the philosophy of will and volition, his uncritical allegiance to the practical power of the idea of unity, and his failure to link dispersion and the priority of the question: these aspects of Heidegger's ethnic identification of German destiny and Greek experience in the application of his thought introduces a play of power and unity in his quest for cultural leadership that mandates the loss of the question in his assertion of its priority. The ecstatic dimension of thinking appears to be lost in a practical German ideal in 1933.

"The world of the mind of a people . . . is the power of the deepest preservation *[Bewahrung]*[7] of the people's earthly strength and the strength of their blood; it is the power of the most inward excitation and most far-reaching trauma *[Erschütterung]* of their dasein. The world of the mind alone guarantees greatness for the people." This world will allow the people to decide between the will to greatness and the luxury of decline and to make this decisiveness the beat to which the people march into their "future history." In the context of this address, the meaning is reasonably clear that the preservation *[Bewahrung]* of the strength of earth and blood, the traumatic power that excites and shakes their dasein, and the greatness they must choose over decline are to come by attentiveness to the intrusion of the question of being, whereby they will rise above their own *Volkstum*.[8] But a subtle shift of emphasis has occurred in the last few paragraphs. There is an insistence on the insistent quality of the German people, a failure to see clearly that the language of will, earth, blood, and power, and the very cadence of the address are of the *Volkstum*, the national, ontic, and ethnic character of the culture. Now those qualities are affirmed, and the expected ontic ecstasis of the essence of the German university becomes for all practical purposes an insistent affirmation of the excitation and elevation of a national culture that feels that it is recovering itself.

Mediocrity and laziness of mind may well be interrupted by Heidegger's proposal, but the everyday interpretations of strength and German identity and the everyday hope for German greatness and destiny become a definitive part of his agenda. Heidegger has moved from a proposal that holds in question values that tend toward universalization and self-elevation to one that takes responsibility without question for a people's privileged calling in Western culture. Instead of an interruption of these values and ideals, there is now a passionate affirmation of them. Heidegger appears to believe that he can move through this affirmation to a "deeper" affirmation that will destructure both the German culture and his present allegiance to it. But that conviction occasions his not maintaining the question in the midst of his strategy; that is, it occasions the kind of oversight that we would expect of everyday life on the basis of his account of it in *Being and Time* without the reversal that moves in the everyday and outside of the monopolizing power of the everyday.

(21) This loss of the question clarifies the increasing emphasis that Heidegger gives to the positive function of the resistance of knowledge and the consequent deemphasis on the *ecstatic* uncertainty of the world. That uncertainty now is interpreted by him in terms of the world's ontic danger. His issue is leadership in the face of this danger and uncertainty, and his account of leadership is one of the points in which his interrupting question of being is especially obscured. The danger is not found so much in temporality and its being forgotten in our concept of time or in the ecstasis of thought—although these are not inconsistent with what Heidegger says—as it is found in the uncritical disciplines of information, interpretation, methodology, and the professions. The Freiburg faculty, he says, "must recoil forward, that is, spring back [*Vorrücken*] to the outposts of danger in the constant uncertainty of the world." His argument is that if scholars resist single-mindedly "in the midst of the essential and oppressive nearness of all things" and if a common question and communally attuned saying arises, then out of this resistance to the insistent world and out of the growing communal saying will come strength for leadership. When one is "empowered by the deepest and destined vocation [*Bestimmung*] and broadest obligation," one is not a solo performer or an isolated individual, but plays a role in a heritage that is community-forming and that arises from what binds individuals together as a people. Such obligation forms the basis for selecting the best and for awakening a following of those characterized by a new mind. That we are involved within an ethos and are not now under the 'leadership' of the destructuring question of being is clear from the ending of the paragraph. We do not need to awaken a new following, Heidegger says. The German student body "is on the march. And *whom* it seeks are those leaders through whom it wills to so elevate its own destined vocation that *it becomes a grounded, knowing truth,* and through whom it wills to place word and work into clarity of interpretation and effect" [second emphasis added].

(22) Out of the *Entschlossenheit*—open resolve?—of the German student body "which stands firm [*standhalten*] with German destiny in its
most extreme distress, comes a will to the essence of the university."
This is the student body that has been organized under the new structure
designed to integrate them into the National Socialist movement. Heidegger
stops considerably short of saying that the student body, as it is constituted,
wills the essence of the university; rather, theirs is a true will "insofar
as[9] the student body places itself under the law of its essence through
the new student code and thereby for the first time circumscribes this
essence." He is using one of the continuing concepts of this address, that
by a disciplined and firm circumscription of purpose and by a passionate
pursuit of that purpose for essential definition over against the easy mediocrity of everyday life, the stage is set for the emergence of a clarity of
vision regarding what is genuine and what is bogus. The division of culture
into what is essential and what is everyday is a first, crucial step in the
direction of proper questioning and spirited mentation. When radical danger
is perceived in a culture and a movement seeks to define it over against
something essential, the following debate can progress to increasingly
proper thought. I doubt that it occurred to Heidegger that a formula can
justify most kinds of dogmatism and closed systems of beliefs, and it surely
did not occur to him that this formula was not in question in the way
he used it in his address. The double edge of his claim was not clear:
"The highest freedom is to give the law to oneself." On the one hand,
this claim sets the university free of the definitive authority of the state
and in a certain sense divides it from political authority. On the other,
it allows for a strictly ethos-dominated redetermination and a traditionally
ethical posture that seeks totalization, unification, and authority over all
fundamental differences, one that tends to the inflation of relative rights
and goods into axioms that seek to govern by suppressing all serious differences and to the inflation of radical differences into opponents of cosmic
proportions. True freedom is contrasted to "the much-heralded academic
freedom" that will be banished from the German university. Academic
freedom is not genuine. It merely allows individual arbitrariness and lack
of restraint. The student body, as well as the faculty, must be placed in
those restraints and services that will draw the boundaries tightly and
form a community of common endeavor for the sake of what is genuine
and proper for the culture. With the proper concept of freedom in tightly
controlled limits, the students will be brought back to their truth. Heidegger
is unmoved by the possibility that openness to the disclosing/concealing
clearing of truth can be facilitated by a maximum allowance of differences
and the severe discipline of allowing practical axioms to fall apart in the
face of what is not integrable by the ethos's highest standards.

(23–26) The three "equally primordial" services or "binding powers"
for students are labor service, armed service, and knowledge service. These
provide the *techne* that will return the culture to its essence. The first

binds them to the community, the second to "the honor and mission *[Geschick]* of the nation in the midst of other people," and the third, which is most germane to Heidegger's purposes, to the intellectual and mental *[geistige]* mandate of the German people. Students in the service of knowledge are not merely trained for professions or given a survey acquaintance with essences and values. "The German people have an effect on its [not *their*] destiny by inserting its history in the openness of the predominance of all world-shaping powers of human existence *[menschlichen Daseins]* and prevailing at every turn in its mental world." That is, the preponderance of technology and subjectivity carry within them the disclosiveness of being and the call back to the originary irruption of the question of being. Only by questioning this state of knowledge will the people find their way back to what is genuine and essential in their heritage. Their forgetfulness of being must come to light in the midst of the forgetfulness. There is no place to stand outside of it. The question of essence in the context of technologies of power will allow the limits of modern culture to be known. Presumably technology will recoil on itself and develop into a self-overcoming movement within the power of the question of essence. If this account, typical of Heidegger, were applied to his own address, then appeals to power and national pride, the use of time's rhythms and cadence, the general ethnocentricity of the address, and the National Socialist sympathies would recoil on themselves and lose, in this address, their vocational authority. But Heidegger's specific claim is that German people must expose their dasein to the most extreme questionableness, and in this process they become a genuinely spirited people, thoroughly housed within *their* destiny. Their destiny is beyond question.

The "leaders and guardians" must be uncompromisingly clear in their "elevated, widest-ranging, and richest knowledge." Students serve this knowledge. Since they are to learn to serve the destiny of the German people, they must be led by those who know the dasein of the people, the dasein that is in severe danger; that is, they must be led by a knowledge that is itself in severe danger and that appropriates its danger in its knowing. This danger appears to be the force that puts knowledge in question. The predominant power of beings makes being questionable, Heidegger says, and forces the people to work and fight for the cause of being; the questionableness forces the people into a state of struggle and search which the professions must serve. The *Übermacht,* the prevailing power, of beings *makes* being questionable and *makes* the people work, fight, and belong to a state. Heidegger's attention is riveted by this *Übermacht*. The posture of genuine knowledge is one of *Standhalten,* a resisting firmness. Now it appears to be shaped not by the welcoming openness of being and the concealing mystery of being, but by the everyday Western hostility to being. The questionableness of dasein here is shaped by its threatened role on the world stage, not by its ecstatic temporality. The truth and essence of the German university is conceived to be under siege, and the initial steps toward defending them are formed in regimental discipline.

What predominates in this part of Heidegger's rectorial address? Where is the move beyond the national self-interpretation of Germany as privileged in the destiny of being? What has overcome the originary question of being and turned it into a question of national destiny? Where is the thinking that proceeds in our questionableness, that finds itself intrinsically in question and not put in question by threatening external forces? How is it that compulsory military service and work service are equally primordial *[gleichursprünglich]* with genuine knowledge in the "German essence"? And why does the German essence uniquely have its privilege in the dispensation of the question of being? Why has Heidegger's question of thought become national and ethical without question?

(27–29) Heidegger is certainly aware of the possibility of misguidance in the academic order that he outlines. All of this will work properly only if the members of the university so dispose themselves that their mental-historical existence is appropriate to the distant predisposition of its beginning. He returns to the language of paragraph 16 and its play on *fügen* and *Verfügung* in order to say that just as the faculty is to arrange itself in a manner fitting to the essence of the German university, so the students, too, must be under this decree and must constitute themselves in accordance with it. The cadence changes. There is now caution and qualification in Heidegger's words. He refers back to his discussion of disciplinary knowledge and its academic orders. He specifies that only that knowledge is intended which defines the essence of the German university, which, he recognizes, is the school that is elevated by its originary mission. It is the knowledge that will teach the German people the power and privilege in their destiny and lead and cultivate them by virtue of their appropriating this essence. This knowledge obligates them to considerably more than objectivity about reality. It makes obligatory the simple and essential questioning that is the basis for any so-called objectivity.

(30–33) We thus have a double movement: The concept of proper disciplinary knowledge must shape the German university by taking hold of faculty and students alike. This concept *[Begriff]* must seize *[ergriffen]* and hold those who make up the university. At the same time this concept must intervene in and transform the defining forms of the faculty and the academic organization. The transforming hold of this concept of disciplinary knowledge, analogous to the resisting firmness by which faculty and students come to and maintain disciplinary knowledge, on the one hand, falls just short of rigidity and, on the other, by virtue of its strict discipline provides a context in which the essence of the university can be approached. The faculty carries out its mission *only* when it shapes the oppressing powers of dasein into "the *one geistige* world of the people." And the organizing body must also tear down the departmental barriers and overcome the stifling aspects of professional training. When the faculties and the academic organization begin to raise the simple and essential questions, "both students and teachers are encompassed by the *same* final necessities and pressing concerns which are indispensable for the dasein of the people and state."

(34–36) This will be a slow process. Not only has it not yet been practically initiated in the university, but we can expect it to take a very long time. The character proper to this mission must be broadly cultivated among all related people. Heidegger mentions rigor, responsibility, and superior patience. The required reorganization and reconceptualization will not occur as minor adjustments. Heidegger is clear that he is proposing a long process that will have revolutionary consequences. "One imprinting force"—that is what he wants the academic community to be in its work, legislation, and administration. The university is to be like a stamp, the kind used by a notary public or, in Germany at that time, by a university official, to give a legitimating imprint to a document. It is to give the imprint of the simple unity of the essence on all who come under the forces of its influence. Strength of will must be nurtured and the form of the imprint slowly forged, while the dispersion of the academic community, its laissez-faire attitudes, its foolish misrepresentation of freedom, its allowance of widely divergent methodologies and disciplinary traditions, and its blindness to the unity of its essence are purged by the emerging piety of simple and single-minded questioning. On the one hand, the present state of things does not fare well in this address. On the other, a bureaucrat's decisive and sometimes presumptive certainty seeps into the imagery and provides a unity and a sterile purity for the context of questioning that leaves very little room for doubt about how questioning is to go on. Heidegger is *so* certain about the unity and mission of the essence of the German university.

(37–38) Heidegger picks up the cadence again. In the midst of emphasizing the simple importance of the essence of the German university for shaping service and knowledge, he begins to highlight words more frequently. He is clearly worried about superficiality and ill-directed enthusiasm among the students, and his anxiety is evident as he summarizes what he has said about the student body in direct, hard-hitting sentences. I surmise that he intentionally reflected the cadence and passion of current student and political rhetoric in an attempt to pick the students up where they were, to fire their imagination for the intellectual and moral discipline that he sees as necessary for genuine education and professional life, and to attract them to a model closer to Plato's guardians than the one he finds in the current, relatively light-headed student leadership. His remarks can also be read as a warning to the faculty in reference to the students. The will to essence must be awakened and strengthened, he says. This will must force itself to rise to the highest clarity and culture of knowledge, and it must integrate its engaged knowledge of the people and state into the essence of disciplinary knowledge. These are unaccomplished tasks, Heidegger says, and reflect perceived and extremely important deficiencies in both faculty and student leadership and exertion. But the mood and beat of the appeal also constitutes an intimate association with a quality of certainty, zeal, nationalism, and ethnic glorification that transformed the nonobjective, nonsubjective, nonvolitional difference of the question of being into a defined teleological march, a march that is circumscribed and stamped by language and feeling that are necessarily oblivious to the boundless danger of the question of being for all quasi-religious ethics and national enthusiasm. "All capacities of will and thought, all strength of heart, and all skills of the body must be unfolded *through* battle, heightened *in* battle, and preserved *as* battle." Karl von Clausewitz, the undisputed authority on the defense and expansion of the German nation, is right, Heidegger says. Deliverance will not come by accident. Presumably deliverance will come by maximum preparedness for war. Given the claims of the address, it is to be a war on the entrenched dispersion of the essence of the German university. Given the rhetoric, separation of the battle over dispersion within the university and a less intellectual mobilization is difficult to sustain.[10]

(39–41) "The battle community," in relation to rigor, responsibility, and superior patience, must also be characterized by exceptional simplicity, toughness, and frugality in the way it organizes its existence. It must understand that those who follow must have their own strength, and it must be prepared for and appreciate the inevitable tensions between those who lead and those who follow. Heidegger foresees a lean organization that encourages austere self-discipline and provides an environment in which spirited and talented people can exert themselves and grow. Spiritedness must be cultivated, not suppressed. As all parties take part in the struggle toward simple and essential questioning and toward clarity of purpose, they will strive, fall short, think again, and pursue again their quest. Thoughtful self-attention must be nurtured by struggle. Self-assertion and careful thoughtfulness go together, for Heidegger is not concerned with change for change's sake, but the change that goes to the originary essence of the university. Without attentive thoughtfulness, there can be no access to the university's fundamental element. Then Heidegger adds another assertion: "No one will prevent us from doing this."

(42–43) This is the same 'no one' who does not notice whether people will properly when the mental and spiritual life of the West fails and falls apart, "when the moribund semblance of culture comes in and drags all that remains strong into confusion and lets it suffocate in madness." Whether the crisis culminates in such desolation depends on whether they— those very people in the lecture hall and the others in the German academic community—will themselves as a people with an historical mission. If they do not so will themselves, if they keep to the course that they now follow, their misfortune is assured. They are in crisis together; they are each a part of the crisis. Responsibility weighs heavily on everyone.

(44–46) Heidegger's closing sentences affirm that "we" *do* will the fulfillment of the German people's historical mission, that "we" *do* will ourselves in a young and recent popular strength, which already outstrips us and sets a decisive direction, and that the splendor and greatness of this awakening depend on the profound and far-reaching presence of mind out of which comes Plato's wisdom in *The Republic,* "All greatness stands in the storm." In the original address, Heidegger concluded with "Heil Hitler," which provided a point of political reference for the context of standing firm, willing themselves, and finding a decisive direction. Plato's reference, on the other hand, provides the context for finding, in the Greek dispensation to the German people, what the essence of the willing and the mission is.

Ecstasis in *Being and Time* is found in thought as thought turns in the mortal, ecstatic temporality of its being: thought is ecstatic, for example, in the processes of self-overcoming that we followed; in the question of being thought is ecstatic as it moves beyond the habits of everyday life and belief; it is ecstatic in the *Vorlaufen* of possibility as well as in the proper appropriation of the *Vorlaufen* of possibility. In dasein's open resolve in its being, the proper moment of presence is not found by reference to firm standing or integrated confidence, but in a process of removal from the firmness of an ordering life-world. This remotion *[Entrückung]* is integral to resolve, is consonant with the ecstases of temporality, and defines the question of ethics as that question develops in *Being and Time*. Dasein is thereby able to concern itself with beings out of care in its being for its being. This ecstasis is found in the ontological difference of being and beings that is constitutive of dasein and that frees one, wrenches one free, from the predominance of ethnic values, hope, and visions. In the question of ethics all that a culture prizes is put in question. The ontic ecstasis that we have found in the Rector's address—the ecstasis of the movement of the German mission in the midst of German decadence—solidifies its hearers in a regional enthusiasm that is punctuated by the final salute. It hides the remotion of time in the forward march of a new state of affairs and solidifies a Germanic politics that is far removed from a 'proper' appropriation of the ecstasis of temporality. The address affirms a government internal to a particular ethos. It is a governance that is instituted by education and that totalizes German ideals in spite of Heidegger's intention to give priority to an essence that cannot be identified with German identity. Without a recoiling self-overcoming movement to put the given discourse in question, the address is destined to be ruled by the morbidity of regional values that are out of touch with the movement of their own temporality. This morbidity expresses itself as an enthusiasm that falls considerably short of ecstatic thought as Heidegger had previously defined it and undergone it.

The problem of succumbing to everyday values and of losing the question is one that Heidegger addresses throughout his writing. It is built into his way of thought. Up until he wrote the Rector's address, Heidegger regularly began a given body of thought in a recognized affirmation of the field that circumscribed his thinking. He would then begin to turn that field of assumptions, concepts, etc. into a different *topos* for thinking, as he did in *Being and Time,* which begins with a regional account of the everyday that is not adequately informed by the question of being, or in *The Basic Problems in Phenomenology* in which he begins with a strict phenomenological method that his inquiry into the concept of time overturns. In these cases the movements of remotion and self-overcoming take place as a torsion that is created when a question that is primordial for the language and to which the language is ill-tuned begins to emerge in the process of the inquiry. Heidegger's discipline is one that allows such questions to emerge and that follows the consequences of the emergence in and for the language and conceptuality in which he thinks. He undergoes this movement in the process of the account that he gives.

In his rectorial address Heidegger is convinced that if he begins with the largely technological knowledge of the German academy, with the cadence and rhetoric of the new politics, and with a predisposition in German culture to get to the ground of things by strict discipline, and if he holds these ethnic qualities in the context of the essence of German knowledge and the German university, he is convinced that a self-overcoming remotion will take place over a period of time that will overcome the banal decadence that dominates both the academy and the German culture generally. But the position that he takes in the address, while speaking about the question of essence and less directly about the question of being, does not invoke the priority of question in the movement of the address. A proper appropriateness of ecstasis, on his own terms, does not occur in it. Rather he articulates the priority of *"Wir wollen uns selbst"* (We will ourselves). And consequently the question of ethics does not take place in the thought and language of the address. Instead of standing out in the free openness of the question of being and the disclosure of being, he takes his stand in a stubborn German resistance to contrary *ethea* and in a glorification of one type of national self-interpretation.

In Heidegger's ethnic insistence we found unchallenged the authority of the principles of unity and leadership. His preoccupation with unity in his writings up to 1933, which is expressed in such elements as his inclination to one authoritative methodology, the predominance of one question, and the unity of dasein, was regularly offset by the recoiling and self-overcoming effects of the questions of time, being, and truth. The ecstasis of his thought occurred in the passing away of this authority even as Heidegger wrote within it. But in his address his preoccupation with unity becomes a virtual obsession with the unity of the German university and culture and finds one of its ethical expressions in the principle of the Führer. The wise philosopher as the king's advisor and as the leader of a culture is not only a Platonic and Enlightenment ideal, but one that implicitly maintains the notions of superior, as opposed to inferior, culture and a privileged, quasi-royal access to the principles of the superior culture. Cultural dispersion and nonsynchronized pursuit of many inconsistent ideals and values feel like anarchy inside this ideal. Granted the value of unity and the attraction of new power in a weakened country, a virile German paranoia, and a reemergence of the Führer principle—without the value of unity in being in question—in addition to Heidegger's own extremely conservative convictions about state and academic politics in this state of mind, he is vulnerable to the situation that he judges to be decadent and to the metaphysics that he wants to destructure.

The self-attentiveness that focuses Heidegger's constructive alternative and the way of thought that he wants to exemplify in his rectorial address do not achieve the *ek-stasis* that is necessary if his thought is to avoid the numbing control of the metaphysical stasis that he had put in question so effectively. Had the value of unity fallen into question in a process of recoiling thought, had the question of ethics emerged in the process of his thought, the Führer principle could not have exercised the power that it did. It would have been overturned in the remotion of its own time and Heidegger would have been left uncertain of the values that most attracted him and of his role as Rector. Presumably the uncertainty would not have neutralized him. Perhaps he would have chosen to fellow-travel with the National Socialist party. But he would have been out of step with his own values as well as with those of the party. The questionableness of his position, its "destiny" and the denial of its "destiny," his goals, his hopes would have found articulation in the torsion of his address: the question of his position, not its certainty, would have set its direction and thought. And in that question I believe that radical tragedy and failure gain voice, not silence. The questionableness of axiomatic values is attuned to loss, outcasting, ambiguity, and suffering. The unquestioned direction of a leader, the satisfaction of being properly led, and the desire for a saving hero are wrenched from their moorings in the question of ethics; and had this question exercised much power, Heidegger would probably have felt far more bereft of hope and far more swayed by mortal temporality and the question of meaning than he in fact felt in his Rector's address. On the basis of what he had already undergone in his thought, the address could have shaken his attraction to National Socialism and its metaphysical-ethical underpinnings. The severity of discipline that Heidegger discusses in relation to the call of conscience, a discipline that leads to a twisting free of the surveillance and authority of cultural identity at the same time that one undergoes that surveillance and authority, is replaced in the Rector's address by a severity of disciplined citizenship in a state projected to be under the constant surveillance of a leader who is unchecked by higher or equal offices, and a state that is under the surveillance and authority of a cultural leader who is answerable primarily to an essence that no one properly understands. *In the head's surveillance and authority, the questionableness of essence loses its power, and an ethic replaces the question of ethics.* In this replacement Heidegger seems tragic to me: he appears to defy the destiny of the essence that he expects to lead him and to occasion an ethnic destiny in his thought that overturns the transformation of learning for which he hoped.

The question of ethics is constituted by a disruption of the control of axioms and values that structure and govern the lives of those who live in a given discourse. A discourse marked by the question of ethics, in its interruption of ethical thought and action, is opened to questions and possibilities to which the discourse has been closed and with which the 'normalcy' of the discourse interplays to create a different situation and horizon of thought. This discourse is also attuned to the travail of excluded differences and the pain of transformation. When ways of speaking and thinking appropriate their own disruptions, the inevitabilities that in-dwell their heritage, and the limits to their life-giving values, and do not resist these elements, but learn to give place to them as well as to self-overcoming, then they will be far more attuned to the atrocities and devastation in which they are implicated. The issue presently is not one of judgment, not one of finding out who is right and who is wrong, but one of learning to be attentive to the destruction that a given way of life makes inevitable, usually without noticing. The combination of nurturance and resistance that marks an ethos, the power of identity within a community to give people a firm place and familiarity, and the drive of an ethos toward continuous repetition of its standards and habits mean that an interruption by fundamental questions and differences that put in jeopardy the ethos's self-understanding will be extremely hard to follow.

I have not found it possible to judge Heidegger's politics without making axiomatic for all practical purposes my own politics. I have not been able to avoid a sense of satisfaction, even though it is a painful one, when I recognize what I judge to be his naive stupidity. I believe that I know better than to fellow-travel with fascist movements, and I believe that my democratic values, which preserve among other things academic freedom, are obviously better than his. I know that I do not understand atrocity or the unspeakableness of massive destruction. I am sure that in cataclysmic upheaval, suffering is not measurable or repeatable in thought and language. I feel a measure of confidence and ethnic identity in these recognitions. But when I make my ethical judgments, I also undergo an erasure of the question of ethics, the question that, had it occurred in *his* address, could have had momentous import for Heidegger's politics. I feel myself relatively free of the necessity of such questioning when I face German National Socialism and Heidegger's relation to it. I am very certain in my rejection of it, and I think that all people should be equally certain in rejecting it. I feel no danger in the values that structure my confidence.

But when I undergo the impact of the question of ethics I find that, in Levinas's phrase, the cry of the other—as other—seems to be audible in the passing interruption of my values. Not the value of the other or the dignity of the other or the autonomy of the other or the right of the other. But the cry of the *other*. In the strike of the question's interruption, the measure is taken of universalization, moral clarity, obvious decency, and right-mindedness: the measure of their muffling their own destructiveness, of their genealogies of power and suppression, and of their availability for atrocity. One cannot repeat, in the sense of cannot speak, or re-cognize, either the destruction or the cry, and with it its ethical truths, which cannot be doubted by those included in its mainstream.

Without the interruption of the question of ethics, I suspect that Heidegger was also closed to atrocities that were part of his ethos, as they are part of mine. Without that interruption I am free for the satisfaction of my judgment and am as closed as I believe he was in the address to the *nómos* of destruction that also helped to make his ethos nurturing.

SIX

"'All Truth'—Is That Not a Compound Lie?"

The Ascetic Ideal in Heidegger's Thought

We have seen that the interruption of an ethos—of the values, ideals, practical and theoretical axioms, and habits of mind and heart—can be an occasion for the entrance of possibilities for thought and action that are either suppressed in or foreign to what is ordinary in a culture. When the issue concerns the suffering, destruction, and oppression that are constitutive of an ethos, an interruption of the ethos can make perceptible, if only obscurely, some of the pathogenic elements that are otherwise invisibly a part of the ethos.

One pathogenic aspect of our Western ethos that we have followed is the ascetic ideal. It is characterized by many types of refusal and denial regarding the manner in which human life occurs, and on Nietzsche's account the ascetic ideal reinforces this denial with a habitual insistence on the continuous presence of meaning in all dimensions of life and being. In our ascetic withdrawal from life we join forces with hopelessness, suffering, death, and helplessness by giving them meaning, in our appropriation of them, that far exceeds their occurrence and that subordinates them within a scheme of meaning and hope. The rule governing the ascetic ideal is found in its incorporation and blind expression of the hopelessness and meaninglessness that it is designed to overcome. This incorporation of what it is constitutes the ideal's nihilism for Nietzsche: the affirmations within the ascetic ideal project their opposites and produce a spiral of unwitting and inevitable violence in the spirituality that they create. The denial of life within the boundaries of the ascetic ideal continuously reestablishes the power of the ideal. But when this movement is broken by a self-overcoming like that in Nietzsche's genealogy of the ascetic ideal, the rule of the ascetic ideal is interrupted and a possibility is opened for life-affirmations that do not suppress the most fearful occurrences involved in being alive.

The joyousness of life without the illusion of continuous meaning, the joyousness that Nietzsche found in early Greek culture, was lost, according to his reading, in the course of the increasing cultural dominance of those whose nerve has failed before the disheartening flow of life. The ascetic ideal expresses this failure in its insistence on meaning and in its persistent manufacture of hope out of illusions bred of the failure. Heidegger is perhaps at his most non-Nietzschean point when in his Rector's address he turns to the Greek division between the everyday and the question of being. This is an ironic moment in Heidegger's thought: he traces the origins of his own move to separate the future of the German university from the German *Volkstum,* (that is, from dominant popular culture) to the emergence of the separation of thought from everyday life in Greek culture. But this move is not associated with the joyousness that Nietzsche uses as his reference in delimiting the ascetic ideal. According to Nietzsche's genealogy we have lost an earthly affirmation of life in the midst of the specific suffering of everyday existence. Nietzsche countenances fully the brutality, the fateful shattering of hope, the disappointments that break people's lives, the individual and social tragedies. The debilitation of minds and bodies is juxtaposed to people's savoring food and drink, enjoying sexual pleasure. It is juxtaposed to friendship, the energy of ambition, the struggle between competitors, the mixture of desperation and exhilaration in efforts of accomplishment. Nietzsche's move is toward affirmation in the midst of chaotic living when he speaks of what is lost in the blind and self-deceived chaos of asceticism that is ordered by the illusion of continuous meaning.

In this affirmation one has an awareness, presumably a full awareness, of the otherness to human interest that radically distresses us. People's attention is delimited by it. Rather than escape or turn away from it, people are delimited by it in their relations with things. Rather than appropriate the suffering of life in ascetic self-denial, human beings stand over against its otherness, its unthinkableness, its density. They need not attempt to embody it in forms that seem to shape it to human and thinkable dimensions. They live in the inappropriable, meaningless dark vacuity, with it and other to it, out of it and in it. They are angel and animal, Nietzsche said. Not to be lost, not to be redeemed, not to be overcome, it is juxtaposed to a will to live, an affirmation with, and not in spite of, the chaos. This affirmation does not promise an end to butchery and chaotic insensitivity, but it does provide an awareness of misery, a region for the fullness of its sounds, that is not to be escaped by ideals, goals, and visions that often define our subjection to what we must consider to be the best way of life. The affirmation that Nietzsche uncovers interrupts those satisfactions that are governed by the ascetic ideal and makes a place for the miserable chaos of life that is at once most feared, furthered, and covered over by the ascetic ideal.

Heidegger's move, on the other hand, is toward a break in Western history that makes possible a questioning, attentive thought which, by the effect of the question of being, is drawn away from everyday life, while nonetheless attached to it, and toward a way of living that appears to be more ethereal than Dionysian. This is how it is perceived by Nietzsche's human, who never leaves the earth, even when transported into ecstasy. The factor of withdrawal from the everyday and earthly is more pronounced in Heidegger's thought than in Nietzsche's, although the conflicting emphases are shaded and not always distinct. Zarathustra, for example, withdraws from human society at the beginning, in the middle, and at the end of Nietzsche's poem. We are not to be trapped by the virtues of everyday living, according to *Beyond Good and Evil*. Better to withdraw than to live happily in the herd. But the zigzagging drive of Nietzsche's thought is nonetheless toward the body and earthly life-affirmation in the midst of continuous dissolution of meaning and sense, that unspeakable other of life vis-à-vis human mentation. Nietzsche's withdrawal is away from a traditional escape from life and toward the earthly life that has been all but lost in subjection to ascetic ideals.

Heidegger's thought suggests connectedness in being which, though neither presence nor meaning, gives the basis for hope of retrieval and preservation of something lost and not yet thinkable. In his rectorial address, for example, the cadences of mobilization and marching are toward a discipline of nontechnical thought that will be far beyond the authoritarian measures initially necessary to galvanize German society to the point of willing the true essence of its culture. This chapter addresses the extent to which Heidegger's thought brings to bear the ascetic ideal, the extent to which it includes a process of subjecting the animal, the chaotic, and the meaningless to something that infinitely transcends them and, by its splendor, humiliates them—in spite of the absence of voluntary participation in such a project on Heidegger's part. Does his thought give priority to a seriousness of mind that is inevitably associated with a will to truth? Is there within it a desire for redemption and salvation in some sense of those words? Is his thought akin to spiritual quest, in spite of its intentions? Is there a self-overcoming of spirituality like that which we found so pronounced in the writings of Nietzsche and Foucault? Is there in Heidegger's thought a silence of remove, a wincing silence, before the chaotic flow of appearances in the midst of senseless cries of both pain and pleasure, a silence that delimits the distance between being and beings, one that finds fulfillment in meditative and preserving attention to the highest things, one that is nurtured by distaste for the corruption that accompanies mortality, taints it, and makes it repellent to a sharply honed Western sensibility? If the ascetic ideal without a movement of self-overcoming is an element in Heidegger's thought, we might discover our closeness to his thought, our affiliation with the ascetic ideal, in what we now find to be his limits. Is it possible that the quiescence of his meditations and the elements of silence that accompany it are already attractive to us in our desire to find a way of life that eliminates evil and that eventuates in a community that preserves primarily our difference from animality and from the meaningless glare of being who we are?

We found in *Being and Time* and "On the Essence of Truth" that the questionableness of our thought and values takes place in dasein's standing out of its presence. This ek-stasis takes place in the occurrence of temporality, which Heidegger interprets as the disclosiveness of human being and the world-openness of human being in which beings occur in their own disclosures. The draw of the question of being includes a withdrawal from (and in) the dominance of ordinary language, meaning, and value. The withdrawal is a necessary part of the interruption and of the questioning thought. In this withdrawal we find a mysterious kinship with being in its withdrawal from presence. One of its effects is a severe delimitation of "the everyday" and of traditional philosophy, whose values, meanings, and interpretations are within the domination of the everyday. To remember that the question of being is forgotten in its own heritage is to begin a process of retrieving the division of thought from the everyday that has given our heritage (or at least the German heritage) its temporality and its destiny. This 'otherness' to the tradition of Western thought, this 'otherness' that Western thought traces by antiphrasis, 'defines' temporality in two senses: it opens human time to its own ek-stasis, to its own radically noneveryday dimension, and its interruption of continuity constitutes the mortality of our inherited 'foundations' for life and truth. Ecstasis thus interrupts mortal temporality, the essence, that is, the *Wesen* or coming to pass, of the Western heritage, as well as the ontological difference between being and beings in dasein's ecstatic occurrence. Dasein's propriety, we found, is in questioning and questionableness, and no account of human being, including Heidegger's, can be taken as definitive and certain and also be proper to dasein's being. We found that because of the meaning of temporal ecstasis in Heidegger's thought, his own work is self-overcoming.

The elements of withdrawal from the everyday, the difference between beings and being, and dasein's standing out in the disclosiveness of being are the very elements that hold ethics in question, provide the basis for recoil in Heidegger's thought, and constitute Heidegger's vulnerability to the ascetic ideal. Does the question of ethics reinscribe the ascetic ideal? Dasein's questionableness, its mortal temporality, is not a selfsame identity. It is not subject to categorization. But it is 'uncontaminated', in Derrida's phrase, by everyday life in its difference from everyday life and it is conceived with a seriousness of mind that complements the most heartfelt endeavors of traditional thought. Is this the spirit of seriousness, in spite of Heidegger's holding 'spirit' in question?

The unbroken seriousness of Heidegger's thought seems to be appropriate to the forgetfulness of being and the disastrous control of calculative thought that accompanies this forgetfulness. In it our heritage is at odds with its own temporality, its *Wesen* or essence or coming to pass. But in this great danger, Heidegger's turn of mind, the turning of his mind, up to 1933 appears to promise a listening that connects with and counters the destructive forgetfulness, an ecstasis of thought that is closer to rapture than to a rupture's spasm. There is a continuity between this seriousness of mind regarding being and its forgetfulness, on the one hand, and the cadences of the rectorial address that are preparatory to essential thinking, on the other. Heidegger's early thought harbors an expectation of single-minded endeavor that is unified by a singularity of occurrence, and in spite of his clear insistence that the question of being and the disclosiveness of the world are steeped in the pathogenic contamination of forgetfulness, in spite of the recoils that occur as he thinks through mortal temporality, *disclosure, error, being, essence,* and *ecstasis* inspire a seriousness that draws him toward not just an avoidance, but a ridding of the contamination of forgetfulness, however subject to failure this elimination may be. This seriousness bestows an insistent quality on his thought far in excess of what we might expect given the abysmal difference of being that puts meaning as such in question.

Is this seriousness itself preparatory? Is it an overbearing prelude to a lighter touch? Or does meaning override meaninglessness in Heidegger's seriousness of mind and revert to the ascetic ideal? Had he thought the 'contamination' of the forgetfulness of being in such a way that it could not stand opposed to thought, especially to essential thought, if the interruption of the everyday world were taken as a disruption of mystery as well as of meaning and not only as provisional vis-à-vis a recovery of essential thinking, and if the question of dasein's propriety were lost in multiple experiences of thought, I believe that the interruption of ethics, which characterizes *Being and Time,* would not have seemed compatible with the unifying force for mobilization that Heidegger invoked in his Rector's address or with his national self-identification.

In what sense could dasein's transformation to *Eigentlichkeit* be ascetic? Although one's relations to others and things change in the transformation, although one opens to one's temporal openness and to that of all others, and although that includes a different relation to bodies, a relation not governed by control, mastery, or usage, there is nonetheless an absence of sensuality, dissemination, and, in Foucault's terms, a play of bodies in Heidegger's language. The unity that he invokes, which cannot be a being of any kind, lacks all connotation of body or of the body's dispersions. It is thinkable on Heidegger's terms at this time of his thought only in movements of mind that are presently not describable except in the effects of destructuring, in a recoiling self-overcoming process, the patterns of clarity that have defined Western thought, and in retrieving the question that interrupted the complacency of our early history.

An ascetic self need not be formed in this process, a self that constitutes itself by denying its pleasures and its lack of meaning. And yet, the ecstasis of dasein does not appear to be attuned to bodily pleasure and distress or to find its propriety in the dark, confusing, and often unsatisfying muck of human life. The pleasure and distress of bodies and the senselessness of life are as secondary in this context as they are in most types of elevated spirituality in the West. Does that mean that suffering bodies are also secondary? I am not sure. Does that mean that the other's cry is best heard when it is 'spiritual' anguish and not when it is merely abused or starved? Again, I am unsure. But Heidegger's thought is often closer to a way of praying than it is to an intermingling of bodies, and this meditative dimension waxes rather than wanes as his work proceeds. Saving and preserving the world in a dimension of care-filled listening before the disclosure of beings is one hope in his thought, and Nietzsche's ghost might well rise up in a passion of suspicion over this seeming presence of serious good faith. The danger of the ascetic ideal in Heidegger's thought will not be addressed until preserving, saving, and meditative thought are themselves interrupted and put in question. Surely, the world, language, and the situation of thought and action are too muddled, too filled with cross-purposes, countervalences, and unsolvable dilemmas to allow any saving power or any intensity of careful, thoughtful, deeply informed attentiveness to give them a cleaner, purer, rapturous return to an ungraspable and originary essence. The retrieval of the question of being is as fraught with danger as the forgetfulness of it is, and I suspect that if we forget this, we shall be easy prey to an unbridled desire for meaning and truth, however they are interpreted, at the cost of the very breakage that Heidegger has introduced so powerfully in twentieth-century thought.

We began this chapter on the ascetic ideal in Heidegger's thought with the double possibility that the interruption of ethics provides an opening to hear what is inaudible in our ethos and that Heidegger tends to close that opening by the thought that is intended to maintain it. The closing element is the work of the ascetic ideal in Heidegger's effort to twist free of the forgetfulness of being, particularly, as we noted, in aspects of his thought of ecstasis. In that thought ethics comes radically into question, and in it the ascetic ideal also appears to recoil back on itself, instead of away from itself, and to reintroduce a new ethics of thought.

We turn first to the "Letter on Humanism" to question thought's relation to ethics and the unfolding of the ascetic ideal in Heidegger's later thought. By following the unfolding of the ascetic ideal in this letter we will be able to see more clearly both the ethical dimension of his thought in his breakage of the hold of ethical thought and the danger of ethics in his thinking.

i. The Unfolding of the Ascetic Ideal in the Unfolding of the Appeal of Being

A. THINKING IN THE DRAWING APPEAL OF BEING

In the first paragraph of his "Letter on Humanism," Heidegger advances a thought that figured in a preliminary way in his rectorial address: thinking finds its essence *[Wesen]* in an intrinsic relation to being.[1] Thinking carries out the appeal of being to the essence of human being. To "carry out" *[vollbringen]* means to unfold something in the fullness of its essence, its *Wesen,* its coming to pass. So thinking may unfold the appeal of being in the fullness of its coming to pass in human being's coming to pass. I have interpreted *Bezug* by translating it as 'appeal'. In its *Bezug* to human being—its relation to or draw on human being—being is more like a call in dasein than something standing over against human being and relating to it. "Thinking does not make or bring about the *Bezug.*" Rather, the *Bezug* of being is handed over to thinking from being; it is like an offering that happens as thinking thinks. A double middle voice is audible: as thinking thinks, being (is). Being comes to pass as human being comes to pass thinking. The manifestness *[Offenbarkeit]* of being is in the coming to pass of thought.

The structure of Heidegger's thought in this paragraph is similar to that in his discussion of *Eigentlichkeit* in *Being and Time.* As thinkers (and poets) "watch over" or take care for being (in the sense of "have a care for"), they come to their essence in the watching or caring. Although thought and being are not identical, a sameness of *Wesen* unfolds, not as the subject or object of an action, but as being happens in regard to itself, that is, in a middle voice. The thinking that Heidegger has in mind is being in the middle voice.[2] Heidegger's emphasis is on the *Bezug* of being vis-à-vis thinking because it delimits and interrupts our inherited interpretation of *human* and provides a basis for rethinking *human.* Our emphasis is on this *Bezug* because it indicates that in the interruption of our ethos by the appeal of being we find an accord that goes far beyond any community of agreement that we might construct. The accord of being and human being makes manifest not an essential or defining structure—an essence in that sense—but a quality of belonging that is not at all clear to our usual ways of thinking, one that is close and intimate, like a dwelling that infuses the dwellers and gives them a space of passage that constitutes them. Although such an accord is not a structural continuity, and although it has an abysmal dimension, nonetheless, as accord, it provides unity in the sense of sameness for being and human being. Although it is not a structure of meaning, is not subject to meaning, and in thinking defers the circumscription of meaning, this accord appears to be suited to the metaphors of dwelling, giving, and offering. The proper role of the thinker and poet is approximate to that of a shepherd or to a careful and devoted guardian who by alert attentiveness preserves the manifestness of being. In this attentiveness one comes to pass in the unfolding, not in the vacuity or dispersion, of being. Heidegger speaks of "the simplicity of the manifold dimensions' rule" (LH 6–7). Being is the element of thought that enables thought and brings it to its essence. Thought belongs to being; and being "bestows essence as a gift," makes thinking possible in being's coming to pass, is thought's "may-be," its finite, ecstatic, temporal coming to be.

A releasing serenity, which Heidegger meditates under the name of *Gelassenheit* in another essay, pervades this thought—a striking contrast to the cadences of Heidegger's preparatory rhetoric in his rectorial address. It is not the serenity of dogmatic certainty or of theoretical clarity, but one of deep, virtually unspeakable propriety of being in which nothing in everyday life is privileged.

The may-be of being means that the full range of finite possibility—death and suffering as well as pleasure and happiness in everyday life—are allowed in the fitting accord of thought and being. Heidegger's play on *mögen* 'favoring' and *mögliche* 'possible', in the term *mög-liche,* or may-be, gives emphasis to the disclosiveness of human finitude in the context of being's giving, bestowing—enabling *[vermögen]*—the essence of human being. Being enables thinking to be thinking and is of thinking's disclosive process as thinking's disclosive process is of the enabling disclosiveness of being. Allowance, even the gift, of life in its simplicity accompanies the despair and ruptures of living as well as its moments of peace and congruence. *May-be* suggests the difference of being in its company with existence. In its allowance and affirmation one lives through the difference and is not totally circumscribed by one's travail and success,

Serene joy in the midst of life is clearly projected by this thought. Being's allowance of life, the sameness of this allowance in all divisions of life and in the midst of life's dispersions, the thought (of) being, this middle voice is not ruptured by life. It gives the possibility of releasing serenity in its difference from everyday life. The thought of *its* ontic rupture would be nihilistic for Heidegger. Being is not to be overcome by the disaster or disruption: it is without the possibility of ontic hernia. Nor do the ruptures of living have any privilege in disclosing being. They show the finitude of existence, and they can provide the shock necessary to give vitality to the question of being. But being is voiced in a primordial accord with thought and language, a quiet power *[stille Kraft]* of favoring and enabling that is quite other than the wreckage or satisfactions of life. This accord is beyond the erotic, consumptive, dispensing, establishing, deposing, nurturing, killing, competitive, impotent, controlling, loving, hating, despondent, suffering, abusing, warring, negotiating, peace-giving elements that constrain us to be human. The accord pervades these elements. It saves them in the sense that they *are.* Rather than a reign of chaos, it illuminates them, gives them moment and voice beyond their discourse. Being in its accord means more than the whole of human meaning. It gives unity beyond the lives of humans. The accord of being thus has a redemptive aspect that bestows "the gift of essence," interrupts mere nothingness, as it were, and saves the being of all beings that are destroyed, consumed, or made static in the world of humans. Or at least so it seems. These are indications whose thought is still beyond us, but they are vaguely audible in our belonging to being as this belonging comes to us in our heritage.

More meaningful for Heidegger's thought than meaning itself. More important than the whole of our values. More hale than our most robust vitality. More affirming than our highest love. Beyond our satisfactions. Saving of essence even in our helplessness and hopelessness. Beyond the limits of identity and causality. This dimension of Heidegger's thought is both ascetic and ideal. It restores a seamless mystery of being in the midst of effecting the sharpest cut into twentieth-century thought. It tells us that human being belongs to being and that being, although abysmal and severe in relation to all that we value, is beyond the travail and limits of our common lives. In Nietzsche's terms, the angel rather than the animal and the rupture of the angel provide the stimulus for thought. There appears to be no chaos in the coming of thought's essence, although there is an abundance of mystery. The withdrawal of being and the non-essence of its event are interpreted in the language of mystery under the aegis of bestowal in this aspect of Heidegger's thought. He speaks of chaos only in relation to the dispersions of life that has forgotten its essence. It seems in essence that the bestowal of essence is *the* thought. There appears to be a continuing triumph of being over chaos, and for Nietzsche that *is* the ascetic ideal.

This much is given and forecast in the first three paragraphs of the "Letter." The stakes are high. Without the accord of thought and being, thinking becomes instrumental (LH 8–9). It teaches, elaborates, explains, and solidifies itself into positions to be defended and expanded. It becomes like an ethos in that it both nourishes identity and closes people to differences that threaten the autonomy that sustains them. Chaotic confusion is the result. People confuse essence with personal autonomy, public openness with the enabling openness of being, role-dominated communication with a speaking proper to the human essence, subjective self-possession with essential relation to being. The essence of humanity is thus threatened, and this extreme danger is not apparent to us because our language, rather than homing in on being's bestowal of humanity's essence, covers over the truth of being and "surrenders itself to our mere willing and trafficking as an instrument of domination over being" (LH 9). The dispersion of human life in this confusion of dominations and manipulations and its resulting demeaning of human life and indeed of the entire world has lost the quiet sameness of being. Heidegger does not project a totalizing society, but rather one in which the differences of beings, their disclosiveness, not the uniqueness of their roles, but their essential relation to being in their disclosures, are heard, attended with gentle care, and preserved in their address by our ways of being with them.

This is far from the pastoral romanticism that some readers find in Heidegger and either attack as obscure or appropriate by cultivating rusticity or early twentieth-century ways of life that are unburdened by some of our conveniences. Just as mortal temporality, according to *Being and*

Time, is the meaning of all events in dasein's world, so the bestowal of essence is concurrent with everything in human life, including its perversions and horrors. But Heidegger's intensity of conviction, his desire to be faithful to the appeal and draw of being, and his prophetic sense of both doom and hope provide a setting for single-minded, even obsessed, concern for the simplicity and sameness of being. One expression of this intensity is found in the rectorial address. Another is found in this letter in which the corrupt dispersion of human life is held in judgmental contrast to what appears to be the purity of being—purity at least in relation to lives that are unclaimed by being. Heidegger's rejection of democracy or any other communal system is not the issue. It is rather his longing for reunion with the lost "claim of being" that propels him toward language and thought that struggle for, not the thought of mere difference or of disjunction without unity, but the thought of being that unfolds in the *fullness* of its essence (LH 11). The demands of this quest drive him to separate from the inessential part of the world in an almost priestly way—in the world, but not of it. Is there an inessential part of the world?

That question raises the further question as to whether the question of essence is itself inessential in the sense that it does not lead to the discovery of anything ultimate or have ultimate value for people and in the sense that it is not the primary question of our tradition. Without ultimate value people and beings are heard in the 'mere' quality of their life struggles. Their hierarchies and roles are at best conveniences in a given way of life. Without sanctity their anguish and happiness can be clearly heard—not necessarily heard, but possibly heard—in the interruption of the inherited claims to ultimacy, claims that suggest a staggered range of importance concerning who is anguished or happy. An absence of ultimate importance levels us all, discloses us all without the sanctions of the many orders of our lives. In such an interruption of ethics, the ascetic ideal of Heidegger's approach to being, *this* part of our Western ethos, is momentarily suspended, and the question of ethics affects the beginning steps that one might take toward retrieving something in our tradition that has been lost. The lostness, our common lack of essence, not what has been lost, affects us and provokes us to think in that moment.

Nietzsche and Heidegger are separated by the issue of whether the simple lack of an ontological 'home' and the consequent question of being and its loss move through and define our history. On Nietzschean terms, Heidegger misreads our common history by his thought of the claim of being. *That* claim and Heidegger's attraction to it give voice to the ascetic ideal, the ascetic force that shapes both the claim and our history in its hope-giving, meaning-giving obsession before the chaos and homelessness of human being. The claim of being overrides the accidents and randomness that riddle our economies, thought, and practices. A being's claim on human being and its differences from human being—such elements are found by

Heidegger to be ontic, and the governance of ontological thought by beings and their many differences constitutes nihilism for him. The issue between Nietzsche and Heidegger at this point rests with quasi-historical claims: for Heidegger, human history is constituted by the claim of being, its manner of thought, and its being forgotten; for Nietzsche, human history is constituted by a conflict between those who can live fully in the meaninglessness of life and those who must hide chaos in order to survive it.

"Man essentially comes to pass [west] only in his essence [Wesen] where he is claimed by being. Only in this claim 'has' he found that wherein his essence dwells. Only in this dwelling does he 'have' 'language' as the home that preserves the ecstatic in his essence" (LH 13). There is something consumptive in these only's. Heidegger intends to set apart human being by virtue of its ecstatic relation to being. "Such standing in the clearing of being I call the ek-sistence of man. Only to men is this way of being proper" (LH 13; emphasis added). This ecstatic relation makes reason—ratio—possible, as well as human essence. Human being is completely unique in this "standing." Rather than ratio joined to animality, the human being is singular in its body: the whole body is found in the relation to being. As Heidegger shifts the terrain of thought from a mind-body dualism, he puts the meaning of animality in question just as he has already put thought in question. It is not a question of adding qualities to animality; it is a question of rethinking human being in the singularity of its essence. The biological sciences, medicine, and psychology are also put in question. We cannot know properly the human mind and body by disciplines that are based in the mind-body division. The human body is not an animallike object. Although the facts of the sciences are not necessarily wrong, their structures of knowledge and interpretation skew whatever they discover by the assumptions about the world and mind that are built into their perceptions and verifications. Heidegger's claim, with which we are now familiar, is that these disciplines must be rethought in reference to the question of essence of human nature. Ek-sistence is the leading thought for this reconsideration, because human being is found only in its Bezug to being. Human being comes to pass only in the clearing of being. The disclosure of being is the truth of human existence.

The only means that humans are separated from other creatures by an "abyss" (LH 15). However other creatures are known, they do not stand ecstatically in the lighting-concealing advent of being. Human being is the provenance of the truth of being. This means, I believe, that although human being inevitably turns away from being (error delimits it in its ecstasis), nothing in the human is utterly dumb to being, nor is being completely erased for any aspect of human being.[3] The human body is singular in its ecstasis. Ecstasis thus eliminates kinship with creatures; an abyss separates us from them. Ecstasis finds part of its meaning in an only that suggests a totally unique relation with being, an only that erases the thoughts of 'no clearing at all', simple darkness, dumb juxtaposition, or meaningless convergence. The abysmal mystery of being thus appears to consume our kinship with other creatures, to imprint human being with an encompassing destiny of being that makes singular every dimension of human experience and provides a pervasive sameness for human being, however that sameness is thought.

Have we moved beyond the ascetic ideal by shifting the provenance of thought from its traditionally dualistic mind-body character? Probably not, because undwellable chaos has been consumed in an assurance of dwelling that, no matter how mysterious and questionable, elevates our cries and our laughter by an ecstasis that finds its fulfillment in a reconceived thinking and saying of being. Is animality rethought, or merely lost? In Heidegger's thought we find our essence in the ecstatic coming of being, in a departure from unspeaking earth that, no matter how mortal, is nonetheless saturated with meaning in meaning's loss. Perhaps the human cry is never like an animal's because it is infused and constituted by meaning. But failure to hear the radical delimitation of meaning in the cry is one aspect of the ascetic ideal, and we wonder about what we are unable to hear in our ethos in which meaning reigns even in our spasms, twitchings, and murmurs of satisfaction. Does the abyss that separates us from the animal constitute an opening in which we might hear mere suffering and death, mere happiness that is interrupted continuously by the abyss, a glow of meaning and a depth of essence that find their intensity by an absence of gift that accompanies them? A strangely equalizing body of sounds in which elevation, enlightenment, and superior cultural sensitivity mean nothing? An equalizing body in which the question of the meaning of being has no suasion over folly, in which the cry cries and pleasure pleases, in which there is neither rank nor governance—the equalizing human body that puts in question the claim of being and the thought of being as meaning and essence come to pass, passing away in the body's earth as it shifts under the impact of whatever cataclysm or nurture befalls it.

B. RECOLLECTION OF BEING AND NOTHING ELSE

The "Letter on Humanism" is like the Rector's address and *Being in Time* in the sense that it is largely preparatory to a language and thought not about being but of being. The clear change from the address to the "Letter on Humanism" is that a nationalistic appeal is no longer part of Heidegger's preparatory strategy. His preoccupation with human destiny and human lostness is important for both works, but his conviction is consistent in both pieces that people are homeless to the extent that their lives and thought are oriented *primarily* by a specific ethos rather than by the essence of their language and thought which becomes manifest in an epoch-making interruption of the Greek ethos.[4] If we retrieve a sense of homelessness in the midst of our familiar environments, we take an initial step back to the forgotten essence that will lead us, as human beings, home. The preparatory work includes an interruption of our satisfactions with our identities and our ethos. It includes the emergence of the question of ethics in the context of the question of being. The ethnic interruption of Heidegger's initial steps toward the thought of being is aligned with the primordial interruption in Greek culture. The interruption's importance is governed by the question of being which, as we have seen, circumscribes the interruption and gives it a quite specific meaning and destiny: that of returning us to the abysmal essence of our language and thought. Our return to essence-giving being in its ungraspable mystery is like a homecoming.

In our heritage the thought and saying 'there is being', which comes to us in Parmenides' fragments, is the one that continuously moves thought (LH 22). Being is not an object to be contemplated or a prime mover, but takes place in the coming to pass of language and thought and in this coming to pass is world-governing. Being clears for beings in the middle-voice sense of clearing clears. Clearing is the region for the appearing of beings. Instead of nothing at all, being (is), and beings are. When thought and language think and speak in an open address with beings and also, at once, are fully attuned to their own clearing event, 'there is being' is said, as distinct from forgotten and left unsaid, in the very process of thinking and speaking. As a person thinks and speaks in this alertness and attunement, he or she is predisposed to allow what is focused to be delimited by the clearing, by the 'there is being'. The ungraspable mystery of being then pervades thinking and speaking that address and relate to beings.

In Heidegger's reading of our heritage, thought began in the clearing interruption of the question of being. We have already felt the impact of the clearing effect that can accompany an interruption of habitual patterns of certainty, most recently in this chapter when we asked if an interruption of the question of being would clear the air for the sounds of human suffering and pleasure that are otherwise drowned out by many valuable things. Heidegger's claim, however, is an explanatory one as well as a descriptive one. Thinking begins in this clearing interruption in Greek thought; this beginning is fateful in the sense that it delimits the future of thought. Thought is forever coming to the interruptive clearing of beings; it emits or sends thought in our heritage; thought is always in the hegemony of the sending and clearing of being; that is, being (is) or gives itself in thought so that beings come to stand as something; and our heritage is made up of the ways in which things come to stand in thought. Human beings thus ek-sists in the "nearness of being" as the dispensation of being unfolds in human history (LH 29). Human being is a continuous process of nearing and falling away from being in this dispensation: it is its own continuous interruption of being's interruptive closeness in the midst of unthinking endurance.

Our language thus serves, protects, and preserves thought to the extent that it allows a 'saying' of this dispensation as it speaks of things. Heidegger's preparatory work is not necessarily a saying of being. It is an attempt to prepare the way for recognition of the importance of thought and language that is oriented to being. It is responsive to the originary interruption of the question of being and the originary bestowal of thought in our heritage. It maximizes an awareness of its own inability to do what it projects as most desirable. It provides a continuing diagnosis of our consumptive endurance and our forgetfulness of our proper essence. And, as preparatory, it steadily undercuts its own prescriptive authority. But we have found that it also does not put in question the originary preeminence of being. The pattern of certainty that accompanies this trusting service to the importance of being, not only in our tradition but in the very movement of thought, is where we have located the power of the ascetic ideal. That being is continuously near is known without doubt in Heidegger's discourse. Hence his language speaks of the thinking that is yet to come, thinking that bears in mind the truth of being as "meditative recollection of being and nothing else" (LH 42).

In this 'nothing else' we have found that the body of desire, mere living, the viciousness and crudeness of ordinary life, the division of bruteness from civility, and the meaninglessness that pervades meaning: all such elements of human living are subjected to the provenance of being. This subjection has a muffling effect in the sense that the giving of being, the continuous 'it gives', casts the mere desire of thought, the ordinariness of thought, and its meaninglessness into the role of a falling from thought proper. Proper thought is to be clear, simple, and clean. It is to be filled with care for being, never aversive in its proper realm. Critical diagnosis, though necessary, bears witness to thought's fall, and the thought of this fall will protect the falling in *its* being and save it from fallen obtuseness. The longing for home that Heidegger thematizes is a longing for essence that always puts dispersion, ambiguity, and discord in their proper place. Dispersion takes place in the process of twisting free from the hold of forgetfulness, but it, too, is retrieved in its being in the process of turning to being, a process that allows a clearing rule of thought, and one that allows dispersion to dwell in the language that is the "house of being" and the 'place' most fitting for humans.

And when we suffer in our mere living, or when we experience simple pleasure? When we only exert ourselves to make something, to carry out an ambition? When we undergo the normal senselessness of everyday dispersion and distraction, or when we merely conform, that is, when we live ordinarily? Does the thought of nothing but being attune us to our ordinary misery and happiness? Only to the extent that it tells us that there is something *much* more important than ordinary pain and the enjoyment of everyday things. We can read Heidegger as saying that everyday things will be elevated by the simplicity of proper thought, but the question is whether they are everyday in their elevation. The 'saving' of the everyday from the everyday, the preserving of what is proper in the midst of the ordinary, appear to eliminate the very thing that is to be preserved and saved: the everyday.

The quasi-sacramental quality of Heidegger's thought regarding being betrays the ascetic ideal in Nietzsche's sense, an ideal that obliterates the meaninglessness of the mundane by an ever-giving, elevated, and onto-logically different essence that destroys much of what it is designed to save in the saving process. When this loss is not interrupted by the ordinary senselessness of life, we are ensnared in a group of values that easily lose the mere burst of hilarity, the everyday struggle to survive, or the cry of simple desperation. We lose them in an effort to elevate them and to give them more than they have: meaning beyond all everyday meanings and truth with a quality of 'ever'.

I doubt that we can hear each other well until we interrupt our senses of privilege and elevation and interrupt as well the meanings by which we perceive salvation from that which none of us is saved: the ordinary meaninglessness of everything that gives us meaning, and the simple disruption of all of our presumed continuities. Nietzsche's account of the ascetic ideal is right in this, that whatever in our tradition saves and preserves seriousness concerning truth and meaning saves and preserves the very elements that are taken to be overcome by truth and meaning in their seriousness, and also that this inaudible preservation makes soundless the senselessness and disruption that it is intended to replace.

There is one paragraph in the "Letter on Humanism" in which Heidegger says that proper thinking is manifest in a part of his letter. This part goes beyond preparatory thought and enters into a more fitting saying of being. Prior to this observation he said that "historically only one saying belongs to the matter of thinking" (LH 42). Essential thinking "lets being be" (LH 42). It guides humans in their ek-static bearing with being into the region where healing arises and beings become hale (LH 43). This healing does not mask evil but makes it all the more apparent. "The essence of evil does not consist in mere baseness of human action, but rather in the malice of rage. Both of these, however—healing and raging—can essentially occur only in being insofar as being itself is what is contested" (LH 43). The nihilation of rage illuminates itself, is cleared, as having an essence, too. Destructive rage is in the history of being, albeit perversely. Its lost essence is the nihilation that belongs to being. Being's nihilation is found in its not being a being; in its essence (it) is not, (is) other than existence. In that sense being's withdrawal is nihilation. It is like a no to every*thing* that is. Everything possibly definitive falls away from being. In its healing favor, however, being grants the fall; and when, in its falling away from being, human being closes on itself and is closed to being's favor, a compulsion to degeneration and calamity takes place. Only if this rage that accompanies forgetfulness of being, the rage that is expressed in a society of consumption and manipulation, for example, only if it is thought in the healing gift of being can it undergo a quiet regeneration by returning to its favoring, never-destroying, granting essence. When falling from being is thought in its fall *from* being, dwelling in the house of being can take place (LH 43–44). Then the rage of separation from being is quieted before the granting that clears even for this rage. Malignant rage is never nothing. It, too, exists. Without the giving of being, instead of rage there would not have been . . .

Because the granting of being is always other than what is granted, the 'evil' that comes with the granting clearing of existence does not, in Heidegger's thought, occasion a contamination of being. For Heidegger, being is not stained. We are seeing, however, that its freedom from contamination constitutes the pervasive stain of the ascetic ideal in the thought of being. This thought of being appears to be impossible without the ascetic ideal.

Further, from human "ek-sisting in the truth of being" can come the human's true fortune and lot in life (LH 44). People can find their directions from the dispensation of being: one "abides" in the truth of being (LH 45). Human economy is ruled by this dispensation which, although it never tells a person what to do, provides the gift of being by which all things can be truly minded. In such minding of being, the human deed exceeds objectification. Thinking then "towers above action and production, not through the grandeur of its achievement and not as a consequence of its effort, but through the humbleness of its inconsequential accomplishment [Vollbringen]" (LH 45). Ek-sisting then can come to language, "for thinking in its saying merely brings the unspoken word of being to language. . . . Being comes, clearing itself, to language" (LH 45). Then, "ek-sistence thoughtfully dwells in the house of being. In all this it is as if nothing at all happens through thoughtful saying" (LH 45).

At this point Heidegger says: "But just now an example of the inconspicuous deed [Tun] of thinking shows itself. For to the extent that we expressly think the usage 'bring to language', which was granted to language, think only that and nothing further, to that extent we retain this thought in the heedfulness of saying as what in the future continually has to be thought, we have brought something of the essential unfolding of being to language" (LH 45–46). The moment of thinking to which Heidegger refers is not preparatory to essential thought, but breaks through separation from being to the thought of being as the words *bring being to language* and do what they say regarding "being that comes, clearing itself, to language." In this deed, this event that unfolds the appeal of being in the fullness of its essence, human being comes to its essence and, by coming to it, thinks and "says" its essence. Its essence is brought to language. We have a moment in which "the *sole* matter of thinking" is thought, a moment that is joined by 'the Same' to essential thinking whenever it occurs in our heritage (LH 47, emphasis added). No evil can dwell in this moment, no technological madness, no misuse of beings. The danger, Heidegger says, is that we confuse the Same with a being, with something self-identical. Then ambiguity and "mere quarreling" constitutes the danger, and essential thinking does not occur. But without this confusion we can be in the dispensation of being in a fitting way: "The fittingness [Schicklichkeit] of the saying of being, as of the proper sending *[Geschick]* of truth, is the first law of thinking" (LH 47). Not the necessity of self-overcoming, not its own dangerousness, but the fit of the saying and the sending of being is the first law of thinking. Although being means for thought a continuous process of self-overcoming and experimentation in the preparatory aspect of thought—an aspect that is largely definitive of the best thought available to us—in the destiny of being, proper and fitting thought in a deed beyond manipulation and objectivation, in this abysslike mystery, there is neither self-overcoming nor corruption nor destruction. Rather, there is saving power, whose saying *[Sagen]* is the first law of thinking.

Further, the knowledge that being's dispensation is saving power, that being is the sole matter for thinking, and that language can be fitting to the self-sending and fortune of being appears to be the lot of the essential thinker. This knowledge has the practical effect of providing certainty outside of the self-overcoming processes. A dispersion of the Same would be no less than the raging madness of language and thought ensnared in forgetfulness of being. That would be the effect of thought out of touch with its own being and proper heritage. The proper thought of being is not subject to dispersion or ambiguity or to any interruption other than that of its own advent. Instead of interrupting his own approach to being or interrupting the thought that being can be thought in a fitting way, Heidegger suggests a strategy of preparation that is based on the secure knowledge that being is the sole matter for thinking. He says that attention to the propriety of thoughtful saying means that we consider carefully when and whether we say anything regarding being. We must time our saying carefully, now assuming that our thought and language give being its proper sway, with reference "to what extent, at what moment of the history of being, in what sort of dialogue with this history, and on the basis of what claims, it ought to be said" (LH 47). The rigor with which we call being to mind, the carefulness of saying, and a frugality with words determine the strategic piety of this thought. Such careful gathering of language into "simple saying" restores thought "inconspicuously" to "the poverty of its forecasting essence" (LH 47). At this point in Heidegger's thought, the die is cast for the indelible stamp of being. A version of poverty, chastity, and humility deeply marks this die.

Heidegger's claims about being seem to place essential thought outside the sway of an ethos. On the one hand, he has relegated values to an activity in which the subject takes priority over being; he has seen that valuing is correlated with warring over the highest and most objective values. The effort to prove the objectivity of values is bizarre and foolish, he says. This effort does not know what it is doing (LH 34). Being is beyond value and valuing and puts ethics as such in question. But Heidegger exempts the thought (of) being from evaluation and judgment. It is set apart from the vicissitudes, accidents, and collisions of its heritage. Nothing intrinsically chaotic takes place in its proper middle voice. Unlike

Nietzsche's thought, Heidegger's is never interrupted by the serious consideration that the essential thought of being is an *error,* that our philosophy has its origin in an error whose only 'value' is the negative one of interrupting the experience and life of the senses.[5] Rather, Heidegger's thought means that humans exist in an openness that has no disruption in its mystery. Its disruption of ordinary life is at once a calling of human life to its totally nonordinary and nonsensuous essence. Being (is) dispensation that sets the standard for interruptions, but is also openness that grants and never vacates.[6] One part of its destiny in Heidegger's thought in the "Letter on Humanism" is thus to forget its mortal temporality and to cast its mortality in a self-denying valuation that holds at bay its own interruption. In this sense, his thought (of) being, in its presumed and unqualified openness, seems to fall prey to its own thoroughly ethnic quality which privileges the Greek and German cultures and which sees no alternative to nihilism if its mysterious difference is traversed by nothing at all. In this dimension it exhibits the anxiety typical of the ascetic ideal.

2. Giving Thought to Simple Oneness

The fine line that we have followed divides the effect of the thought of being in human effort, in Heidegger's account of it, and the continuous sameness of being as he speaks of it. In its withdrawal from any specification, being is like nothing at all and is like (an) abyss. In that sense it is also like chaos. It escapes meaning and has the effect of putting all specifying thought regarding it in error. Human being loses being, is always on the verge of being and nonbeing, and is at once abandoned and given by being.[7] Being, in its oblivion, leaves room, as it were, for straying, forgetting, and, as we saw, the malicious rage of living as though being were not. The oblivion of being calls for a radical dismantling of our tradition which has thought of being as a being and puts in question all of our values and concepts which develop in this tradition. But the oblivion of being also is subject to recovery in essential thought, and the language that Heidegger uses regarding being in its recovery does not appear to incorporate a recoil away from being and its question, but rather to intensify its mystery, withdrawal, closeness, dispensation, and otherness. Being remains in question in its verge, but it also attracts an uninterrupted certainty and asceticism regarding it in Heidegger's thought. The withdrawal of being at once preserves being from dispersion in its dispensation and highlights the mortality, separation from being, forgetfulness of being, and closeness of being for humans. The retrieval of the question of being, however, invokes a voice that is not circumscribed by human being. It is an ecstatic voice in which being as clearing openness, as disclosedness, is revealed in a highly disciplined and ontologically alert way of thinking. Both this way of thinking and being as (it) comes provisionally to Heidegger's language incorporate the ascetic ideal as Nietzsche described it. How is one to live in this provisional and questing thought?

Toward the end of "Building Dwelling Thinking" Heidegger speaks of the loss of accord *[Bezugsverlust]* with things that occurs in states of depression.[8] This loss of accord does not represent our abandonment by things or a void in the midst of things to which depression makes us alert. Things in their very essence are with us, and we in our essence are with things. Disclosedness constitutes a sameness pervasive throughout the world. In a delicate elaboration of being-in-the-world, Heidegger speaks of human dwelling as an abiding with things and locations. To dwell is to be, and to be is to be with things in their disclosures. When we are depressed, he says, we lose our rapport with things. We are still essentially with them and they with us, because human being *is* being with things. The feeling that we are closed off from things and that everything is at a great distance from us does not properly manifest human being. Human being "stays" with things, and depression includes a "failure" of things to concern us and to speak to us in their continuing disclosures. Feeling severed from things, we are quietly at odds with our being in our depression.

Nietzsche, on the other hand, found the anxiety and depression of those in need of the ascetic ideal to indicate a negative attunement in life in its threatening, severed, and meaningless dimensions. Their loss of vitality is a failure of nerve before the totally uncaring quality of vitality. Rather than lacking insight, they saw and heard clearly the chaos and absence that pervades all of life. Life-affirmation is not a retrieval of being and presence, not discovery of nurturance and sameness at the heart of things, but is rather a will to will in the midst of a process for which dismemberment is as revelatory as affiliation is. For Heidegger a depressed loss of rapport with things is stayed in (indwelt by) the disclosedness of present things. For Nietzsche, a depressed loss of rapport with things opens onto discord and strife that discloses no option to discord and strife. For Heidegger, depression is able to overcome by retrieving the rapport. For Nietzsche, depression is overcome by an affirmation of the discordant conditions of depression. Although Heidegger speaks of human being as verging on both being and no being at all, his emphasis falls heavily on the ecstatic, continuing, giving disclosedness of being—its sameness— which makes appropriate human renunciation of the primary importance of the ordinary, broken, sensuous world. Being is always the guiding star. *Dwelling* is one name for human communal life when it is guided by alertness to being as people build and think together. In it there is no cause for depression or madness. Its proper affection, we shall see, is that of serenity in association with a strict and critical attitude toward the ordinary world.

Dwelling for Heidegger thus names a basic way of life in which human living is guided by the dispensation of being. He raises the question of dwelling in this essay in 1951 at a symposium on Man and Space. It was a time of concern over the housing shortage in postwar Germany, a time when many people were homeless. His clear conviction is the war that has caused homelessness has its roots in a homelessness that is far more pervasive of Western culture than Germany's specific plight.[9] Homelessness accompanies human inattentiveness to being and a consequent fixation on production of goods, usage space, and satisfaction of needs that arise in deafness to being's gift. Human being belongs to being, finds its home in a play of being's dispensation and in a virtually unheard longing for being that arises in this originary kinship. To learn to dwell is to attempt to appropriate this kinship in the relations of humans to things. Dwelling is found as humans home in on and preserve the disclosedness of things in building their structures of communal life.

Although Heidegger gives no hint of the exaggerated hope for total cultural mobilization and transformation that motivated his Rector's address, his purposes are nonetheless practical in this essay. He is addressing people who are concerned with the problem of housing and with rebuilding the bombed-out infrastructure in the German cities. He wants to provide a direction for planning and an exemplary way of thinking in the process of assessing and planning.[10] They must rethink the usual approaches to solving social problems if they are to avoid the pathology that has led to the destruction of homeland. They could simply use the resources available to them to produce houses and buildings. They could once more clear the rubble and fill up the space with structures into which people would move with their furniture and equipment. But then nothing essential would have been changed. The environment would continue to appear ready for exploitation. Blueprints and traffic patterns would guide construction, and no thought would be given to the gift of being that makes possible the gathering of things and spaces into a region of communal life; *communio,* the sameness that makes a human environment, would seem to be a body of elements that are defined by human need and desire. Heidegger's purpose is to rethink the sameness that makes possible a human community in which being, not our forgetfulness of being, not practical and charitable anthropocentricism, infuses the meaning and significance of building and dwelling. He is attempting to influence the reconstruction of Germany by tending to being's gift of disclosure and to make more likely a society that is dedicated to its own disclosedness by its preservation of things in their disclosedness. It would be a society that does not destroy itself by a mordant, if well-intended, consumption of things for the purpose of further consumption. It would maintain itself in care of the simple oneness that gives all being in common.

This project entails a return to essential words that speak in alertness to this oneness, hold quietly a lost awareness, and withhold that awareness in their ordinary usage: "For with the essential words of language, what they genuinely *[eigentlich]* say easily falls into oblivion in favor of foreground meanings. . . . Language withdraws from man its simple and high speech. But its primal call does not thereby become incapable of speech; it merely falls silent. Man, though, fails to heed this silence" (LH 326). Heidegger's plan is to heed the silence of the primal call of being in a few essential words as he assesses the environment out of which and to which he speaks, to give way to the saying of being that is hidden in them, and to uncover, by his language and thought, being's dispensation of dwelling. The question of ethics continues. There is no normative group of values or way of thought that is able to set unquestioned standards. But the language of being also does not fall into question, and we shall find the ascetic ideal operating where the rule of self-overcoming and questioning leaves off.

If we mortals do not preserve our ecstatic kinship with being in the ways in which we build things and form spaces, Heidegger says, we will cultivate neither ourselves nor the things around us. The issue for him is one of advancing the growth and flourishing of things. Instead of marshaling the passions of conquest, ambition, and pride, through which Heidegger in his rectorial address hoped to lead the German people to the ecstatic transcendence of the question of being, he now appeals to desires for freedom, growth, and peace with the intention of giving priority to "the primal oneness" of being. Underlying his words is one of the fundamental questions of *Being and Time,* namely, how mortals are to care for their world. And, consonant with *Being and Time,* his conviction is that proper care can develop only if we give priority to the simple and unseamed disclosedness of being which both gives the world its clearing for life and in its difference from beings makes questionable all of our values and goals. Mortals are always of being—in the 'voice' of being—and in the loss of being. So how they maintain the question of being will define their way of dwelling. In maintaining this questionableness, this mortality, they take care of themselves and of things by not disturbing, covering over, or using up the disclosures that make up the world. They preserve the ecstatic relation of being that constitutes their mortality, that is, that constitutes their living. Mortality is being in the loss of being. This means that mortals most properly are "sparing" of the ecstatic occurrence of disclosure. Both the German word that Heidegger uses, *schonen,* and the English word, *spare,* that translates it indicate a relationship in which one preserves something by not using it up. *Using up* in this context means taking something over and giving it its definition by the way it is used. The frugality that Heidegger has in mind is a matter of letting things be, conserving them in their disclosedness, as distinct from relating to them primarily in their everyday usefulness. They are not primarily valuable; that is, they do not have their being by reference to either positive or negative valences. Before valuation, they *are,* and their care is found in efforts to be with them in our common being and loss of being.

"The fundamental character of dwelling is this sparing" (LH 327). By sparing things we leave them to their own disclosure, respond to them in their disclosures, and preserve their free openness for relation. The word *dwelling [Wohnen]* has taken us to its own essential meaning: to leave things in the peace of their essence as we live and build with them (LH 325–27). We build with things in the manner that we dwell with them. We stay with them, allow them their place, with a strict discipline of sparing them, or saving them, in their being. In that staying we find ourselves at home in the world. Our dwelling then stands out from the concerns of daily life into the disclosures of things that mandate an allowing, restrained forbearance with things. Mortals then live in a fallen ecstasis of being—with being to spare.

This proper releasing of openness, an elaboration of *Entschlossenheit* with words that cannot be heard as indicating strength of will, finds its space in the "primal oneness" of earth, sky, divinities, and mortals. The measure of propriety is the "simple oneness" of these four elements, a simple oneness that gathers into a space the nurturing earth, ethereal sky, presencing and withdrawing divinities, and humans who can die. This unfolding onefold that gives the space of dwelling is spared by human devotion to earth, sky, divinity, and mortals in their essential accord with being. We are to preserve their yielding and giving space, to devote our building and making to their dispensation of clearing space. An opposite to this devotion is found in primary concern for what we find ourselves wanting, our desires to project our physical and social needs onto the world in an insatiable drive to fill the vacuum that divides us from being. In *that* desire we use up, clutter, expropriate, and consume our resources. We build by filling spaces with no rapport with the yielding fourfold. We spend or accumulate resources rather than preserve disclosure. We make ourselves homeless in the strife and conflict of getting, expending, and owning. We lose the poverty of our mortality, our humility before disclosiveness in its yielding and withdrawing, and the chasteness of all things in their accord with being.

Heidegger leaves no doubt that life dispersed by energy given over to the many competing claims of existence, life insensitive to its own ecstatic essence, will occasion depression and homelessness. The abstemious and gentle option that he proposes, one that is filled with reverence for being in its simple oneness and its primordial divergence from anything specifiable, tends toward resolution of the question of ethics by single-minded devotion to being. Such devotion allows restitution of simplicity and unity to life, not by an excellence of virtue, but by an allowance of being in all relations. The severity of his judgment concerning ordinary relations is itself redeemed as things are saved in their essence from the mordant effects of anthropocentric values. Our economy is to be measured by a dispensation of being that can teach us how to live not primarily with virtue, but with reverence in which our mortal difference from being is honored and preserved in all actions. Until that devotion and reverence is approximated by our holding our being always in question, we shall not know how properly to think or act. Everything but our reverence for being is provisional. By that reverence a simple oneness can become audible beyond the fragments of our lives, like a call, finally, to home.

The gentle nurturance of Heidegger's projected world accords with the nurturance he ascribes to being. Being's withdrawal means that the home of mortals is a place of suffering and death as well as a place of care-filled attentiveness to the being of all things. But the yielding, giving provenance of being has absolute priority in Heidegger's language. Exploitation, aggression, mere division and separation, erotic passion for its own sake, unconscious devices and manipulations to arouse interest and intensity in life, cruelty, the mindless drive for autonomy and self-esteem, indifference, simple will to survive: such living 'things' are to be understood only within the jurisdiction of being's mysterious grace. In Heidegger's language, being gives all such things their essence, their essential space in time, and it gives essence so thoroughly that even the language of causation fails to address adequately the radicality of being's gift. Dispersing and aggressive things show the withdrawal of being, their fall from being, but their power of disclosure is negative in the sense that for Heidegger they open onto what they conceal and fall from. His thought can respond properly dispersing and aggressive things only when it thinks them in being's dispensation, a dispensation in which they in their fall are continuously subjected to their 'essence' in the course of being's magisterial withdrawal. In Heidegger's economy, whatever does not nurture the disclosure of being departs from its essence as it lives out its nonnurturing drive. This way of thinking thus appears to hold within it a well-concealed despair over life outside of being's priority. Without the simple, nurturing sameness of being, could life be worth living?

3. A Simple Conjunction

Being's rule in Heidegger's thought, we have found, is shown in two distinct ways. On the one hand, no formulation about being is final or complete and ethics is perpetually in question. Conversation and thought regarding being are never definitive and are always subject to reconsideration. On the other hand, the priority of being is not in question, and its priority provides Heidegger with a type of knowledge that tends toward a piety of certainty regarding the mystery of being and proper responses to this mystery. We turn now to Heidegger's thought specifically regarding mystery by considering the relation of revealing to concealing. We shall find that it is a relation of conjunction that partially defines being's mystery. It is mystery of simple unity without internal scission. This thought on Heidegger's part is an elaboration of an ontological position that is informed by and supportive of that part of the ascetic ideal that emphasizes conjunction and unity. We shall find that the concealment of being does not put in question simple oneness, but rather is interpreted by reference to simple oneness. Being's abysmal aspect is seamed by conjunction. Although human beings come to pass in the question of being, *our* questionableness, when properly appropriated, opens us to being's clearing disclosedness and to the inadequacy of human being to grant being or to comprehend it. Being, however, is not transgressed by fall or dispersion. Although being is beyond translation and full embodiment in this world, it is transcendent in its simple oneness. This oneness is shown in Heidegger's use of the word *and* to connect revealing and concealing.

We shall consider the 'beyond' of being in its simple oneness in the context of Heidegger's meditation on Heraclitus's sixteenth Fragment. Three issues are before us: In what sense will being not travel over and come to proper translation except by recognition of its concealment? How are we to understand the connection of concealment and unconcealment? And in what way does this connection address the question of how we are to live? We are raising the issue of the ontological connection between concealing and unconcealing, on the one hand, and between concealing and unconcealing and human dwelling, on the other, in the context of the remnants of the ascetic ideal in Heidegger's thought.

Being, in its nearness, we found, is beyond human grasp. Although it can come to its own saying in language and thought, it cannot be translated (carried over) into any kind of objectivity or subjectivity. Our claims about being are thus properly subject to continuous rethinking. Essential thinking also requires a radical transformation of what we traditionally call thinking into a singular kind of commemoration of the question of being as it has had an impact on and has escaped from our heritage. In this commemoration being remains appropriately beyond any specificity that we might apply to it. It is beyond translation.[11]

In his discussion of Fragment 16B, Heidegger emphasizes that he is not looking for an "objectively correct" interpretation of Heraclitus.[12] He intends to follow Heraclitus's language as it points to the appropriating event *[Ereignis]* of concealment and unconcealment. *Lanthanomai,* for example, points to the conjunction of concealment and unconcealment. It says, "I am—with respect to my relation to something usually unconcealed—concealed from myself" (AH 108). He further indicates by a middle-voice formulation that the sameness of an event in this conjunction is expressed by *me . . . pote:* "something does not . . . ever . . . (what then?) . . . come to pass otherwise than as it comes to pass." That is, something comes to pass of itself and out of itself. In the case of this phrase, the *me,* the negation, comes out of the event of coming to pass, reverts back to that event, and indicates an obscure sameness. Further, *kruptesthai* speaks of the self-concealing of *phusis* and elaborates its *philia,* its love, of self-concealing (AH 113). The self-rising of *phusis* and its self-concealing both complement the phrase "the not setting ever" in the context of his discussion. Both *phusis* and "the not setting ever" are, in their middle voice, occurrences in which concealing and unconcealing mean 'the Same'. Conjoined by *and,* concealing and unconcealing mean that "never entering into unconcealment, it *[phusis]* is the enduring rising out of self-concealing" (AH 118). In the case of both Heidegger's and Heraclitus's phrase "thoughtful wonder," unconcealing and concealing are meditated and released as they take place in and through their own event. This releasing meditation, in its middle voice, shows in its turn both unconcealing and concealing in the sameness of their event. It is thoughtful and alert, but also obscure and beyond the reach of categorical thought. Thoughtful wonder is a way of being that Heidegger contrasts to the self-showing but self-forgetful choosing and grasping *[elesthai]* that characterize the middle voice of the subjectivity of ordinary living. Concerning these instances of the middle voice, Heidegger speaks of "the purely appropriating event" that gives rise continuously to the question of lighting and making obscure, that is, to the occurrence of *aletheia* prior to our fixing assertions and certainty-giving choices regarding objects. Concealing and unconcealing are pervasive in the very issuance of activity and receptivity, and yet in their sameness they are beyond the reach of activity and receptivity.

Heidegger uses middle-voice structures to translate Heraclitus's Fragment 16B so that it speaks now more clearly than it could in a language that excludes the middle voice. But Heraclitus's thought is nonetheless beyond translation and is concealed in two senses: one is the concealed dimension out of which unconcealing ever rises, and the other is the untranslatability of Heraclitus's obscure wonder. Both concealments are pervasive in the thinking and speaking in which Heidegger and Heraclitus mutually engage. By returning to the middle voice, Heidegger is able to say that concealment conceals (of itself) in the occurrence of unconcealment, without suggesting either activity or passivity in concealment and unconcealment. Only in this middle voice does the full wonder of concealment and unconcealment come to bear and does Heraclitus's thought come home to us.

When we say that concealment is beyond translation, *beyond* indicates distance that is not to be overcome by any means of approximation. That is a nonrelational distance, one that does not call for conjunctive connection, but rather one that traverses and transgresses translational relations without incorporation or appropriation. Concealment has this quality, but Heidegger also qualifies this sense of distance when he speaks of concealment and unconcealment not as contraries or differing powers, but as belonging together in their difference as Same. For example, he says that Heraclitus means by the *to me dunon pote*—the not setting ever—that "both revealing *and* concealing—(are) not . . . two different occurrences merely jammed together, but (are) . . . one and the Same" (AH 112–13). This nearness is of the very event of self-showing, not as a formal essence or as a consequence of some pre-fixing action. As the occurrence of ever-rising, the Same is a nearness that reverts to itself in concealing and unconcealing and in its event is ever beyond translation.

Heidegger interprets this nearness of concealing and revealing in the language of sheltering and preserving which can be taken as elaborating the thought of *beyond*. Self-showing is sheltered and preserved in self-concealing. Self-showing "belongs" to self-concealing. There is a quiet with-holding that suffuses the occurrence of self-showing, a holding back which yields the 'ever' quality of self-showing, which gives it place and pace. This self-preserving, saving aspect is of the self-showing event. It is the same in the event with self-showing, and it means that self-showing enjoys a reciprocity of revealing and concealing, a conjunction that happens as the event's own given voice. Self-showing never goes into concealment. Conjoined with concealment, unconcealment is ever rising out of conceal-ment.

On this reading the bestowal of presencing is composed of an almost unthinkable "intimacy" of concealing and revealing. Heidegger interprets this conjunction in the metaphors of love *[philia],* joining, an ever-rising movement toward one another, an ever-living fire of rising without extinc-tion (AH 115–18). The meditative thinking that follows the ever-rising of self-showing is interpreted in the metaphor of gathering. "The meditative fire," in the context of Heraclitus's thought, "is the gathering which lays everything before us (into presencing). *To pur* is *O Logos*" (AH 118). In this thinking the world occurs as lightened and sheltered: 'the not setting ever' sets no more in this meditative thinking than it sets in the unconcealing of all other beings. A "consonance" runs through not only Heraclitus's words, but through the near-rapturous, always ecstatic clearing that yields presence (AH 118). This consonance or joining, in its sameness of conceal-ing *and* unconcealing, does not have the voice of fracturing or fragmenting. In the conjoining voice of *and,* no transgression traverses the Same. Concealing and unconcealing suffer no wound or injury, no intensified 'yond' in their event. Although they are beyond translation in their nearness, they are borne so intimately together in Heidegger's thought that there is no scission in their voice, no distance, no splitting difference.

This is a voice that moves always toward a serenity of releasing and open dwelling. In such dwelling, presencing in its concealment is both commemorated and bestowed; self-concealing is recalled with alert and sensitive restraint and humility. Commemoration and sensitive restraint themselves yield presencing in self-concealment, and the circle of Same continues to speak in its voice of Same beyond identity and difference. At this point in his discussion, Heidegger asks,

Did Heraclitus intend his question as we have just been discussing it? Was what this discussion has said within the range of his concepts? Who knows? Who can say? . . . The fragment does say [the sort of thing we have said] provided a thoughtful dialogue may bring it to speak. The fragment says it, and leaves it unuttered. (AH 120)

The unuttered remains, in its own voice, in question, Heidegger says. And these questions always invoke only such things as were manifested long ago on those paths under diverse disguises.[13] That distance and its disguises that Heidegger thematizes occur in our everyday and self-assured oversight of the mystery of revealing and concealing. People turn away from the yielding of presencing and toward "what is present" (AH 122). The familiarity of our ordinary connections voices a distance from the logos that gathers the presence of all connections. The middle voice of unthoughtful choice *[elesthai]* is that of separation from its own presencing, a voice of stupidity that lacks intimacy with what is closest and most bonded with it. The untranslatability of the concealing and unconcealing of presencing is not carried over in the occurrences of ordinary life, and the nearness of ungraspable mystery, of this splendid obscurity, is beyond the disposition of our ordinary predispositions and values.

Heidegger's thinking, and Heraclitus's thinking on Heidegger's account of it, are processes of translating *this* beyond that transpires because of our traditional ways of living and experiencing. Heidegger is not translating revealing and concealing as such, but their nearness and distance. The voice of revealing and concealing with its untranslatability is retrieved by the middle-voice structures that replace our usual inclination to transform everything into subjects and objects. In its retrieval its untranslatability is protected, but the yielding, bearing, sheltering nearness that Heidegger retrieves also has the voice of untransgressed Same—a "wholesomeness," a "self-keeping," "self-restraining," "self-veiling" voice (AH 123). This is a voice without fragment. Nothing un-dwells in it.

Heidegger's thought is a questioning one not because revealing and concealing un-dwell in scission and fragmentation, but because being is always other to mortality and because our Western experience is constituted by forgetfulness of this otherness and the seamless, ungraspable occurrence of concealing and unconcealing. Our thinking is thoroughly seamed by the beyond of revealing and concealing. Our lives are ruled by the perversity of our historically developed indifference to being's untranslatability. We live fragmentary lives, choosing hay rather than gold, in Heraclitus's words, holding on to all that we can grasp in our distance from what is nearest to us. But the destiny of this distance is found in the dispensation of the obscure Same of revealing and concealing. It is a destiny that recalls us to dwelling *in the connection* of the concealing that yields presencing and of the revealing that gathers whatever is.

Heraclitus's "not setting ever," however, occurs in a fragment. The fragment's historical setting, which Heidegger emphasizes early in his discussion, is one of vague recall, a group of phrases repeated from other fragments and scraps of hearsay. We have Fragment 16B because of the survival of Clement of Alexandria's *Paidagogos,* in which Clement folds it into a Christian metaphor for divine life and presence. Heidegger unravels this weave and, instead of divine presence, finds in the fragment the thought of undecidable conjunction in concealing and unconcealing. The fragmented, piecemeal aspect of the transmission of this thought does not invade what is thought or the truth of the thinking event. The consequence of ignoring the dispersed and fragmented transmission is that an *and* rather than a slash connects concealment and unconcealment. Instead of a fragmented juxtaposition of revealing and concealing, Heidegger elevates the saying of the fragment beyond its fragmentation and gives to it conjunction without division. As a result, wholesome dwelling in commemoration of being, beyond and with the fragmentation of human life, is obscurely forecast by Heidegger's questioning thought. The language of suffering, radical darkness, unthinkable transgression, madness, mindless separation, silent indifference, near and inappropriable difference—this language arises from our traditional and constitutive falling away from being, not from being's fragmented quality, but from the Same of revealing *and* concealing. Our suffering is a voice of this human falling away, not of a fragmented and demented quality of presencing and truth.

Shall we say that Heidegger's translation of Heraclitus overcomes the possibility of any transgression in revealing and concealing? Has Heraclitus the obscure shown us in Heidegger's retrieval of him a way of dwelling with and beyond fragmentation by recalling the fragmentation of our ordinary lives? Has Heidegger's Heraclitus gone beyond his own fragmentary presence in our language and thought? Or shall we say that Heraclitus's fragments provide the space of both Heidegger's and Heraclitus's thought, that this space transgresses the conjunction that Heidegger adds to it? That the fragment interrupts the presumptive joining of revealing *and* concealing and, as the voice of fragment, makes unthinkable the conjoining *and* and Heidegger's dwelling with it? That *fragmentation* and not *Same* name the voice of revealing/concealing?

By dividing the Same of concealing and unconcealing in Heraclitus's thought from the transmission of this thought in fragments, Heidegger separates the translation of Heraclitus's fragment from its historical transmission. In Heidegger's translation, concealing and unconcealing 'are' Same and 'are' consequently quite beyond the broken words and fragments that gather 'their' thought. Unconcealing gathers words and fragments, but its concealing protects it not only from the exhausting mortality of historical circumstances, but also from the fragmentary manner by which unconcealing comes to us. Concealing and unconcealing neither flow nor fall apart in the breakage of historical life. Unconcealing is ever rising. The same voice of concealing and unconcealing has untranslatable distance in its historical life, forever beyond and with the fragmentation in whose voice we come to hear their obscurity. By thinking this fragmentation in the context of concealing we find a serenity that appropriates the fragment in its gathering and singular occurrence. The circle of Same is retained in the withdrawal of fragmentation. We read the *and* in this withdrawal. The conjunction restores the Same out of differentiation while bestowing the distance that traverses the thinker's language. While Same is not translatable, the *and* is quite translatable in the retrieved distance between Same and language regarding it. 'Concealing' and 'unconcealing' are not Same because of the *and*. Yet the conjunction obscurely retains in Heidegger's thought the untranslatable Same and preserves it from the fragmentation of a slash.

And yet. The *and* indicates by its double preservation, if not knowledge and justification of the Same, at least the restoration of concealing to unconcealing in our thought of it. This is a fragmented action, this restoration, an obscure retrieval of Heraclitus's thought in the midst of the divisions of language and transmission. I find in Heidegger's thought no voice for this restoration other than that of arbitration among the fragmentary possibilities that have formed the transmission of his thought. The voice of the *and* is one of interpretation in which are preserved the full range of fragments and divisions, only one of which gives the possible thought of Same. In this sense fragmentation seems to occur in the voice of Same as it comes to us in both Heidegger's and Heraclitus's thought. Heidegger's projection of Same beyond fragmentation reveals a multiply fractured process of transmission which his thought submits to the rule of simple being.

The Same of concealing and unconcealing has in its destiny a piety that gathers differences into Same by a disciplined recall of the concealing nearness of unconcealing in the fragmentation of speaking and thinking. The signature of fragmentation—cycles of creation and destruction, exhaustion of meanings, ceaseless play of endings, departures without origins, the impulses and imagination of contentious eros—such things that Heidegger knew well, leave the Same unmarked and suffer a distinctive humiliation in his thought by virtue of the Same's intimate withdrawal. The near difference to Same on the part of dispersed things means that a kind of poverty runs through the riches of ordinary life. No sense of eros excites Same. We have already noted the serene gathering of differences that characterizes the truth of this dwelling, and in this serenity is gathered as well the language of our tradition—destructured by Heidegger in its theological import—by which we recall the unspeakable mystery of Being and its yielding in the midst of all that is speakable and graspable. Concealing and unconcealing as Same are not subject to the breakage of fractured life. The conjunction *and* means that unconcealing is ever rising without breach. There appears to be no basis for destruction *in* the ever-rising of unconcealing: the ever-rising is the measure of the destruction of ordinary excess, pride, and valuation. Distance from the ever-rising, however, occasions loss of Same. This loss is part of the meaning of that dwelling by which the loss is recovered in alert attentiveness to the concealing of unconcealing. This recovery demands the asceticism of proper living, its gentle renunciation of the power of all that is only pleasurable, contrary, self-assertive, lustful, violent, retentive, and given to the world of competition and ambitious conflict. But the Same does not appear to generate our ordinary distance from it. It gathers in its severe distance, and in that sense the conjunction of concealing and unconcealing is apart from the movement of ordering life's self-overcoming. It withdraws from this movement and is protected from it. The *and* conjoins where the movement of self-overcoming fractures.

Can we push Heidegger to the thought that concealing gives rise ever to the fragmentation of the very thought of unconcealing, or that fragmentation is the truth of unconcealing? Probably not, because for Heidegger the conjunction of revealing and concealing is beyond fragmentation. And this means that the *and* of concealing and unconcealing stands as a fragment over against the fragmented self-overcoming of every fragmented thought in a way that invites further questioning. If this conjunction stands over against the fragmented self-overcoming of fragments, then we may wonder whether dwelling in the thought of this conjunction might advance the nihilism of the ascetic ideal, whether it rules without question in a continuous humiliation of fragmentation without putting itself sufficiently in question to overturn the Same of concealing and unconcealing. In that case, the *and* of concealing and unconcealing would call for destructuring by the obscure force of the space that transmits it, fragments it, and turns it as a conjunction into an ungathering slash that leaves unjoined the concealing and unconcealing that it is designed to protect.

4. The Rule of Being in *Gelassenheit*

If our claims are correct, that Heidegger unjustifiably separates the Same of revealing and concealing from the fragmented process that makes the thought of Same possible, that the Same is a thought projected by the ascetic ideal, and that one of its purposes is to provide unity and an eternal (ever-rising) source of life and meaning in the midst of the world that otherwise gives no privilege to life and meaning, then the kind of dwelling that Heidegger idealizes appears to have as its basis the value of the Same. This basis has the valence, the power, to direct people away from meaningless fragmentation and toward gentle communion together in association with all things. The danger is that such gentle communion will also have the unappropriated power to fracture and fragment, to become a nurturing ethos that projects its opposites as perverse and unworthy, the power to defeat them by humiliation and a type of surveillance and conquest that are consistent with the ethos. We shall look first at *Gelassenheit* and its attractive possibilities for developing a human ethos. We shall conclude by considering the limits of its rule and ask about the fragments of voices that in its insulation it drowns out.

A. A STRONG CASE FOR CLEARING RELEASE [*GELASSENHEIT*]

In the context of the question of ethics, Heidegger's thought is a region of language—we can call it an *ethos*—which develops out of transformations of metaphysical thinking. It overcomes the priority of subject and will by maintaining the unresolvable question of being, obliviousness to which yielded the priority of subject and will. The effect of Heidegger's thinking takes place as one undergoes the transformations of metaphysical thinking that occur in the process of his discourse. These transformations are forecast by the transformation that takes place in *Being and Time:* time is rethought in an open and free resolve regarding the continuous mortality of human being and of the human world. A different discourse develops out of this rethinking, a transformation of thinking regarding origin, purpose, and being. Interest in overcoming mortality or finding something deathless for thought and hope becomes less functional. The thorough historicity of being and thought can be reconsidered without the metaphysical polarities of time and eternity, relative-absolute, or contingent being and necessary being. Heidegger's thought is moved by questions that have been traditionally suppressed and that show the deep uncertainties, the fearful projections, the gaps and severances that constitute our tradition of thought. In the movement of the question of being, that question, which is constitutive of the meanings and connotations of our philosophical history, explicitly moves thinking. Instead of being obscured by words and thought, in *Being and Time* the question of being is made manifest by words and thoughts. Two things happen. First, the language and thought that carry the question of being explicitly have themselves been formed in resolutions that override the question of being. Language and thought are changed in their functions and meanings in the processes by which the question of being is developed and maintained in *Being and Time.* Second, the language and thought in *Being and Time* also tend to cover the question of being with their meanings, which developed when the *question* of being was largely ignored. The simultaneous obscurity and manifestness of the question of being occur again in this language, but now as an explicit and formative part of the language. A different way of thinking begins to come out of this obscurity and manifestness in the thought of being, and in Heidegger's work the direction of this thinking is toward a way of thinking in which the very thought of being seems to be undergoing transformation, transmutation, and passing away.

Something similar though much less developed happens in his writing regarding the question of ethics. This issue is closely associated with the question of being, but it is not so clearly thematized. The question, we found, occurs in studies related to authenticity, truth, dwelling, and difference. In the present context we can state the question in this way: How have we human beings been separated from each other in our world in such a way that our divergences of language and thought have resulted in dispute and destruction? I state the question this way in order to highlight the significance of our tradition's experiences of *ethea* which we discussed in the last chapter. We are formed of cultural differences on which depend our senses of belonging, our particular senses of being. But they are also differences in the absence of a *nómos* that transcends an ethos or a confederation of several *ethea*. The question of ethics thus arises in the severance and nomadism that are constitutive of our commonalities. We have noted that some of the most cherished values of our ethos are kept in Heidegger's language, such as affirmation of thinking, peace without destruction, and nonmanipulative enhancement of differences. But another dimension of his thinking puts these values in question. At the center of his thought is the ontological difference between being and beings. It is a difference that is traditionally affirmed. The thought is that being is not a being, but in Heidegger's work this ontological difference gives in our tradition a continuous fissure in attempts to think or to apply in everyday life the essential unity or identity of being. The pervasiveness or nearness of being in our traditions means, in its difference from beings, the pervasiveness or nearness of gaping and severance, not unlike mere space or complete silence. "Dif-ference" pervades our talk, thought, and practice regarding life and its commonalities. This constitutive gaping, indicated by the ontological difference between being and beings, means not only the absence of one *substantia,* but also the ethnic discontinuous quality of our various nurturing fields of axioms, rules, and principles. If one tries to overcome the strife-yielding differences among beings by appeal to the nature of being, one perpetuates those differences by setting a group of axioms, rules, and principles over other groups that will, in turn, fight for their ways of belonging. Being will not translate into values that are universal for human beings. This is a descriptive claim: that ethical solutions to problems of destructive differences tend to perpetuate destructive differences by ways of thinking and acting that ignore or blindly attempt to override the inevitable fact that, in our traditions, commonalities are partial and regional. There appears to be no basis in the heart of our history for a continuing harmony provided by an essential identity pervasive for all differences.

If we accept this description as accurate, we might work within an ethos that has the goal of allowing differences and developing a "dia-logos" out of the allowing processes. The inevitability of *ethea* and their many ways of dwelling is allowed. This inevitability is affirmed in the intention to hear, speak, and think without an overarching field of principles for establishing right or goodness. But this is far less than we have been taught to hope for, and it suggests that even our best hopes, when they look for a final *nómos,* carry destructive separation from the fragmented bases for human community.

Heidegger's effort to allow the priority of differences to emerge with awareness in his thinking has become possible in large measure because the priority of the difference between being and beings was thematized in his early work in the *question* of being. One result of this question is that in Heidegger's thought the thoroughgoing fragmentation of Western culture is given thematic focus. Heidegger's thinking itself must be seen as a fragmenting focus in which ethnic belligerence becomes optional as this thinking holds itself in question. The ontological differences of being and beings mean that a peculiar distance, a cut, a fundamental difference vis-à-vis what exists and the essential possibility for existence is in our language regarding all things. If we follow differences, ontological distances, unfathomable mysteries, and above all the relations of domination and violation, we follow the destiny in our culture of the ill-considered ontological difference of being and beings. We have seen this cut already in the structures of *ethea,* structures that are both of belonging and of hostile violence.

As Heidegger brings to awareness the significance of this difference in our language and thought, he develops a way of thinking that does not constitute one more ethic that aspires to superiority and dominance. He develops with his discourse awareness of the pervasive strife of difference in the history and structure of his own discourse. His is to be a kind of thinking, a dwelling place, that anticipates its own overcoming. By giving priority to difference, to conversation that makes difference its space for dialogue, and to self-overcoming, this way of thinking provides conditions that might erase the dimension of violent hostility that has constituted many types of traditional ethical thinking. The options in our traditions that most attracted Heidegger were focused on dwelling. He attempted to let the freeing, homing aspect of ethos restate itself in a way that erased the belligerent stubbornness in its development. The language of Western mystics, distanced from the imposing structures of creed and worship, helped Heidegger to dislodge the dominance of the ethnic subject in the history of Western experience. The possibilities of dwelling with things in the language of disclosure, not of calculation, helped still more. He found, particularly in early Greek thought, the possibility for speaking and thinking in which things are allowed to be in their own self-showing ethos, a language and thinking that give way to the clearing release of beings. These possibilities give hope that one might think without the domination of one ethos and without the consequences of that domination: the privileging of self, judgment, calculation, and representation.

These possibilities are to be pursued only with the greatest tentativeness. The assertiveness and hard-nosed certainty that we intuitively demand when we feel ourselves to be at our best constitute rejection and suppression of the language and thinking that begin to emerge in Heidegger's work. The possibility exists to appropriate the ontological difference in our heritage in such a way that differences are addressed without interest in domination. That kind of address cannot be carried out in the discursive functions, emotions, and intentions that develop with the dominations of ethnic rightness and goodness. This is a quandary, because without control in an ethos of well-chosen values, we are surely doomed to nomadic violence of the worse kind. But another kind of nomadic violence on a grand scale among large, overpowering *ethea* appears to be inevitable in a heritage in which ethnic rightness and goodness mean that those who live in *that* ethos have the right to overcome others by disputation, conversion, or the imposed control of law.

If the "free space of opening" could give us our thoughts and names, perhaps a world appropriate to our own deepest history and experiences might emerge, a world that appropriates being's abysmal difference from beings and appropriates as well the consequent privilege of differences in relation to founded, universal values. But how is one to begin? How is one to face this dark obscurity, the free clearing, in common with other people who live according to very different values? One modest option can be found in a way of speaking together.

Is it possible to converse in the domain of free and open clearing as distinct from a region that is circumscribed by a given body of meaning and value? If we are able to let the dominance of will pass away, for example, without the intentions of asceticism or self-sacrifice, without the idea of God or the patterns of universal law or the way of Christ, but let the dominance of will pass away in the puzzling experience of things coming to presence, do words and thoughts then form that carry with them not only their own release but the "release of presence" by language and thought? Can "dif-ference" happen with alertness as people converse together so that beings are released to their differences without ethnic judgment? Will a way of being together develop in which the priority of valuing and judgment changes to a very different kind of affirmation, one that is appropriate to the granting of being in its difference of beings? Heidegger's essay "The Conversation on a Country Path" engages in such an experiment.[14]

This is a conversation among three academics who pursue the possibility of speaking and thinking without giving priority to willing or representation. They develop a slow, careful rhythm of finding words and names for nonvolitional occurrences. They work together to keep in mind primarily the word *Gelassenheit* 'clearing release', which names what they come to suspect is a dimension of speaking and thinking that can take place in ways about which they are unclear. They release themselves easily from Meister Eckhart's Christian assumptions and language, which gave context to *Gelassenheit* in his writing. They emphasize the word now by assuming that they do not know exactly what they are talking about when they use it. The word and what it names are, however, equally available. They say the word in a variety of contexts and cultivate a waiting sense, listening to what the word can say in the contexts. They develop among themselves a state of mind characterized by uncertainty and waiting without despair or definite expectation. The image is one of being on a path, like wanderers. The path is already there, and they are already on it when they notice it, but it is not defined by a specific destination, as a highway or a road would have. They feel alert and in the open, and the path they are on accentuates the openness around them. This openness is not like an infinite expanse, but is like a region in which the path goes its way. The region pervades and rests in its path, its countryside, its fences and fields and buildings. It is like a language or a way of thinking that pervades whatever is said and thought.

The three people use a variety of words to speak of this pervasive allowance: sheltering, abiding, resheltering, withdrawing and returning, coming to meet us, regioning, release. They find that their own releasing uncertainty about thinking and *Gelassenheit,* their bearing of alert waiting and exploring, put them in touch with the dimension of clearing release in their own conversation. Their lack of prescriptiveness attunes them to the nonprescriptiveness that takes place in speaking and thinking. The more they are released from demanding or insisting thought, the more a dimension of speaking and thinking emerges that is different from the language of force, drive, intention, system, or subjectivity. Their own attunement is puzzling to them. It increases their uncertainty and their alertness. It draws them into the conversation, encourages their speaking and thinking, gives them an issue for which their best prescriptions and methods are ill-suited. Their *gelassene* attunement returns them repeatedly in their conversations to the *gelassene* region of thinking and speaking, and they do not know what that means. Something abides in their conversation that they can neither will nor represent. It neither solves nor resolves. It does, however, seem to bring them together through release and to occasion increasing interaction.

What the three academicians attempt to think happens among them. In the process of their conversation, they find themselves increasingly attuned to each other through or in something else for which they are trying to find fitting words. They find themselves getting closer to the nearing effect of language and thinking, and by the end of the conversation they are in sufficient accord with each other and their subject matter to complete appropriately each other's thoughts and sentences. They find that their ideas are formed in the situation of release, uncertainty, and the clustering of fitting words. The transformation that develops is a process of which they find themselves a part. But the transformative process in this conversation is not like that of transvaluation in Nietzsche's discourse or "de-structing" in *Being and Time.* The conflict and overcoming that characterize those processes are no longer present. This conversation is gentle in the sense that transvaluation and de-struction have themselves been left aside. The overwhelming, undercutting transmutation and the often violent recasting of words and thought that occurred in the transformation of metaphysical thinking have been released in this interaction, and this experience of release seems to open into a dimension of thinking that was as closed to transvaluation and de-struction as it was to their progenitor, metaphysical thinking. The conversation has no element of strife to overcome. It lacks the desire to cut (or slash) through disagreement or to establish definitive word combinations.

The pressure for academic success is gone. There is no need to establish dominance or to carve out an excellent achievement. There is no fear of thoughtful closeness and intimacy. Something else is taking place. Instead of being like a process of bifurcation, the time of the conversation is more like a nearing of differences. Instead of mortal care, the being of this conversation is like an open way to wait. Instead of the metaphors of seeing, those of hearing seem best suited to the released waiting. The activity of the three people, which is hard, concentrated work for them, does not reflect back on itself, but is more like the effort involved in stepping back from one's characteristic, intuitive hold on things so that something else can take place with more freedom and attention than is otherwise the case. The three participants find that words come together in this process and that different thoughts form that indicate the situation of release rather than a situation of determined and well-intentioned effort.

Heidegger's way of thinking in this conversation is unmarked by the determined struggle that characterizes his own and other ways of thinking that struggle to overcome metaphysics. In that sense, his conversation is beyond both metaphysics and its overturning. When one thinks within this conversation, the differences among *ethea* become occasions for dialogue without dominance or recalcitrance. The participants continually differentiate, seek no center, and find thinking to be like a shapeless clearing, like being in the midst of beings, that gives presence and occasions the demand of learning how to speak and think beyond the limits of self-interested ways of life. This modest option cannot quiet our fears of living beyond ethical thought. But it can be taken as one beginning in which our culturally dominant solution to the problem of differences among *ethea* has begun to be rethought without the violence bred of the dominant classical 'solutions' to sharp differences of value and meaning.

B. THE LIMITS OF BEING'S RULE

Being does more, however, in Heidegger's discourse than provide the ontological difference and the question of ethics. Its dispensation is found in the 'it gives' of every temporal moment. Even in *Time and Being,* a text in which the prominence of being fades, the 'it gives' and allowance of presence continue the emphasis that Heidegger consistently placed in being's dispensation. In this emphasis Heidegger has sought a transformation of Western culture with its inevitability of destruction. This inevitability constitutes the traditional priorities of subjectivity, will, judgment, calculation, use, and consumption. Heidegger's thought made cultural transformation a continuing goal from the time of his rectorial address. To rethink the question of being is to approach a way of life that recognizes our unhealable distance from being and that struggles to find ways whereby humans can retrieve a transforming care for the being of all things. The allowing of presence—a love of presencing—is one of the moving passions in Heidegger's discourse. It is one that calls for both radical dissatisfaction with our culture and transformation of our communal lives. The rule of being calls for a society of almost monastic restraint before the human ability to invade, destroy, and use up. Everything but the yielding of presence is dangerous.

In this sense, Heidegger's thought reinstates the ethical at a "higher" level: the rule of being with its call for judgment regarding the everyday and the transformation of traditional patterns of life is beyond question. It 'gives' the entire question of ethics, and in its giving reinscribes an authority beyond definition and control. The rule of being functions like a countenance before which we are always falling and failing and before which we live and die. It has a surveillancelike quality in Heidegger's thought: it yields life and death, is the coming to presence of those states that most contradict it, inspires awe and anxiety in its difference and withdrawal from human existence, and is the concealing disclosure of everything. It gives us nothing to do that is universally narrative, but its nearness in our existence is inescapable. We do nothing without being's nearness, and its intimacy is awe-inspiring as we fall from it, forget it, or violate it. Its violation means nihilism. Our forgetfulness of it means destruction and severe loss. Falling from it means suffering. Appropriating its "nearing nearness" means saving power with people and things. Recognizing its withdrawal means hope for disciplines of life-giving restraint. Commemorating it properly releases human beings to life-processes that are nurtured by being and to a life deeply attuned to its own 'essence'. By appropriating our forgetfulness of being we find renewed life before the primal, acausal, ever-concealing, ever-rising origin that we can never be, but in the commemoration of which we are beyond ourselves in a destiny that comes to pass outside of our comprehension, and yet comes to pass as the home of our dwelling.

In the context of the question of ethics and the nurture/hostility syndrome of any ethos, the rule of being in a life dedicated to clearing release gives emphasis to the allowance of differences in their disclosedness. This emphasis is Heidegger's strongest response to the defensive hostility that characterizes an ethnic structure. Preservation of disclosure is the hallmark of *Gelassenheit*'s own disclosure. The sameness of being regulates the propriety of this way of being. Instead of hostility to other's values, an attunement to the sameness (not of human nature as one or another ethos defines it, but to the sameness of being that transcends ethnic difference) regulates people's perception and reception of meanings and values. An affirmation beyond value is the guiding affection that we saw operate in the conversation on a country path.

This claim, however, means that 'affirmation beyond value' is not itself a value or an ethnically developed power. Although one aspect of Heidegger's thought makes being *the* thought of Western culture, his stronger claim is that being is not ethnically dependent, but is the ethos-giving, presence-yielding mystery wherever *is* can properly be said. This universalizing tendency can be seen in the boldness and confidence with which Heidegger turns away from the possibility that the sameness of being is but a fragment of chaos. The issue is not one of sameness and unity, but of the jurisdiction of sameness and unity with regard to their absence. The questions we are raising are whether in this rule its own strife and difference can be heard, whether the mere sensuality of pain and pleasure can be heard adequately, whether the cry of the other in its meaninglessness can be heard through the voice of being's sameness.

To incarcerate meaninglessness and absence of sameness—mere dispersion—in disclosiveness, to suppress the sounds of what is most thoroughly excluded by being's rule, namely no being at all, undwelling, and fragmentation of being's sameness—to miss these sounds is to cultivate insensitivity to what we, in the heritage of ascetic ideal, most desperately want to hear. I am not sure that clearing release on a country path can be attuned to the singularity of human meaninglessness and can respond to it and in it except by distortion and blind affiliation with it. Heidegger clearly could not put *Gelassenheit* in question. Neither he nor I know what that means. I (and probably he) fear the consequences of that questioning. Can we live in dispersion without a final sameness? Can we live without the ever-rising countenance of being, veiled and magnificent in perpetual withdrawal and perpetual affirmation? Can we be unshepherded, unherded, as we yield in the it-gives? Can we be lost to order in our orders? Lost to disclosure in our disclosures? Lost to sameness in our 'essence'? Can we hear our own question as we affirm with confidence the sameness of being?

5. "We Need Desperately to See in the Dark"

The ascetic ideal is one of our clearings, perhaps our most effective one, in which and by which we see things connected, manifesting their meanings, and evoking from us those sacrifices that keep the clearing inflamed by light and truth. The sacrifice is no more manifest than in the distance that writing maintains from everything but the written. We have joined Heidegger in this sacrifice, that the written has held our fixed attention, and the unwritable is either held at bay or is transformed by writing. Consider, in the context of what is most feared in the ascetic ideal, what cannot be written: darkness that is merely there and refuses light and the circumference of light; emptiness without figure, sound, or movement; disordered confusion beyond the reach of grammar; sensations in their moments of pleasure and suffering; satisfactions of taste; a passing stirring scent; a rumble in the belly; loss of presence as a meaningful thing evaporates in our experience and our experience becomes a vapor. In writing about such things, and also in thinking them, a different world begins to form whose distance means not only a sacrifice of the thing written about, but a new (or slightly new) order, certainly fragile and filled with discord and ambiguity, but order nonetheless. The power of the ascetic ideal and the attraction of texts cannot be separated: the power of the lighted text, the power of words, the attraction of ordered lives that, in their order, allow their disorder but keep away the darkness of no light at all, and that inspire an obsession to write and read again and again, a reader's/writer's compulsion to know in the truth and light of script. We have not escaped the ascetic ideal in our writing of it.

But the sacrifices of the ascetic ideal go beyond those of the text's distance from the nontext. We have found what we can now interpret as a certain desperation in Heidegger's thought, a questionableness that could not be eradicated by his obsession with the question of being, and a desperation that he held in common with the ascetic ideal. Darkness demands illumination, and not by a fragile and tentative light, but by one that is ever-rising and that is conjoined with—that illumines—its concealment even as it withdraws in concealment. This desperation does not find its origin in illumination, but in the question of ethics in which our sense of life and death comes to pass and fades away. How are we to live with *this* anxiety? By turning it against itself and producing thought that gives the comfort of ceaseless being? By turning the event of wonder into a kinship with the 'essence' of life? This anxiety produces enormous effort to eradicate whatever undercuts the saving sameness of being, whatever symbolizes radical fragmentation and mere difference. On Foucault's account, madness projected that anxiety in the seventeenth century. And in our time, would it be a totally noncommunal aspect of human life? A complete absence of the worshipful? An absence of the Same? The destructive dimensions of heroism? The hopelessness of human life? Would the marks of such things enrage us, enflame us, in our clearing release, our bonds of love, our common humanity, and cause us to contain or eradicate them in the thought of ever-rising, abysmal being? In the clearing release of thought?

And if the *question* of ethics persists to such a point that the question of being and the conjunction of revealing and concealing are fragmented in their authority for thought, would we have found an opening beyond the ascetic ideal's horizon, beyond the boundaries of the Western ethos of being's rule to an uncertainty whereby the mere cry of the other could be heard? If we appropriated and gave rein to this uncertainty of ours, would other holocausts occur? Would we care less? Would we be more attuned to the dangers of our highest values? Would we take delight in strife? Would we be less desperate before the darkness of human life?

Would desperation transpire, as Nietzsche thought, into a joy of life that gives affirmation no ontological privilege?

I do not know the answers to these questions. I suspect that in coping with them, as we maintain the question of ethics, we will find that our values and their evaluation have generated blindly some of our worst pain—because of the desperation by which we have sought to see in the dark.

Notes

2. THE QUESTION TURNS ON ETHICS

1. The examples here are taken from *Devavanitravesika, an Introduction to the Sanskrit Language,* Robert P. Goldman with Sally J. Sutherland (Berkeley: University of California Press, 1980), 31.

2. W. D. Whitney, *Sanskrit Grammar,* 12th ed. (Cambridge: Harvard University Press, 1971), p. 293.

3. Although the English phrase "I was born" looks passive, it would seem to indicate a middle rather than a passive voice. Perhaps it and other expressions such as "I was caught," "the dishes dried," "this reads like a novel," and "the cup broke" derive from the ancient middle voice.

4. See, for example, *Being and Time,* trans. John Macquarrie and Edward Robinson (London: SCM Press, 1962) sections 7, 74, 75, 78, 80; and "Différance," *Margins of Philosophy,* trans. Alan Bass (Chicago: University of Chicago Press, 1982), pp. 9–10, where Derrida writes of temporizing, differing, and deferring.

5. Jean Pierre Vernant, "Greek Tragedy: Problems of Interpretations," in *The Structuralist Controversy: The Languages of Criticism and the Sciences of Man,* ed. Richard Macksey and Eugenio Donato (Baltimore; John Hopkins Press, 1972), pp. 276–77. I am indebted to Charles Shepherdson, with whom I have discussed this and most other features of both the middle voice and of middle-voiced events and who first called my attention to the significance of the middle voice in the context of Heidegger's thought.

6. Vernant, "Greek Tragedy," p. 279.

7. The following discussion reworks and places in a different context material from chapter 2, section 4 of my *Language of Difference* (Atlantic Highlands, N.J.: Humanities Press International, 1987). I have used it here because the self-overcoming aspect of the idea of will to power in Nietzsche's discourse best shows how self-overcoming takes place at the most elemental level of his thought.

8. "The ascetic ideal for a long time served the philosopher as a form in which to appear, as a precondition of existence—he had to *represent* it so as to be able to be a philosopher; he had to *believe* it in order to be able to represent it. The peculiar, withdrawn attitude of the philosopher, world-denying, hostile to life, suspicious of the senses, freed from sensuality, which has been maintained down to the most modern times and has become virtually the *philosopher's pose par excellence*—it is above all a result of the emergency conditions under which philosophy arose and survived at all; for the largest time philosophy would not have been *possible at all* on earth without ascetic wraps and cloak, without an ascetic self-misunderstanding. To put it vividly: the ascetic priest provided until the most modern time the repulsive and gloomy caterpillar form in which alone the philosopher could live and creep about" (GM III 10).

9. The techniques of this turn are discussed in GM III 17–19: the hypnotic muting of sensitivity to the feeling of being alive so that the pain of meaninglessness, mortality, etc., are made tolerable; mechanical, absolutely regular activity such as that of rituals and unthinking obedience, the cultivation of "petty pleasures" that advance the cause of consolation and its communities, and the advance of "orgies of feeling" which maximally deaden the pain of life.

3. ETHICS IS THE QUESTION

1. *The Use of Pleasure,* trans. Robert Hurley (New York: Pantheon, 1985),

pp. 10–13, hereafter cited as UP. "On the Genealogy of Ethics," in *Michel Foucault: Beyond Structuralism and Hermeneutics,* Hubert Dreyfus and Paul Rabinow, 2nd ed. (Chicago: University of Chicago Press, 1983), pp. 238–43.

2. "The Subject and Power," in *Michel Foucault,* ed. Dreyfus and Rabinow, p. 209.

3. "On the Genealogy of Ethics," p. 231.

4. "Polemics, Politics, and Problematizations: An Interview," *Foucault Reader,* ed. P. Rabinow (New York: Pantheon, 1984), pp. 388–89. In this part of the interview Foucault develops the interpretation of problematization that I have summarized and his account of the history of thought from which I shall draw in the following discussion.

5. Ibid.

6. "The Subject and Power," p. 231.

7. Ibid., p. 208.

8. "Preface" (by Foucault), *Anti-Oedipus: Capitalism and Schizophrenia,* Gilles Deleuze and Felix Guatarri, trans. Robert Hurley, Mark Seem, Helen R. Lane (Minneapolis: University of Minnesota Press, 1983), p. xiv.

9. "Le retour de la morale," *Les Nouvelles,* June 28, 1984, p. 37.

10. Foucault uses the word *archaeology* to characterize his work in, for example, *The Order of Things* (New York: Random House, 1973) and *The Birth of the Clinic,* trans. A. M. S. Smith (New York: Random House, 1975). He tended to use that word to refer to the study of structures and to use *genealogy* to refer to the study of the lineage of power-effects. This convenience obscured the fact that for him there is no clear division between structures and power-effects and also led to serious misinterpretations by those who read his 'archeological' studies as a hybrid of structuralist methodologies. Although Foucault was later critical of his own insufficient attention to the power-effects of systems of knowledge, none of his 'archeological' studies can be accurately read to suggest that there are structures of knowledge that make up a kind of reality in their own right as though there were structures that are independent of institutional, political, and broadly cultural interplays of ordering and subjecting power. Such an interpretation also encourages one to overlook the powers that play through his own discourse in these studies and to think that they are works within the broadly humanistic and historicist traditions. We shall see, for example, that in *The Order of Things* the powers of the various systems of knowledge are at work in Western societies and that their work constitutes one of the major issues of the book. Consequently I shall use *genealogy* to refer to the study of formations and deformations of knowledges as well as to studies of the effects of institutional powers. I shall emphasize the power-effects of formations and deformations of knowledge and the close relations of Foucault's 'early' work to his 'later' in which genealogy includes studies of knowledges, practices, and selves.

11. MC 115–116. Foucault's work on transgression in the context of Bataille's writings provides an image for the play of madness's silence through *Madness and Civilization:* "Transgression forces the limit to face the fact of its imminent disappearance, to find itself in what it excludes (perhaps, to be more exact, to recognize itself for the first time, to experience its positive truth in its downward fall . . .). Perhaps it is like a flash of lightning in the night which, from the beginning of time, gives a dense and black intensity to the night it denies, which lights up the night from the inside, from top to bottom, and yet owes to dark the stark quality of its manifestation, its harrowing and posed singularity; the flash loses itself in this space it makes with its sovereignty and becomes silent now that it has given a name to obscurity" (LCM 34–35). *Madness and Civilization* is transgressed by the silence of madness. In this metaphor, madness's silence is the

lightning flash that marks the imminent disappearance and the downward fall of rational discourse. The density of such a discourse is shown in its darkness by the lightning's space in its radical divergence from common knowledge and good sense. The density of rationalization is broken for a moment by the stark clarity of madness. Madness's silence in our recent civilization reveals the obscurity of what we have taken to be our enlightenment. In this reversal by which the darkness of delirium illuminates the boundaries of civilized life, the dark folly of rational containment becomes clear for a moment and defines a space for a kind of speaking and writing that strikes us as radically other as the *Übermensch* is to the last man. *Madness and Civilization* is transgressed by the silence that it cannot speak. By knowing itself as transgressed, it is both repelled and sprung from the obscurity that it proposes as its best knowledge.

12. "Since the end of the nineteenth century, the life of reason no longer manifests itself except in the lightning-flash of works such as those of Hölderlin, of Nerval, of Nietzsche, or of Artaud—forever irreducible to those alienations that can be cured, resisting by their own strength that gigantic moral imprisonment which we are in the habit of calling, doubtless by antiphrasis, the liberation of the insane by Pinel and Tuke" (MC 278). We note that Foucault's emphasis is not so much on liberation as on the counter-memory that reinherits the caesura of unreason. The liberation of the insane from moral confinement is not a liberation from madness any more than the liberation of people from pastoral power frees them from the brokenness and death that pastoral power both cultivates and deeply fears. No ethic is intended. Rather, Foucault recalls the feared and suppressed aspect of the tradition, thinks it through, writes and speaks in its reinheritance, and holds open the field of thought for what the counter-memory makes possible: the end of 'man' and man's world, the beginning of different discourses.

13. This is also a problem for both transcendental knowledge and the project of self-constitution. When self-constitution, for example, intends to establish a unified being who realizes universal human nature or universal values, it perpetuates discontinuity in its project, and its identity establishes its difference from universality. The identity of both the transcendental field and the self that constitutes itself makes a difference. We shall see that this quandary of perpetuating discontinuity in the effort to eliminate it involves a refusal of the dispersed temporality of both the transcendental field and the self.

14. With reference to the problematic of representation, Foucault asks, "How is it that thought has a place in the space of the world, that it has its origin there, and that it never ceases, in this place or that, to begin anew?" (OT 50). This is a question integral to his thought as well as to modern thought. He rethinks this issue of place and space in part by recasting time in relation to space under the aegis of the dispersion that recent Western thought has produced but ignored.

15. "For if exegesis leads us not so much towards a primal discourse as towards the naked existence of something like a language, will it not be obliged to express only the pure forms of language even before it has taken on a meaning? And in order to formalize what we suppose to be a language, is it not necessary to have practiced some minimum exegesis, and at least interpreted all these mute forms as having the intention of meaning something? It is true that the division between interpretation and formalization presses upon us and dominates today. But it is not rigorous enough: the fork it forms has not been driven far enough down into our culture, its two branches are too contemporaneous for us to be able to say even that it is prescribing a simple option or that it is inviting us to choose between the past, which believed in meaning, and the present (the future), which has discovered the significant" (OT 199).

16. See *The Care of the Self,* trans. Robert Hurley (New York: Pantheon, 1986)

p. 239. The processes of problematization and vigilance that characterize the formation of the ethical subject now recoil on that formation in Foucault's account
of it.

4. THE QUESTION OF DASEIN'S MOST PROPER BEING

1. Although Foucault, in his last interview, stated that Heidegger was, with
Nietzsche, the major influence on his thought and that he read Heidegger continuously during his career, Nietzsche, not Heidegger, defines the horizon from which
Foucault most often takes his departure. Heidegger's influence is apparent throughout Foucault's writing, but it is found in a more Nietzschean context. The element
of Heidegger's thought is different from Foucault's element, and Heidegger's style
of seriousness of mind defines not only his difference from Foucault and Nietzsche
but also the element that, we shall see, most inspires and problematizes his thought.

2. I take the term *twisting free* from David Farrell Krell's translation of
Herausdrehung and from John Sallis's use of the term in "Twisting Free: Being
to an Extent Sensible," *Research in Phenomenology* 17 (1987): 1–21.

3. Does this mean that the being of dasein is a transcendental reality that
is independent of its history? I discussed this question in detail in chapter 3 of
The Language of Difference (Atlantic Highlands, N.J.: Humanities Press, 1986).
The short answer is that the being of dasein, in the terms of *Being and Time,*
must be historically formed and transcendent in its disclosiveness vis-à-vis everyday
identities and selfhood. *Being and Time* begins a process whereby the issue of
historicity and transcendence and the terms of the debate concerning them are
recast and decisively changed by the priority that Heidegger gives to disclosure.

4. We said that in Foucault's account of surveillance, the power to observe
and judge is also a power to incarcerate. One developing claim in *Discipline/Punish*
and toward the end of *The History of Sexuality* trilogy is that the state's manner
of enforcing its interests in the welfare of its citizens changes as government changes
from regency to forms of democracy. Authority is internalized. Instead of an external
state's surveillance, an interior surveillance forms whereby we become incarcerated
by a body of values to which we are taught to give voice: the power of conscience
in this sense of the word is the power of a hierarchy of values. Genealogy is
the approach Foucault uses to break this power in his writing. Instead of a different
authority that counteracts the authority of modern conscience—and hence the authority of modern self—genealogy counteracts conscience by means of disclosing
the power-interests that invest self and conscience in the context of those values.
So, for example, our predisposition to distaste and disgust regarding dissemblance
recoils against the dissemblance that constitutes the values of sincerity and nondis-
sembling honesty, the very values that generate our predisposition to disgust regarding dissemblance. In this way the modern conscience and self are in question
in his writing.

Although Heidegger, in contrast to Foucault, uses *conscience* constructively
in his analysis, we may also appropriately ask who is looking and judging in the
context of his description of conscience. His direct answer is 'das Man', the anonymous one of our inherited structures of value. In the function of conscience, however, in its distance from its contingent religious and moral contents, and in the
ontological function that Heidegger ascribes to call, language, and guilt, he finds
neither a normative self nor the priority of meaning and value. He finds the articulation of dasein's difference vis-à-vis its daily and traditional observations. *Conscience*
names a movement of dasein that has no surveillance and no judgment, and by
conceiving it that way one is in a movement of twisting free from the everyday

that puts the priority of value-judgment in question. How are we to think outside this priority?

Nietzsche's account of the ascetic ideal claims that philosophical reflection as such originated in an ascetic, priestly contemplation that removed people by its activity from alertness to earthly, fragmented existence. Nietzsche's thought recoils in the strain that it puts on itself as thought and always diminishes itself in the metaphor of will to power and eternal return. Heidegger's thought, in the context of conscience, diminishes no less its own conscience regarding dasein's forgetful and banal life. The contents of everyday conscience, its clarity regarding right and wrong, its fearful guilt, its concern over metaphysical security and peace of mind, its predisposition not to question its axioms for conduct—its forgetful banal life—are in question by the recoiling movement whereby it puts itself in question by the values that it holds. This wrenching motion is an aspect of the conscience of *Being and Time.* It is in question in *Being and Time* no less than Nietzsche's philosophical reflection is in question in his reflective account of the ascetic ideal. If the wrenching, recoiling movement is emphasized, rather than the specific and static claims that Heidegger makes regarding the ontological status of conscience, we find the process in which both the subject of the description and the subjectivity of describing are in question.

5. In pathological grief, for example, a person is often traumatized by the interruption of death, and the grief is less over the specific loss than over the mortality that infuses the other and one's relation with the other.

6. This movement of transformation and self-overcoming is found in Part II of *The Basic Problems of Phenomenology,* trans. Albert Hofstadter (Bloomington: Indiana University Press, 1982) in which Heidegger's discussion moves from an invocation of strict phenomenological method to its *Umschlag,* its transformation, at the end of the book. We take up this movement in section 5 below.

7. For an elaboration of this question, see David F. Krell's *Intimations of Mortality* (University Park: Pennsylvania State University Press, 1986), chapter 3.

8. See the third edition of *Vom Wesen der Wahrheit* (Frankfurt a.m.: Klostermann, 1954).

9. Both this translation and the research on *éthos, nomós, nómos* are found primarily in Charles Chamberlain, "From 'Haunts' to 'Character': The Meaning of Ethos," *Helios* 11:2 (1984). I have also used H. Frisk's *Griechisches Etymologisches Wörterbuch,* vol. 2 (Heidelberg, 1960–61), and *A Greek-English Lexicon,* 2 vols., H. G. Liddell and Robert Scott (Oxford: Oxford University Press, 1925).

5. THESE VIOLENT PASSIONS

1. *Die Selbstbehauptung der Deutschen Universität; Das Rektorat, 1933/34,* (Frankfurt a.m.: Klostermann, 1983). "The Self-Assertion of the German University. The Rectorate 1933/34; Facts and Thoughts," trans. Karsten Harries, *The Review of Metaphysics* 38 (March 1985): 467–502. See also "The Self-Assertion of the German University," trans. Cyril and Liliane Welch, *Proceedings of the 20th Annual Heidegger Conference,* ed. Manfred S. Frings, DePaul University, 1986. Although I consulted these translations and frequently used their phrasing, I often chose different words and phrases that I found to be more appropriate to Heidegger's text and that make an important difference in the interpretation.

2. *Review,* p. 490.

3. *Geistige* means intellectual, spirited, or spiritual in the sense of 'of the whole mind'. At times *intellectual* can be used in spite of the obvious inadequacy

of the word. *Spiritual* is not usually an appropriate translation, although philologically entirely correct, because of the generally religious and quasi-religious overtones of the English word in ordinary usages. Given the wide range of meanings for *mind,* an adjectival form of that word would be much better, if an acceptable adjective existed for this context. *Intellectual* does not capture the powerfully synthetic connotation of *geistige* nor the German word's ability to indicate a history of culture-forming development and fateful determinations. On the other hand, *intellectual* points to the mission of the university to form the minds of people by disciplined study. That mission, of course, must be transformed, and *intellectual* is no less in question than *spirited* and *spiritual.*

4. Jacques Derrida, *Of Spirit: Heidegger and the Question,* trans. Geof Bennington and Rachel Bowlby (Chicago: University of Chicago Press, 1989).

5. Heidegger uses *Versagen* for the failure of knowing. That word is in contrast to the *Spruch* or saying concerning the "creative importance of knowing."

6. Instead of *Einlass* 'welcome', modern existence is characterized by *Verlassenheit* 'abandonment' regarding the question of being. The difference between welcoming the question of being and losing it constitutes the crisis of academic knowledge.

7. It is a preservation that conserves the revealing and concealing of being.

8. Compare paragraph 9 above, which describes the Greek rise above ethnic obscurity and relativity.

9. The English misleads by translating *sofern* as 'in that' instead of 'insofar as' or 'inasmuch as'.

10. If Heidegger had not quoted Clausewitz, one could more easily translate *Kampf* as 'struggle' rather than 'battle'. Heidegger's claims can be taken to argue for 'struggle'. His rhetoric, however, favors 'battle'.

6. "'ALL TRUTH'—IS THAT NOT A COMPOUND LIE?"

1. *Über den Humanismus* (Frankfurt a.m.: Klostermann, 1947). "Letter on Humanism," *Basic Writings,* ed. David Farrell Krell (New York: Harper & Row, 1977), pp. 189–242. The German text is cited in text as LH.

2. Heidegger phrases this occurrence in this way: "Das Denken . . . lässt sich vom Sein in der Anspruch nehmen, um die Wahrheit des Seins zu sagen. Das Denken vollbringt dieses Lassen. Denken ist l'engagement par l'Etre pour l'Etre . . . penser, c'est l'engagement de l'Etre" (Thinking . . . lets itself be claimed by being so as to say the truth of being. Thinking unfolds this allowance in the fullness of its coming to pass. Thinking is the engagement by being for being . . . thinking is the engagement of being), LH 5.

3. Medard Boss has put this claim to work in psychoanalysis by showing that every aspect of the human body is pervaded by one's appropriation of being. In this way he rethinks psychosomatic medicine and the psychological meaning of physical impairment. See *Grundriss der Medizin* (Bern: Hans Huber, 1971), Part I. B.

4. LH 236. Compare Nietzsche: "Origin in something else counts as an objection, as casting a doubt on value." "'Reason' in Philosophy," section 4, *Twilight of the Idols,* trans. R. J. Hollingdale (New York: Penguin, 1968). This "degenerate" idea, according to Nietzsche, is companion to the ideas of 'highest concept', unity, and the unconditioned. Heidegger eliminates the idea of *causa sui* without question, but do these other "last fumes of evaporating reality" pass away in Heidegger's thought?

5. Ibid., section 5.

6. We may say that being 'vacates' by its withdrawal, by its continuous aban-

donment of human being in its difference from beings. In that sense humans are bereft of being in the granting closeness of being. But *that* abandonment protects and preserves being in its difference as well as in its granting nearness, its purity vis-à-vis beings. Being continues to enjoy an unquestioned privilege.

7. See David Farrell Krell, *On The Verge* (Bloomington: Indiana University Press, 1990), chapter 6.

8. "Building Dwelling Thinking" in *Basic Writings* (New York: Harper & Row, 1977), p. 335. "Bauen Wohnen Denken" in *Vortraege und Aufsaetze* (Pfullingen: Neske, 1959), p. 158. Unless otherwise noted, quotations in this section will be taken from the translation.

9. "The real plight of dwelling is indeed older than the world wars with their destruction. . . . The real dwelling plight lies in this, that mortals ever search anew for the essence of dwelling, that they *must ever learn to dwell*" (BDT 339).

10. "But that thinking itself belongs to dwelling in some sense as building, although in a different way, may perhaps be attested to by the course of thought here attempted" (BDT 338).

11. The *yond* of *beyond* may have the sense of 'border' if it is taken adjectivally as 'at the farther side'. Or it may connote the presently unreachable if it is taken as 'more distant'. The prefix *be* intensifies *yond* and carries the meaning of 'out of reach'. As a prefix it indicates in our context an intensification of surpassing distance that pre-fixes the space of transmission. It also gives the sense of 'throughout' or 'thoroughly', of bordering distance that characterizes a situation throughout that situation. Whatever is beyond translation is beyond throughout the process of traveling over and transmission. Improving the translation intensifies the beyond rather than overcomes it. Hence, in discussing Heidegger's interpretation of being vis-à-vis revealing and concealing, I emphasize being's ecstatic event with the phrase "beyond translation." In being near, it translates itself by concealing itself.

12. "Aletheia (Heraklit, Fragment 16)" in *Vortraege und Aufsaetze,* (Pfullingen: Neske, 1959), pp. 257–82. "Aletheia Heraclitus, Fragment B16" in *Early Greek Thinking,* ed. David Farrell Krell and Frank A. Capuzzi (New York: Harper & Row, 1975), p. 106. Noted quotations are taken from the English translation and cited in this chapter as AH.

13. As Heidegger faces the limits of his own interpretation and gives priority to the text's questionableness, as he suggests the questionableness of his own reading, he links *revealing* and *concealing* with a hyphen rather than the accustomed conjunction *and*. Does the fragment of Heraclitus's thought prompt the replacement of the *and* by the hyphen? He speaks of the "revealing-concealing lightning" in two places (AH 119, 120) and of the "revealing-concealing gathering" on two other occasions (121, 122). But otherwise, when *revealing* and *concealing* are used as nouns and not as adjectives, the conjunction *and* joins them. So we are forced by the grammar to believe that the hyphen connects the words in a proper joining of two adjectival functions without suggesting a beyond that separates them. The emphasis on belonging together never wavers. And he says that the beginning and the end of the fragment name "revealing *and* concealing" (121, emphasis added).

14. *Gelassenheit* (Pfullingen: Neske, 1959). *Discourse on Thinking,* trans. John M. Anderson and E. Hans Freund (New York: Harper & Row, 1966).

Index

Active voice, 18–21, 24–25, 26, 34
Aeschylus: *Agamemnon*, 144
Aesthetics: and ascetic ideal, 36
Affirmation, 5, 10–13, 15–16, 36, 212; and will to power, 30, 37; of life, 25, 31, 34, 43, 45–48, 94, 116, 174
Ambiguity, 2, 5, 21–24, 104, 170
Anxiety, 6, 8, 17, 98, 166, 211; in ascetic ideal, 43, 47, 49, 190, 191; of dasein, 101, 109, 135; of questioning, 5, 57; of reason, 66, 69; ontological, 117–18; psychological, 117–19
Aphrodite, 64
Archeology, 53, 214n10
Aristotle, 113–15, 124–33
Artaud, Antonin, 215n12
Ascetic ideal, 2, 4, 5, 13–15, 25, 27, 33–48, 51–52, 53, 94, 95, 106, 196, 210, 211; and religion, 36, 46–48, 50, 175, 178, 187; and suffering, 111, 119, 173, 210; and transcendence, 14, 33, 173, 175; and will to life, 42–43, 175; and will to power, 28, 42; in Heidegger, 2, chap. 6; in Nietzsche, chap. 2, 181, 217n4; polluting effect, 15, 37, 51; recoil of, 18, 30, 35, 37, 43, 45; reversal in, 42–45; self-denial in, 41–43, 45, 177, 213n8; suppression in, 25, 30, 38, 45–46, 50, 173, 174. *See also* Genealogy
Asceticism, 91, 95, 119, 201, 206; ascesis, 89–90; *askésis*, 9, 94
Athens, 22–23. *See also* Philosophy
Authority, 163, 216n4; and ascetic ideal, 40; in Heidegger's language, 149–50, 169, 209; questioning of, 16, 64, 80, 93, 104, 115, 145, 164; within a heritage, 38, 60, 70. *See also* Ground
Autonomy, 6, 148, 150–52, 159, 163

Bataille, Georges, 214n11
Being, 10, 12, 17, 81, 105, 107, 123, 175, 177, 190, 194; and language, 185, 188; and the everyday, 186–87; and thought, 179–80, 184, 185; appeal of, 179, 183; as presence, 108–109, 146; concealment of, 141, 147; forgetfulness of, 177, 178, 187, 189, 209; images of, 33, 66; in question, 7, 108, 136, 164, 190; 'it gives' of, 11, 186–87, 208–10; oneness of, 195–96, 200; priority of, in Heidegger's thought, 195–96, 203–204, 208–10; question of, 7, 104, 109, 110, 124, 129, 140–43, 146–47, 148, 158, 161, 164, 167, 169, 175–77, 185, 186, 190, 193, 196, 203, 205, 209, 211, 218n6; reverence for, 194–95; saying of, 187, 189, 193; unity of, 74,

193; withdrawal of, 181, 187, 190, 195, 209, 218n6, 218–19n6. *See also* Presence
Beings: concern for, 122, 139, 168, 179; disposability of, 155–16, 134, 193–94; engagement with, 136–39; flourishing of, 139–40, 193
Belonging, 143–45, 179, 180, 204, 205
Beyond (*über*, trans), 18, 31–32, 33, 180–81, 219nn11, 13; of dasein, 121; translation, 196–99, 201; transmission, 200–202. *See also* Horizon
Blanchot, Maurice, 35
Body, 175, 218n3; and ascetic ideal, 35, 42, 44, 48, 177; and desire, 74–75, 186; and disclosure, 79; and ethos, 64–65; and mind, 183–84; in Heidegger's thought, 177–78, 186
Boss, Medard, 218n3
Buddhism, 142

Caesura, 65–71, 215n12
Causation, 24, 82, 195
Christianity, 49, 95, 157, 200, 206
Clausewitz, Karl von, 167, 218n10
Clement of Alexandria: *Paidagogos*, 200
Community, 123, 139, 146, 171, 176, 204; university, 159, 162, 163–67
Concealment, 140–41; conjunction of, with revealing, 195–202, 211, 218n7, 219n11, 219n13; of beings, 156
Confinement, 66–68, 215n12, 216n4
Conscience: in Heidegger, 106–107, 109–10, 170, 216–17n4; in Nietzsche, 16, 27, 35, 48. *See also* Understanding
Contemplation, 39–41, 43, 45, 217n4

Dasein, chap. 4, 216n3; and care, 118, 122, 193, 209; and knowledge, 154; and middle voice, 120–21; attestation of, 102, 111; difference from self, 99–100, 102–103, 105; everydayness of, 128; ownmost being of, 97–101, 105–11, 112, 119, 134, 176, 217n5; running ahead (*Vorlauf*), 97–103, 106–108, 110, 120, 122, 135, 139, 168
Death, 11, 37, 66, 84, 85, 105, 124, 184, 211; being to, 97–101, 103, 110, 139
Democracy, 150, 157, 171
Demosthenes, 144
Depression, 123–24, 133, 191, 194
Derrida, Jacques, 10, 11, 151, 176, 213n4
Desire, 74–75, 76, 84, 85, 89, 90, 95, 186
Destiny: of being, 184; of German people, 149, 152, 156–57, 161–65, 168–69; of knowledge, 155–56; of thought, 171
De-struction, 96; of identity, 151, 153; of time,